TELL ME I'M FORGIVEN

To Maggie
with love
Alison Child
xx.

TELL ME I'M FORGIVEN

THE STORY OF FORGOTTEN STARS
GWEN FARRAR AND NORAH BLANEY

ALISON CHILD

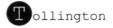ollington

First published in 2019 by Tollington Press, Machynlleth, Wales, UK
Reprinted 2020 with minor amendments
www.tollingtonpress.co.uk

ISBN 978-1-909347-15-1

Cover photograph of Gwen Farrar and Norah Blaney by Dorothy Wilding
© William Hustler & Georgina Hustler / National Portrait Gallery
Cover design by Andrew Kay
Edited and typeset by Helen Sandler

Printed in Wales by Y Lolfa, Talybont, Ceredigion,
on FSC-certified paper

FSC

Contents

LIST OF ILLUSTRATIONS

Kind permission has been given by the following to reproduce illustrations:
Derek Hunt (DH); Sir Andrew Watson (AW); Mary Evans Picture Library
(ME), which represents Illustrated London News Ltd (ILN); National
Portrait Gallery (NPG), and others as listed.

Parts I & II
Norah aged eleven months (© ILN/ME)
Norah onstage at the piano (DH)
Margate Concert Party (DH)
Gwen as a small child (Bodleian Libraries)
Welcome Home at Chicheley Hall (Royal Society)
Gwen's 'Gibson Girl' sketch (AW)
Gwen dressed for riding (AW)
Norah and Gwen in *Tatler* (© ILN/ME)
Caricature of Norah and Gwen in *The Punch Bowl* (AW)
Gwen's drawings of 217 King's Rd (AW)
Gwen's sketches of life on tour (AW)
Gwen's sketches of herself, Norah and the Prince of Wales (AW)
Marriage of Norah Blaney and Philip Durham (AW)
Caricature of Norah and Gwen by Nerman (© ME)

Plate Section One
In *Pot Luck* at the Vaudeville (© ILN/ME)
Gwen and Norah publicity photograph (© NPG)
Cover of *Popular Music and Dancing Weekly* (author's copy)
Cover of 'Come Back' sheet music, photo by Dorothy Wilding
   (© William Hustler & Georgina Hustler/NPG)
A Musical Comedian at Home (© ILN/ME)
Caricatures of *The Vagabond King* (*Stage*)
An Audience of Stars (© ILN/ME)
Gwen and chorus, *Shake Your Feet* (© ILN/ME)
Gwen throwing a shape (© ILN/ME)

Parts III to V
Una Troubridge and Radclyffe Hall (© ILN/ME)
Joe Carstairs with friends on her yacht (© Classic Boat Centre
   Trust Collection)
Arthur Roberts (author's copy) and Radclyffe Hall (© NPG)

Foreword

In 2014 I discovered the revue stars Gwen Farrar and Norah Blaney on a grainy piece of silent movie footage someone had posted on YouTube.[1]

Clowning around on a golf course in 1924 were two young women demonstrably in love. Their mutual attraction was on show for the camera, but there was no mistaking the authenticity of their bond.

Here was a romantic friendship captured on film: funny, touching, playful, spontaneous. The chemistry between Gwen and Norah looked remarkably like the appealing rapport of today's lesbian YouTubers. It was flirtatious, confident and knowing, in strong contrast to the secrecy and shame that has so often characterised depictions of lesbian love.

I was enchanted and immediately embarked on a research project that was to take up five years of my life and result in the book you now hold in your hands. I set out to discover everything I could about Gwen Farrar and Norah Blaney, visiting archives in London, Lincoln, Stratford-upon-Avon, Birmingham, Paris and New York. I had conversations with people who remembered them. I travelled to Johannesburg to see Gwen's childhood home and walked through London tracking the places they lived and the theatres they filled.

Gwen Farrar was born to wealthy parents in 1897 in the West End of London – right in the middle of what would become her world. Four years earlier, bouncing baby Norah had been born to rather humbler parents in the suburbs of the capital. The two girls grew up in different worlds but by their early twenties they had become 'partners and pals'.

They both began as musical children with exceptional ability and drive. Norah played the piano and sang. Gwen was a cellist. When they got together Gwen was nineteen and Norah twenty-three. Performing together and sleeping together, facing life side by side, they encountered a world of new possibilities. Singing the popular songs of the day to each other, to their own accompaniment – and, crucially, not taking themselves too seriously – they became enormously successful with an act that had wide appeal across regional and class divides.

'The partnership they formed knew no bounds. They became the vogue in London and the provinces and starred in the most successful shows.'[2]

Then impresario Florenz Ziegfeld whisked them off to perform in New York and Palm Beach. They met the richest men and women in the world and the biggest stars.

Navigating their lives and careers to avoid bigotry and homophobia, the duo played careful public relations games and were as bold as they dared be about their closeness. They occupied a space in queer subculture that brought them in contact with a diverse array of lesbians: Natalie Clifford Barney, Romaine Brooks, Djuna Barnes, Una Troubridge, Radclyffe Hall, Joe Carstairs, Noel Streatfeild, Pamela Travers, Naomi Jacob, Miriam Margolyes, as well as bisexual women Adele Astaire, Tallulah Bankhead, Daphne du Maurier, Beatrice Lillie and Gertrude Lawrence.

To understand the Blaney/Farrar act, I transcribed the lyrics of the songs they sang while composer Sophie Aynsley reproduced the accompaniments. With my partner, Rosie Wakley, I put these songs onstage. We couldn't begin to do justice to Gwen and Norah's musicianship. We were just very happy to have found a lesbian story to celebrate and share in an accessible way.

One night local Surrey historian Jeremy Palmer came to our show and introduced himself. Ever since, he has shared his meticulous research in a wonderfully generous and modest way. Together we have speculated and searched, followed through on hunches and unearthed the material that forms the basis of this intriguing, funny, sad and celebratory story.

There is no surviving correspondence between Gwen and Norah, but the lyrics of the songs they chose to sing, commit to memory, share and fill with meaning, provide an insight into their relationship. Praised for their diction and interpretive skills, Gwen and Norah could raise a laugh or romantic frisson through a combination of words and carefully worked out harmonies. When apart they rehearsed down the telephone. When they fell out and became solo artists, the songs they chose contained deliberate messages of one-upmanship. Later, when Gwen sang, 'Tell me I'm forgiven for daring to show the rest of the world I love you so,'[3] she was deliberately appropriating a song from a male colleague and putting it on record for Norah.

Since Gwen and Norah first sprang to my attention through a visual medium, it feels right to tell their story through some astonishing pictures: photographs, caricatures, press clippings and production shots. I hope they will bring to life these two women who have been so present to me since I first found them.

Audio evidence has been equally vital. This book would have been impossible without Derek Hunt, who heard Norah's records in 1972 and sought her out, becoming her helper and friend. More than forty years later he entrusted me with six fragile tapes. I found a cassette player, inserted the first brittle plastic casing and pressed PLAY in trepidation, fearing the tape would snap. I listened in rapture as the reels revealed a series of conversations in which Derek delicately interviewed Norah about her childhood, her musicianship and her life with Gwen. Her delight in reminiscing is palpable, her story-telling technique fine-honed and her warmth and humour infectious. These are qualities I have tried to bring to the pages of this book.

Norah and Gwen were intimately linked for twenty-seven years. Their story is not without its share of guilt and blame. What tale of twentieth-century queer life could escape it? Standing out from Norah's narrative and from Gwen's whole life is a sense of love, forgiveness and the desire to be forgiven. Today we can exonerate them, posthumously, from guilt about their sexuality, and celebrate their partnership in ways they would never have thought possible. It is up to the reader to decide whether to forgive Gwen and Norah for the way they treated each other.

Sources

There are four key sources that form the basis of this book. They are: the interviews Norah gave in 1976 to Derek Hunt and 1981 to Roger Wilmut; the respective personal archives of Norah (in the V&A Theatre & Performance Archive at Blythe House) and Gwen (held by family members), containing cuttings and photographs; and the vast and valuable resource that is the British Newspaper Archive online.

Then, there are four smaller collections that each throw light on a specific area of the story. Viscountess Muriel Lowther's unfinished typescript on the life of her father, Sir George Farrar (amongst family papers in the Bodleian Library, Oxford), provides a delicate and measured reflection on the childhood experience of the three eldest Farrar girls. From deep in the well-guarded Parisian archive of Natalie Clifford Barney (in the Bibliothèque Littéraire Jacques Doucet), the letters Dolly Wilde wrote in 1937–39 offer a one-sided but intriguing account of a peculiarly dysfunctional triangular relationship. The BBC Archive at Caversham contains contracts, internal memos and, in Norah's cursive hand, a number of surprisingly frank letters from the early 1950s. Finally, the letters Norah wrote to Derek Hunt from Denville Hall show all the contradictory elements that characterised her from the start.

A note about pronouns

I have used gender pronouns in the way that Gwen, Norah and their friends used them.

PART I
EARLY YEARS
1893–1917

Norah at the age of eleven months

~ 1 ~

THE CHAMPION BABY

Norah received her first rave reviews at the age of eleven months. If the journalists reporting on the 1894 Knightsbridge Baby Exhibition had been doting relatives of the winning child, they could not have described her in more loving detail. Only a royal baby could have occupied more column inches or attained greater nationwide coverage. Her 'abundant curly brown hair and big dark eyes and exceptionally nice manners' were proclaimed in the *Pall Mall Gazette* and syndicated across the land.

'The successful candidate was a Miss Norah Mignon Cordwell, who weighed 25lb. loz., and was born on the 16th of July, 1893,' one reporter announced, adding, 'I had the honour of an interview with her just when she had received news of her success.

'"Well, how old are you?" said I.

'"Gr-r-r," said she, laughing, "Mum-ma!"

'... Then she threw her biscuit at a bystander.'[1]

It is tempting to see in the infant Norah already that tension between the purposeful and the flippant which marked everything she did in life. Certainly she presented as a serious contender and despite the tongue-in-cheek style of the reporters, there was no doubting the impression she made.

'When Norah Mignon Cordwell, aged eleven months, at teatime on Saturday last was brought into the judging ring, all the other competitors looked very glum.'[2]

Norah was an only child. Her middle name, Mignon, meaning 'cute' in French, was also the title of an immensely popular opera of the 1870s.

The professional name she later adopted came from her maternal grandmother, Joyce Blaney, originally a domestic servant from Shropshire who married a labourer and had ten children. Their second daughter, Molly, was Norah's mother. A spirit of ambition and adventure drew Molly to London where, in her early twenties, she married Walter Cordwell, an insurance clerk. Walter had been brought up in a family of boys by his widowed mother. It was not a musical family, but a doctor recommended sickly Walter's lungs would benefit from regular practice on a wind instrument. By sixteen he had left school and was a dock clerk but he kept up the oboe and persevered with night-time practice. In his mid twenties, already married to Molly, he won a scholarship to the Royal College of Music. He became a professional bassoon player.

Molly looked after the small amounts of money Walter began to earn from orchestral playing. She kept house at 30 Godolphin Road, Hammersmith – a neat, new, terraced property in the fast expanding suburbs to the west of the capital – and took in other musicians as lodgers, cleaning their rooms and cooking for them. Norah's triumph at the Knightsbridge baby show confirmed Molly's faith in the importance of appearances and was an auspicious confirmation of the faith she had in the family's potential for success and respectability.

When Norah was six, the Cordwell family moved a short distance to 226 Hammersmith Grove, sharing the four-storey terraced house with another family, the Hammonds. There were no servants. Norah's father, Walter, continued to eke out a living as a musician, making and selling oboe reeds as a sideline.

Speaking in 1976, Norah's recollections of her childhood were very happy ones. Her father had a terrific sense of humour, blowing raspberries on the bassoon and entertaining her with the little jokey lyrics musicians made up to fit classical tunes. Her mother was firm but fun. Norah remembered her singing a song made famous by the music hall star Ellaline Terriss, whom she was said to resemble: 'Just a little bit of string, such a tiny little thing.' Her mother's sisters were doting and entertaining; Annie, the eldest, being a particular character, who lived with them for a while at number 226. With no siblings or cousins nearby, Norah's deep attachments and loyalties were all to adults. She developed a strong sense of duty, an eagerness to please and a commitment to their shared aspirations for her. Norah became precociously proficient on the piano. In her own words, she was:

> a small, dark haired, dark eyed little girl with a pony tail down her back sitting at the piano, beating her tiny fingers on the keys. Most of my time was spent at the piano, not always as a willing student.[3]

There were local excitements. In 1900 the Prince of Wales, soon to be Edward VII, opened Shepherd's Bush station, inaugurating the Central London Railway, offering a direct route underground into the heart of the capital. The following year the solemnity of London's crowds at Queen Victoria's funeral marked the end of an era. It is likely Norah was taken to watch the procession. She was always deeply impressed by royalty and aristocracy.

The Cordwells had little cash to spare but Walter was well connected in the music business. A cellist friend was a member of Henry Wood's Orchestra at the Queen's Hall where the Promenade Concerts were a regular summer fixture. As a perk he had two season tickets which he gave Molly. Norah recalls that she and her mother went every night of the week, except Monday, which was Wagner night. Her mother didn't like Wagner.

For her sixth birthday in July 1899 Norah was taken up to the gallery of the Royal Opera House, for a shilling, to see Nellie Melba sing Mimì in Puccini's new hit opera, *La Bohème*. She cried at the beauty of the singing, but remained unconvinced that the portly Miss Melba was ideal casting as the consumptive heroine.

Another artist who made an impression on Norah was Yvette Guilbert, whom she was taken to see when she was ten.

Dressed in her signature bright yellow dress with long black gloves, Guilbert was an expert on French folk songs. Norah never forgot her intense delivery of the grimly melodramatic '*Mon père m'a mariée á un bossu*', in which a young woman, forced into an arranged marriage, takes the law into her own hands. Norah could still impersonate this intense performance with great conviction well into her eighties.

All her life Norah was generous in her praise for women artists, finding pleasure in their performances and, with the exception of Melba as Mimì, appreciating the way they looked.

The Bradford-born star Gertie Millar, reigning queen of Edwardian theatre, dazzled Norah at the Gaiety on Aldwych in 1902, in one of a run of 'girl'-themed musicals, *The Country Girl*. Her influence on Norah's repertoire and performance style was to be huge. 'She was so lovely,' Norah later recalled, with feeling, 'she remained my goddess for a long, long time.'[4]

Of the pianist Irene Scharrer, Norah said, 'I looked upon her with rapture because I thought she was so pretty to look at and I loved her playing. She was very brilliant, glamorous and exciting, looked lovely. I used to watch her and Myra Hess thinking how wonderful they were. To me, they were goddesses.'

Margaret Cooper was another of Norah's role models. Born in Peckham, the daughter of a baker, Cooper attended the Royal Academy of Music, before her lucky break came and she was picked to perform her 'songs at the piano' at the Palace Theatre. She was an instant and overwhelming success.

At just the same time – May 1906 – twelve-year-old Norah sat for a piano scholarship at the Royal Academy. Her hands could scarcely have been large enough to achieve the big stretches demanded by the repertoire. Four hundred contestants applied for this valuable, four-year endowment. 'And I thought, "I'm going to win it!"'[5] she later recalled.

The distinguished Polish pianist Jan Paderewski was one of the examiners and he presented Norah with a signed photograph and warm congratulations when her confident prediction came true and she won first place.

Her teacher was the German *émigré* Oscar Beringer. His *Daily Technical Studies for Piano* is still sold in paperback. A glance inside at the repeated phrases, with minutely detailed modulations, shows just how demanding and repetitive Norah's studies must have been. She was absolutely determined to make the most of the opportunity she had won for herself and she flourished on hard work in the warm but disciplined environment Molly and Walter provided for their beloved only child.

Oscar Beringer had been a pupil of Clara Schumann who, throughout her sixty-one-year career on the concert platform, always played from memory. Norah was proud of her link to this legacy and, as well as working at her technique, she strove to learn all the pieces she played by heart. At one time she could play eleven concerti from memory.

Like Clara Schumann, Norah showed very early promise in composition. She wrote her own words and music for a charming, witty song, 'Are You There, Mr Bear?', which she sent to Chappell's Music Publishers. She was overcome with delight when it was published and her idol Margaret Cooper made it part of her repertoire:

> She sought me out and got to know me and she was kind to me and sweet. She was a beautiful pianist and she became a sort of doyenne to me because she used to say, 'Norah, I think you will take my place when I'm gone.'[6]

On Monday 15 February 1909, Norah performed at a concert by RAM students in the prestigious Queen's Hall, then home of the Proms,[7] playing the piano part in the Andante and Finale from Brahms' Piano Quartet in G Minor.

As Norah was still only seventeen, Beringer recommended that she now compete for an open scholarship to the Royal College of Music, the 'rival firm' as Norah put it. She won the scholarship, beating into second place a woman who would go on to have a brilliant career as a concert pianist (and become a friend for life), Kathleen Long.

At the Royal College, one of its founding professors, Sir Charles Stanford, recognised Norah's gift for composition and arranged for her to set some Shakespeare lyrics to music for his former pupil, the actress Phyllis Neilson-Terry. Norah enjoyed what she called her 'collaboration with the Bard' and especially remembered finding Terry 'very lovely to look at'.[8]

While so many ladies looked lovely to her, Norah seemed oblivious to young men. Years later, the famous organist and composer George Thalben-Ball stopped her in the street to say how much he had been in awe of her talent when they were students together, but Norah was embarrassed to find she could not remember him at all.[9]

Norah onstage in Margate in 1914

~ 2 ~

ONE PER CENT TALENT, NINE PER CENT LUCK AND NINETY PER CENT HARD WORK[1]

In 1911, Molly and Walter Cordwell, now more financially secure, moved across the Thames to their own smart semi-detached house on a new development in Lonsdale Road, Barnes. At number 65 they were able to give Norah a beautiful, spacious bedroom, overlooking the long garden, with views of orchards beyond.

Walter proudly took his daughter along to parties and rehearsals so she could observe and learn from the finest conductors and soloists. When a keyboard player failed to materialise at a Sunday morning rehearsal of Tchaikovsky's 'Nutcracker Suite' in the Royal Albert Hall, Norah saved the day by stepping in to play the 'Dance of the Sugar Plum Fairy' on the celeste, under the baton of respected pianist and conductor Landon Ronald.

Walter and his bassoon were also regular guests at the musical salon held in a studio at 19a Edith Grove, Chelsea, at the home of the inspiring American salonnière, Muriel Draper, and her husband Paul. In attendance were the greatest classical musicians of the day: cellist Pablo Casals, violinist Jacques Thibaud, pianists Arthur Rubinstein, Benno Moiseiwitsch and Myra Hess. Paul Draper was the brother of the monologist Ruth Draper, whose self-penned solo shows were to influence some of the twentieth century's greatest actors. In these early days, if Paul Draper announced his sister would do a recitation, some of the audience were indignant at the idea that an act by a relation was being imposed on them, interrupting the music they had come to hear. But, as Rubinstein recalled, as soon as Ruth Draper had finished one of her mesmerising character studies, the entire room, 'enchanted and excited, shouted... bravos and praises'.[2] Norah thought she was marvellous.

There were other comedy moments. Myra Hess would play a Beethoven Sonata with great seriousness and authority, then promptly put an orange on the keyboard and play 'God Save the King' by moving it around with her nose.

On another evening at Edith Grove, Norah was struck by rising star Benno Moiseiwitsch's exquisite performance of a piano suite by Debussy. They got into conversation afterwards about their studies, comparing notes about their teachers, and sharing their frustration that they weren't allowed to play jazz.

Despite this early sign that she was tempted by music outside the classical repertoire, an event occurred at the salon which stood out as the absolute highlight for the rest of Norah's life. The room was so full on this occasion that Norah was sitting on the floor. Guests sat spellbound while the Spanish cellist Pablo Casals played the unaccompanied Bach suites that had been his life's study. Described as the greatest cellist there has ever been, Casals had played for Queen Victoria and Theodore Roosevelt. Here he was, at close quarters, playing with complete mastery and superb artistry, while coolly smoking a cigar. Perhaps this was the moment when Norah made a spiritual connection with the cello; the long, sonorous body of the instrument, resonating at the same familiar pitch as her father's bassoon, the vibrations coming straight through the floorboards from Casals' bow, and the sight of dextrous hands on the fingerboard, stretching up towards the bridge. All these sensations combined with the earthy aroma of the cigar which so nonchalantly rested between the great man's lips. Something extraordinary happened next.

Casals finished playing and asked his host, in broken English, who was the girl sitting at his feet.

'That's our bassoon player's daughter,' Paul Draper replied. 'She's a piano student.' Then, to Norah's complete astonishment, the great Casals asked if she would like to play. He and violinist Jacques Thibaud wanted to run through the Beethoven Piano Trio in B-Flat Major and their regular collaborator, Alfred Cortot, was absent. Draper found the sheet music and the three of them began to play. For Norah it was a glorious forty minutes of ensemble playing, with two of the world's greatest musicians, in front of an attentive audience of appreciative experts and her father, looking on with pride.

At the end, Casals declared that she had a great deal of talent and congratulated Norah on her marvellous sight reading. She didn't let on that she knew the piece backwards, having played it dozens of times at the College.

'Everybody has a high spot,' declared Norah seventy years later. 'And that was mine.'[3]

In just one night Norah had surpassed her wildest dreams as a classical artist. But, rather than consolidate her determination to be a professional pianist, there is plenty of evidence to suggest that at this point she turned her attention to acting and singing. She was astonishingly versatile. Not many concert pianists are also blessed with acting skills, comic timing, great diction and the ability to sing and dance.

What Walter and Molly thought, we do not know, but since Norah was prepared to continue her piano studies alongside her new career, perhaps they were content to wait and see where it would all lead. Soon Norah was moonlighting from the Royal College. At Christmas 1910 she made her professional acting debut at the Court Theatre (now the Royal Court) as Bo Peep in *Little Boy Bluebeard; Or The Boy Who Couldn't Grow Down*.[4]

In Norah's first recorded provincial performance she appeared at the Buxton Opera House in September 1911 as Princess Alice in *The Dollar Princess*.

In February 1912 Norah was at a special event at Chaloner Hall, Guisborough, to celebrate Mrs Hunt, Pioneer of the Ladies' Orchestras, which made professional performing careers for women a reality. Norah played her own compositions, 'Variations in F Sharp Minor' and 'Mister Bear'. While the song survives and is still in print, the Variations have been lost. The *Yorkshire Post* reported the next day, 'Miss Blaney unquestionably possesses gifts. Her sense of humour is so marked that it is not difficult to imagine her making a great "hit". But the best feature of all is her appreciation of what is poetic in music.'[5]

Norah's professional career was a testament to her belief in women's rights, but she stopped short of militant activity. When ninety-six women were arrested in London for smashing windows and causing damage on 4 March 1912, Norah was very likely playing the dutiful daughter at home. Being an only child brought with it special expectations of conformity and good behaviour. She was politically conservative and self-interested enough to choose her battles with care, fighting only the ones that were the most urgent and personal to her.

One good cause she worked for was the National Sunday League, which made quality music available to working people through low-priced concerts. In early 1912 Norah took part in concerts at the King's Theatre, Hammersmith, and the Croydon Empire (now both demolished).

She was engaged by the conductor of a certain provincial symphony orchestra to play a different piano concerto every night for a week. Her fee was the not-so-princely sum of nine shillings. She spoke warmly of the man. He had spotted her playing in student concerts and given her encouragement and opportunities. She was less impressed when, just before a concert, he exposed himself to her in the dressing room. 'It was like an aubergine!' she said. 'All I could think of, looking at him on the podium, was an aubergine.' Forever after that, she was inclined to refer to a man's penis as his 'nasty'.[6]

She spent the 1913 summer season at the Southwold Assembly Rooms, Suffolk, in the Royal Pierrots Concert Party led by famous banjo maker and ukulele performer, Clifford Essex. The Royal Pierrots were every bit as distinguished as the name suggests. Twenty years earlier, in 1891, Essex had introduced a French-style Pierrot show to Henley Regatta. The concept had been an immediate hit, quickly gaining the patronage of the then Prince of Wales (later Edward VII). By 1913 every seaside resort had its own troupe of white-faced, clown-like musical comedy artistes.

However much Norah's parents disapproved of her dalliance with popular culture, they must have been consoled to see she was working with and learning from the very best in the business.

Astonishingly, throughout this time, she was still enrolled at the Royal College, and not slacking at all. She won both the Challen Gold Medal and the Hopkinson Silver Medal for piano playing in 1913. With the money from these prizes and her performance earnings Norah was able to spend a term at the Paris Conservatoire.

There a wealthy sculptor took Norah under her wing, making sure her protegée was welcome at her salon when Rachmaninov played and the conductor Toscanini turned up with musicians dressed, bizarrely, as babies. Norah recalls the freedom of Paris and her excitement at being made to feel so welcome.[7] Her benefactress may have been Misia Sert, who later had an affair with Coco Chanel. Another candidate is Winnaretta Singer, Princesse de Polignac, a lesbian and salonnière like her great rival, the legendary Natalie Clifford Barney. (There is no evidence Norah moved in Barney's literary circles, though she was certainly a keen observer in their musical equivalent.)

Norah came home with new French pieces in her repertoire. On 11 February 1914 *Era* magazine noted, 'Two piano solos by Debussy were capitally performed by Miss Norah Cordwell. She played with great brilliancy and had some very hearty recalls from the audience.'[8]

Norah officially left the Royal College of Music on 1 April 1914, the proud recipient of the Dannreuther Prize, awarded to her by Sir Hubert Parry, who said in his address:

> We shall miss Miss Norah Cordwell, who occupied the
> interesting position, rare so far, of being the scholar
> daughter of a former scholar. We often have had occasion
> to delight in the sensitiveness and the poetry, and
> the charming interpretative gifts she displayed in her

pianoforte playing and we hope she will find plenty of opportunities to afford to intelligent people outside the College the same pleasure she has afforded us.[9]

Did he know she was dashing off that very night to do a turn at the Margate Pavilion? His reference to 'intelligent people' may have been a snobbish rebuke.

Stanley Kirkby, a well-known and highly accomplished baritone, led the Margate troupe. He was a neighbour of the Cordwells in Barnes so very likely knew Norah and had hired her. Clifford Grey, the group's chief comic turn, collaborated with Norah on a song, 'Mabel's Pigtail', sung from the point of view of a little girl who misses the fun of romping with her big sister, when she starts taking an interest in men. Norah's delivery on a recording, decades later, was all coy campness, evoking gales of laughter in her listeners.

When Norah celebrated her twenty-first birthday in Margate on 16 July 1914, the world was in limbo, halfway between the assassination of Archduke Franz Ferdinand and Britain's declaration of war on Germany. It was an atmosphere of uncertainty mixed with jingoistic fervour, echoed at holiday resorts around the coast, and later satirised so effectively in

Margate Concert Party 1914 (L to R): Stanley Kirkby, Clifford Grey, Norah Blaney, Albert Lyne (behind), Fred Wildon, Louise Trimble

the musical *Oh, What a Lovely War!* The photograph of the 1914 concert party makes a feature of Norah. Kirkby and Essex stand to her right; Albert Lyne, the other pianist, to her left. There is something about the proximity of novelty violinist Fred Wildon to Norah in this photograph which suggests an enforced intimacy. Norah's nervous gesture, touching her right ear with her hand, betrays an unease that is absent in her later publicity shots.

Norah and Lyne were the youngsters of the group. He was twenty-five and the youngest son of a large working-class family from London. He had received his early musical training with The Band of Hope[10] and spent previous summer seasons at the Olympian Gardens, Bognor, building a reputation as an excellent accompanist, noted for his 'perfect playing'.[11]

They became friends and allies during this blighted summer season and, when it was over, on Wednesday 7 October 1914, Albert Charles Lyne and Norah Mignon Cordwell were married in Margate Register Office. None of their parents were present; indeed the registrar drafted in one of his own relatives to act as a witness.

Norah never spoke publicly about this marriage. Even those who got to know her well much later in life had no idea that she had once been Mrs Albert Lyne. Fred Wildon was a name Derek Hunt heard mentioned in connection with some emotional upset for Norah in this period, but not Lyne. It remains a mystery how this relationship came about, except that Norah was away from the protective embrace of her parents for the first sustained period and war had just been declared. However, this was not, as one might assume, a case of love-struck youngsters getting hitched to enjoy a night of passionate consummation, on the eve of his departure for the Front. From the evidence of newspaper listings we can see that Albert continued his performing career in the UK for another two years, but, notably, separately from Norah.

It seems they initially moved in together to a flat at 5 Digby Mansions, Hammersmith – a large, smart block, right next to Hammersmith Bridge, overlooking the Thames. They had room for a piano, but probably not two. Apart from having to take turns at practising, there were the neighbours to consider. The flat was on the end of the building, so the piano was placed against the outside wall. Daily work was so ingrained in Norah that she would still spend hours at the piano each day, either at the flat or at her parents' house, a short walk away in Lonsdale Road. She was determined to continue to build on her training and make an independent living.

German music was banned from concert programmes. London's Bechstein Hall was forced to rebrand as the Wigmore. Norah was due to give a concert there, consisting of music by Beethoven and Brahms, but it had to be cancelled. So, instead, over the winter she focused on playing Rachmaninov, Saint-Saëns and Grieg, as well as developing what she called her 'silly little songs at the piano'.

Easily, she could have taken a back seat and retired from work altogether. Marriage was the perfect excuse. It was also, potentially, a trap. When her contemporary, Dora Labbette,[12] a prize-winning scholar at the Guildhall School of Music, had married a handsome captain in the Royal Engineers and had a daughter, he insisted she abandon her career. A familiar story. For all the millions of women who submitted to this treatment, Dora was a rare individual who defied convention when she packed her things in a handcart, walked out of the house and left her husband with the child.

Would Norah have had the single-minded determination to take such a step in the same circumstances? She was not going to get herself into a position where she needed to find out. At some point in her life Norah had an abortion and this may be when it occurred. Her heterosexual encounters after this time are practically non-existent so it is tempting to locate the event in this youthful period of sexual naivety. Perhaps this putative pregnancy was the result of an encounter with Fred Wildon. Or maybe Albert would have been the father. All we know is that Norah took a short break from performing, then threw herself into an intense period of rehearsals in the winter of 1914 as she prepared to take her career to a new level.

In the spring of 1915 Albert went on a tour of northern provincial venues in a show called *Mind Your Own Business.* Meanwhile, in what was theatrically her most exciting career development to date, on 15 March Norah made her debut at the newly built Victoria Palace Theatre, London, with her 'Songs at the Piano'.

In the summer, Norah was a fixture at Devonshire Park, Eastbourne, while Albert returned to his regular audiences at the Olympian Gardens, Bognor. It seems curious that these newlyweds, both in demand as versatile performers, could not have contrived to work together as they had at Margate, or at least in closer geographical proximity.

Norah's intensive rehearsing paid off and, on 30 June, the *Eastbourne Gazette* praised 'the virile and resolute brilliancy of her style'[13] in the fiendishly difficult Concerto in G Minor by Saint-Saëns.

By contrast, Albert spent the remainder of 1915 touring the UK as accompanist to juvenile singing sensation Stella Carol. Her repertoire of florid, light operatic soprano pieces, with undemanding piano parts, would become, perhaps, rather grating and repetitive to Albert. But life could be worse, far worse; his contemporaries were being killed in their thousands on the battlefields of France and Belgium.

Along with over half the eligible male population, Albert had chosen not to volunteer. If the Government was going to bring in conscription, unmarried men would be called up first, so he was not likely to be summoned immediately. However, as the war progressed, and the casualty numbers soared, men of fighting age performing onstage were becoming the targets of scorn. It was not uncommon for them to be taunted by young women with white feathers as a symbol of their perceived cowardice. The West End star Basil Hallam was targeted most cruelly in this way until he joined up against doctor's orders.

Certainly Albert felt the growing pressure to enlist and no amount of charity performances to entertain the troops could disguise the fact that he was not in uniform.

By December 1915 Norah's reputation as a musical comedy

performer had earned her the role of the Princess of Hearts – opposite male impersonator Winifred Ward as Jack Horner – in the Christmas pantomime at the huge Marlborough Theatre, Islington. In the show, Ward, dressed as a Tommy in a kilt, sang a love duet with Norah, 'Same Sort of Girl, Same Sort of Boy'. This was a rare chance for Norah to act a role, as opposed to appearing as herself, and it was a thrilling initiation into panto's queer cross-dressing possibilities.

Meanwhile Albert was performing twice nightly in Wolverhampton. He and Norah were destined to spend Christmas apart. To Albert's delight, *The Follies Are Here* was booked to play at the London Coliseum at the end of January, marking, at last, his debut in the West End. His parents, Eddie and Martha, travelled in from Willesden to see him onstage, but even if she had wanted to, Norah could not attend Albert's first night. She was topping the bill at the Pleasure Gardens, Folkestone.

Meanwhile, the pioneering activist and theatre artist, Lena Ashwell, had succeeded in persuading the War Office to allow her to organise concert parties in France to provide some entertainment for war-weary troops. Performers needed to be personally recommended to Miss Ashwell and have impeccable reputations. Norah evidently fitted the bill perfectly. Her parents, Molly and Walter, waved her off with mixed emotions as she set off for France in April 1916. Who would have imagined that she would be the first of the six members of the 1914 Margate Concert Party to leave for the Front?

In January 1916 the British Government introduced conscription for single men aged eighteen to forty-one. To further keep pace with the mounting casualties, within a few months they extended this to include men who were married. Albert volunteered before the conscription papers arrived, knowing the call-up was inevitable. In what spirit of dread did he enlist? He would have known, from word of mouth and casualty lists, far more of the realities ahead than had the eager recruits of 1914.

Albert joined the London Scottish Regiment, whose

recruiting station was in the West End. Several actors and aspiring performers had already signed up, along with a very high proportion of white-collar city workers: clerks and bankers. His training commenced in Winchester in June. For six months he would still be based in England, with the odd leave and the chance to see Norah, but there are no records or mentions of such meetings.

Meanwhile, Norah toured Ripon, Darlington and Hornsea to great acclaim:

> Her dainty, vivacious, finished, and expressive style, and
> her accomplishments both as player and singer, did not fail
> to evoke very emphatic appreciation. On Saturday evening
> Miss Blaney was recalled again and again.[14]

There was nothing of the conceited diva about Norah. Seven years of conservatoire training might have taught her to refuse to play an inferior piano, or made her snobbish about unsophisticated audiences, but this was far from the case.

Her three weeks in April with the Lena Ashwell Concert Party in France had proved she could be resilient and adaptable. She recalled one particular story about this trip:

> At one camp we had to sing out in a field, while the men
> in their steel helmets sat all round. The piano was a very
> ancient relic with no top to it and I had to transpose the
> key with my left hand to make it tune with my right.[15]

In the midst of one of her songs, the rain came down. 'It began in a little drizzle, and soon developed into a downpour, but not a soldier moved.'[16]

It was Norah's first experience of singing in the pouring rain but, she thought, 'The soldiers don't mind it, so why should I?' And though they were all wet through at the finish, she thought that concert went off as well as any they gave. It was at the close of this concert that the woman driver of their car handed Norah a little leaden ring made from shrapnel and a bit of bullet. She told Norah that one of the soldiers had brought it up saying: 'Will you give that to the comic lady? Ask her to wear it from me.' He said the ring had been his mascot, but he wanted Norah to keep it because, as he put it, 'He hadn't had such a good laugh since before the war!'[17]

Norah built rapport very quickly with her audiences and she knew how to tease the officers sitting near the front to raise laughs from the lower ranks at the rear. One lieutenant wrote about her in a letter home:

> A most versatile... girl entertaining at the piano and making all sorts of people on the front row uncomfortable by making remarks during the pauses in her song. Such as 'Dear Bright Eyes' to some solid Hindenburg-Liner of last week. Miss Norah pulled my leg too... and one fellow said he would prefer to be shelled with 5.9s any day than go through the ordeal.[18]

Norah's experience enabled her to judge these situations well, to read audience responses and adjust accordingly. She was sensitive when visiting hospitals:

> Singing in the wards is quite the most difficult part of the whole tour. You get such a choky feeling in your throat: the last thing you want to do is to sit down at the piano and bang out some noisy ragtime. You just have to pull yourself together or it is all up with you.[19]

At one of many performances Norah gave for wounded soldiers, an onlooker noted:

> Miss Blaney sang with such wit, piquancy and charm, that after her first appearance, it seemed that she would be compelled to monopolise the programme; while on her second appearance she made her audience sing with a vigour that would have been remarkable anywhere. In a hospital it was wonderful.[20]

Norah was very flattered when a doctor praised her morale-boosting work:

> You're doing wonderful work. It is just as necessary for the men to be cheered up as it is for them to be nursed. A good concert takes them out of themselves, makes them forget their own troubles. Always remember that, Miss Blaney.[21]

~ 3 ~

THOSE MADDENING BITS WE COULD NOT REMEMBER

While Norah was growing up as a Cordwell in lower middle-class suburban London, two and a half thousand miles away in Johannesburg the daughters of Sir George Farrar were enjoying the fruits of their father's millions. George had started life with something in common with Walter Cordwell. He, too, was the son of a hard-working mother single-handedly raising boys: Helen Farrar, whose widow's weeds disguised the fact she was (at her own instigation) a divorcée.

George and his three brothers were brought up as the poor relations of their mother's siblings, the Howards of Bedford. After Bedford Modern School he entered his uncles' engineering firm and, aged twenty-one in 1880, was sent to look after their interests in the new minefields of South Africa. He was optimistic, athletic, hardworking, and adventurous. Before long, on a hunch, he struck gold. Literally. Then, on an ocean voyage, he met beautiful and vivacious Ella Waylen, travelling with her newly married sister. Ella's childhood had also been disrupted by divorce, with parenting in the sole hands of a resourceful, determined mother, ambitious for her children. George and Ella married and set up home in a relatively luxurious tin bungalow in Johannesburg. A girl was born, whom they called Helen, after George's mother.

But their idyllic family life was about to be shaken to its core. In 1896, when Ella was pregnant with their second child,

Gwen as a small child

Muriel, George was imprisoned, then sentenced to death, by South Africa's harshest judge. His crime was joining the Jameson Raid, a badly thought-through rebellion against the Boers. His sentence was commuted to a fine and he was released, but Ella never felt at home in South Africa after that. She and her daughters travelled endlessly backwards and forwards across the Atlantic, until 'they knew nearly every ship and every captain on the Union Castle Line'.[1]

In London on Wednesday 14 July 1897, Ella gave birth to the couple's third daughter. Gwen[2] was born in a large rented apartment just off Park Lane, in the West End,[3] right in the middle of what would become her world.[4] To the east were the theatres she would play: the Duke of York's, the Savoy, the Vaudeville (resplendent with new electric lighting by 1897). To the south, across the eastern edge of Hyde Park, lay the wealthy, artistic Royal Borough of Kensington and Chelsea, where she eventually would make her home.

But in 1900 the Farrars acquired the tenancy of a stately home in the countryside, ten miles from George's birthplace at Bedford. Chicheley Hall is an eighteenth-century red brick mansion tucked away in eighty acres of parkland. To this day it still has its stable block (now converted), woods, lake, parish church and graveyard.

Very early on, Helen, Muriel and Gwen were expected to entertain their mother's guests. A large budget was available to ensure the three girls were decorative, well mannered and accomplished, a credit to their parents. Nannies, French maids, grooms, footmen, ponies and music teachers were engaged, allowing George and Ella time for their own projects, not least the overdue task of producing a son.

Hopes must have been high in 1901 when Ella was expecting a fourth child.

When the census enumerator arrived at Chicheley Hall on 1 April, he noted, 'Father and Mother away from home temporarily,' and went on to record the ages of the three girls – Helen, six, Muriel, four, and Gwendoline, three – and the particulars of no less than twenty-two servants. This was not unusual. The Farrar children were apart from their parents more often than not.

When another baby girl (Marjorie) was added to their ranks in August, Nanny Elsden, awe-inspiring in starched white uniform, joined the staff to work alongside the governess, Miss Berry. These women uneasily shared responsibility for the girls' welfare, rarely agreeing with each other. Muriel, in her unpublished memoir, reported that they never had a day off, which can hardly have helped. Nanny Elsden doted on baby Marjorie to the exclusion of the older girls, making the new arrival unpopular with her siblings. Helen, Muriel and Gwen became a close-knit trio after this, often in trouble and unsure whose rules they should observe: those of the nursery, or the schoolroom, or their skittish mother, who might suddenly indulge them with her company or whisk them away to be shown off to her friends. While the children sometimes reacted badly to this inconsistent adult behaviour, there were certain treats and opportunities they never took for granted. Muriel recalls:

> If the three of us were taken to a musical entertainment, we went to bed like the three bears in identical beds and would not go to sleep until, between us, we had pieced together the whole of the show we had seen.
>
> If there were any gaps we could not fill in, we pestered our mother to take us again, because we simply could not go to sleep until those maddening bits we could not remember had been filled in.
>
> We played musical games in bed, eternally thumped out tunes with our hands on our up-raised knees for the other two to guess. If the three of us heard a new tune for the first time, when we went to bed we could piece it together like a crossword puzzle.[5]

Miss Berry, the governess, was a good pianist. The girls did not have a great deal of respect for her teaching, but she was appreciated for her ability to play piano accompaniments. Employed by the family for more than twenty years, she clearly had a significant influence on the girls' musical education. Early on, Helen and Muriel took up the piano and the violin. Gwen was a reluctant piano pupil and rejected the violin in favour of the cello, chiefly because she could play it sitting down.

The Farrar family could soon make its own music and, since Miss Berry travelled with them between England and South Africa, there were opportunities to perform and watch performances, especially on board ship. These ocean voyages put Gwen in touch with a wider range of people than usual and gave her an early taste for popular entertainment – not an outcome her parents and governess had in mind.

They shuttled between Bedford and Johannesburg, stopping just long enough to get settled before their mother's whims, or political upheavals in South Africa, necessitated another month-long journey in the opposite direction.

Fortunately, these voyages, in the heyday of the ocean liner, were marvellous adventures, full of on-board entertainment and excitement. Gwen and her sisters would slip away from Miss Berry and Nanny Elsden and explore the whole ship. There were frequent trips to the butcher's and the dairy, below decks, to see the Farrars' unfortunate cow (brought on board to ensure the family had fresh cream daily). In another part of the ship, on one trip, they met a cowboy who taught them to lasso. For the three-week duration of another voyage, they were best friends with The Lazy Juggler. He began his act expertly, then made everyone laugh by losing interest and letting china plates smash all round him.

From an early age, Gwen was ready to perform at the ship's concert – either a recitation or a tableau with her sisters or, later on, a cello piece. Their mother sang, and on one voyage was accompanied by the composer Arthur Somervell in a fast-paced rendition of his famous song, 'Come into the Garden, Maud', which made the girls giggle with embarrassment.

In her nephew's possession is a blurred, over-exposed, scratchy photograph, kept by Gwen all her life, showing small girls in knee-length white dresses with parasols. They are on a makeshift stage, on deck, on a hot day. A large Union Jack is flying. A pale, dark-haired woman, in a white apron and nurse's cap, perhaps Nanny Elsden, looks on severely. Miss Berry, the governess, is out of camera shot. Perhaps she is playing the piano. The children are observed respectfully and curiously by a large audience of men, mostly in flat caps, one in a chef's hat, another with a handkerchief knotted at each corner to shade his baldness. The flat space at the stern of the ship makes a natural stage, with passengers on the decks above sitting or standing behind railings to observe the performance. Some have even climbed the mast for a better view. Crew members and passengers mingle together in a surprisingly democratic, informal gathering.

Muriel says this spirit of camaraderie on board was intoxicating but ephemeral:

> During the last few days of the voyage the temperature
> changed. People began to draw apart. They became
> different and when the ship docked and they went on
> their way, with a curt goodbye, they were quite different
> to the people we had known on the voyage. To us it was
> disillusionment with a big D. The Lazy Juggler had been our
> bosom friend but he hardly bothered to say goodbye and
> we never saw him again. We also walked down the gangway
> into another world.[6]

From Cape Town to Johannesburg the family travelled in a special coach attached to the back of the train, with its own kitchen, saloon, sleeping berths and an observation car on the back. The journey took three days, crossing the Cape flats and the Karoo desert. Occasionally they stopped to get out and stretch their legs. On one of these breaks they accidentally left Helen in the desert and had to delay everyone on board by reversing the train to go back for her.

They would stay for a while in Johannesburg, but, because it was six thousand feet above sea level, it was not considered a healthy place for the children to be for more than six months at a time. They were supposed to become irritable and highly strung. This was a supposition the girls were more than happy to live up to. So then they would move again.

During the Second Boer War, to be safe from the fighting, they took a house near Cape Town, called Trovato. It was a brand new mansion, designed by Herbert Baker, and is now a South African National Monument. The children loved the Cape: the sea and the mountains, the bright light and the deep shadows, the silver trees, the leaves as soft and silky as rabbits' ears.

Then one evening their father gave them each a red leather prayer book with their initials stamped in gold across the corner. With the prayer book he gave them a list of hymns they were to learn while he was away. They knelt down beside their beds with him and prayed that he would come back safely. The next day, off he went to the war.

Trovato became a base for wounded officers sent away from the action to recuperate. Remarkably, the wealthy ones were visited by parents and families from England, and Muriel recalls the atmosphere being very sociable and fun. Her mother attracted the attention of admirers: Colonel Pole-Carew taught her to stand up on her saddle like a circus rider and Lord Basil Blackwood wrote her love poems.

At Trovato the girls were close enough to the coast to visit the seaside resort of Muizenberg. For twenty miles they could ride their horses along the beaches to the other side of the bay with nothing except the surf, the sand and the blue of the distant mountains.

The distinguished author Rudyard Kipling regularly enjoyed the summer here with his wife Caroline and small children, Elsie and John. Kipling was at the height of his fame having published *The Jungle Book* in 1894.

Muriel remembers:

> We were slightly in awe of Mr Kipling. He wore spectacles
> resting on the end of his nose and he had beetling
> eyebrows and a bristling moustache. He used to make us
> sit in a circle on the grass and he sat cross-legged in the
> middle, but he never told us stories from *The Jungle Book*.
> Week after week, he assembled us and said, 'I will teach
> you a password which you must never teach to anyone else

and which you must always remember. No one except Elsie and John and you three children will ever know. It will be your secret code for ever and ever.' And so we sat and laboriously learnt the six words until we were word perfect: Spitzborken, Herborken, Vongrinefaifle, Gobblegoonstadt, Kocksitzen, Kickenveldt, Whiteedorf. This is not the full interpretation because you have to whistle, in one word, click your tongue on another and snort through your nose on the last one. It was extremely difficult to accomplish but all these years have gone past and I have never forgotten it. But it took us ages to learn them perfectly.

We snorted, we whistled and clicked with our tongues. We took it all very seriously. There was nothing light hearted about our lesson. We went on and on until Mr Kipling was satisfied that we had mastered the click, the whistle and the snort in the right places with exactly the right innuendo.

All through these lessons he sat cross-legged, glaring at us through his spectacles, unsmiling and dead serious.

I never remember him smiling. It was Mrs Kipling who came to say that tea was ready and, with a smile and a flurry, broke up our tense circle.[7]

By 1902, George Farrar was a war hero. He had received the Distinguished Service Order for his action against the Boers and he was now engaged in the creation of a new United South Africa as the leader of the Progressive Party of the Cape Colony. As an engineer and an agricultural land owner he was demonstrating his faith in the future possibilities of South Africa, unlike some of his fellow mineral magnates, who were only too happy to take their riches and return to England to enjoy the profits there. His vision, deeply colonial in its outlook, nevertheless stood in principled opposition to Afrikaner nationalism and the forces that would later cling to statutory apartheid.

George's military honour was shortly followed with a knighthood from the King. Lady Farrar, delighting in her new title, became a society hostess par excellence. Although she had vowed never to settle there, it was in South Africa that she particularly shone as a socialite.

On land Sir George already owned just outside Johannesburg he commissioned Herbert Baker to design a magnificent house. Lady Ella altered the original plans to make it even more grand – a place to entertain, rather than a family home. It was a copy of an old Dutch house with white gables, a terracotta tiled roof and a pillared stoep or veranda. It was known as Bedford Farm, later Bedford Court – and it still stands today, in grounds much reduced, in the Johannesburg suburb of Bedfordview, to which it gave its name, not far from O.R. Tambo Airport. It has been a girls' boarding school ever since the Farrars left.

Ella was determined to be an asset to Sir George's career. She delighted in planning parties, sitting on committees and knowing everyone's names. At one election she paraded the girls up and down on their ponies outside polling stations with large banners bearing the slogan, 'Vote for Daddy'. She had a very shrewd judgement of character and Sir George had great respect for her opinion.

He also had a great sense of loyalty to his family. He wrote every week to his mother back home in the original Bedford and he kept in close touch with the older brothers, Sidney and Percy, who were managing the family business in London. He made an effort to spend time with his daughters and (unlike their mother) never expressed any disappointment in front of them at not having a son.

He had energy, vitality and good health and kept himself exceptionally fit with regular exercise. He taught the girls to ride, swim and play tennis. It was part of his weekend's enjoyment to 'train them to be athletes'.[8]

In both countries the girls had ponies to ride and their own groom, Mr Pringle, who travelled back and forth between countries with his wife. In his watchful care they could trek for miles on their ponies and enjoy the glorious South African countryside. Muriel said she, Helen and Gwen sometimes wished they could live with the Pringles in their little house rather than submit to the regime of the nursery and the schoolroom.

It was, of course, not uncommon for women in Lady Farrar's

position to remain at arm's length from their children. She enjoyed the girls as accessories to her brilliant, blossoming social life. She had them dressed exactly alike and treated them alike and never referred to them singly but as 'the children'. Helen, Muriel and Gwen called themselves 'The Three Bears'. They were never singled out for individual attention – everything they did, they did together. They slept in the same room in identical beds, all in a row. They got up and went to bed at the same time, they did their lessons, rode and played together and were never separated.

The only exception to this was if one of them had done something wrong and was sent to bed early. This was the usual punishment and it varied from half an hour to an hour, to fit the crime. It was a punishment they hated. It meant isolation from the others and a miserable time tossing and turning, unable to sleep. If they remonstrated with their governess and maintained their innocence, claiming they hadn't got into trouble on purpose, Miss Berry's reply, 'Everyone is born in sin,' made them wonder what was the point of even trying to be good.

Serious talks from their father, patient and calm, were much more effective deterrents than any of the punishments Miss Berry or Nanny Elsden meted out.

In 1903 Sir George and Lady Farrar took off together to see Victoria Falls, a major trek through difficult terrain – lion territory. Like her husband, Lady Farrar crossed the Falls, wearing waterproof trousers, in a canvas seat suspended from a cable. It was the adventure of a lifetime and on her return she wrote and published a book about her trip before slipping back into her familiar role as hostess.

The *Johannesburg Star* reported:

> Lady Farrar's garden-party gown was of Brussels lace
> flounces and her lace hat had a wreath of pink roses, and a
> veil of tinted pink chiffon; a cluster of pink roses was worn
> in the corsage of her gown. The little Misses Farrar were
> dressed in pretty broderie anglaise frocks, with pink ribbons
> and their linen hats had pink ties.[9]

Even the 'garden boys' were smartly dressed – in blue uniforms with red berets. Not many of the other wealthy white families bothered that the Bantu people they employed, accustomed to warmer winters than in the Transvaal, were often miserably cold. Providing uniforms was a paternalistic gesture, in keeping with the Farrars' colonial outlook.

In May 1907 a fifth girl, Kathleen, was born to the Farrars at Bedford Farm. The baby must have quickly grown used to the sounds of music making.

Gwen's cello lessons were delivered by a Mr Kofski. According to Muriel his clothes were shabby, he was always hungry and he was a marvellous teacher. A Mrs de Kock taught the older girls the violin. Both teachers were brought out to the farm twice a week, teaching the girls not only to play, but to love music. They both had stormy temperaments but were also enthusiastic. They drew them out and built them up; the girls suffered the long hours of practice until the tone deepened and it was no longer just a parlour trick. Music flowed into their fingers and bows. To Gwen the cello became an inseparable part of her life. It was something that, for the first time, set her apart from her sisters, giving her an excuse to neglect her other studies. In houses full of siblings and servants, it gave her licence to be alone, with the music of Mendelssohn, Brahms and Bach and with this vibrant, melodious instrument that she so enjoyed learning to master.

Return trips to England often took place towards the end of the year for the recreations Sir George most enjoyed: hunting and shooting. It was a chance to catch up with his brother, Percy, a great outdoorsman and mountaineer who was married to Mary Beswick, the first woman ever to climb Mont Blanc. They had one child, Joey, whom Gwen and her sisters looked forward to seeing more than anyone else. To them he was an immensely kind older brother figure.

Another visitor to Chicheley was Helen's godfather, Frank Rhodes, who had been in prison with George Farrar after the Jameson Raid.

> He was a great favourite of us children. He had grey hair
> and a grey moustache and a twinkle in his eyes. His face

was a network of deep lines and he used to entertain us
by making faces. He could contort his face like pressing a
rubber ball into the most extraordinary expressions. He was
a great friend of my father and it was always a red letter day
when he came to stay.[10]

Red letter days were celebrated in style at Chicheley Hall. Sir
George often made the ocean journeys independently from his
wife and it seems he was made particularly welcome on the
occasion when not only his family, but a new acquisition awaited
him – the very latest thing – a motor car! Banners proclaimed
'Welcome Home' and Marjorie sat on her pony in readiness for
his arrival. Lady Farrar posed at the wheel for a photograph,
with her mother-in-law, Helen Howard, sitting behind in her
customary black. Gwen eyed her mother enviously.

She would have to wait a while before convincing her
parents to let her loose behind the wheel. In the meantime she
perfected her horse-riding skills, outdoing her older sisters in
the saddle just as she did with her music. A cutting from the
Transvaal Leader shows she was also unbeaten against the boys,
coming first in a contest for 'Pony, 14 hands and under, ridden
by a boy or girl'.[11]

Just two weeks earlier, the *Johannesburg Star* had observed:

A surprisingly good interpretation of the Allegro Maestoso
from the Goltermann 'cello concerto was given by Miss
Gwendoline Farrar, who is making rapid progress in the
handling of her instrument and shows remarkable breadth
and power in her playing. She had quite the reception of
the evening and merited the enthusiastic applause which
she received.[12]

Another critic noted she was not a prodigy but, better still:

a healthy, unassuming English child, who showed evidence
of careful training, and exhibited, particularly in her
encore, a touch and tone which predict for her an ability to
become a thoroughly capable performer on the instrument
of her choice.'[13]

At another event the eldest girls sang Gilbert and Sullivan's 'Three Little Maids from School', resplendent in Japanese kimonos, after which:

> The final item was a scene from *Alice in Wonderland*, the characters being Alice, Tweedledum, and Tweedledee. The two latter, acted by Miss Muriel and Miss Gwendoline, created roars of laughter, their comedy being splendid; and many were the congratulations offered to Sir George and Lady Farrar on the cleverness of their charming daughters.[14]

Sir George was created a baronet on 2 February 1911. This new title was hereditary and could be passed on through a male heir. Much was at stake as Lady Farrar, six months pregnant, returned to England, leaving Sir George and the girls in South Africa to await news of the happy event.

'Welcome Home' at Chicheley Hall c.1911 (L to R) Marjorie on her pony, grandmother Helen Howard, Lady Farrar at the wheel, Gwen, unknown men either side

Gwen dressed for riding at Chicheley Hall around 1914 and (inset) her copy of a drawing by Charles Dana Gibson

~ 4 ~

WELL DONE MISS GWEN!

A male heir was not forthcoming. In April 1911 another girl was born and was named Ella, after her mother. Sir George and Lady Farrar now had six daughters and the eldest three were in their teens. Chief chronicler Muriel does not mince words as she recalls family life at this juncture: 'Our growing-up pains made us difficult to control and intolerable to have around.'[1]

Gwen appears to have been the most troublesome of all. Relations with her mother were so poor that for most of 1913 she was sent to live with Sir George in Johannesburg while he dealt with labour problems in the mines. She practised the cello, rode horses and played tennis with her father and his friends. She also filled her sketch book with ink drawings of women, copying the fashionable, idealised 'Gibson Girls' drawn by American artist Charles Dana Gibson.

Pringle, the groom, had returned to England suffering from alcoholism – brought on (Muriel thought with hindsight) by the stress of answering to the conflicting demands of Miss Berry, Nanny Elsden and Lady Farrar.

It was the first time that the close-knit trio of Helen, Muriel and Gwen had been split up. 'The Three Bears' were no longer an item. Helen was attending finishing schools, first in Paris, then Munich; and Muriel was at boarding school in Berkshire. Sir George wrote to them every week. His letters show a close attention to detail and contain splendid advice:

Thank God every morning when you wake up that you
have something to do that day which must be done
whether you like it or not. Being forced to work and forced
to do your best will breed in you temperance and self-
control, diligence and strength of will, cheerfulness and
content and a hundred virtues which the idle never know.[2]

On 4 July 1913, white miners, objecting to the possibility of
black labourers being brought in to break their strike, raised a
mob in Johannesburg. Sir George received a telephone warning
that they were marching on Bedford Court with riotous intent.
Gwen later recalled, in a newspaper article:

My father and I were alone in the house with one or two
servants. We all passed a very anxious night doing picket
duty. Fortunately either better counsels prevailed with the
mob or they got headed off by the police. But their threats
were not idle ones in those days. That night they burned
down the *Johannesburg Star* offices.[3]

Alarmed by news of this event, Lady Farrar wrote from Chicheley
Hall suggesting that Gwen consider continuing her studies in
England with a view to taking a cello-playing diploma. Now
sixteen, Gwen made the ocean voyage from Cape Town alone
and arrived at Chicheley Hall in late September 1913. She and
her mother had been apart for seven months. All reports from
George about her behaviour in that time had been good and
Ella was optimistic that she was a reformed character.

She greeted Gwen warmly with news of the summer she
had spent chaperoning Helen in her 'coming out season' as a
society debutante. Instead of reacting with enthusiasm, Gwen
scoffed. She told her mother that under no circumstances was
she ever going to be presented at court. In fact, if her mother
insisted, then instead of performing the required curtsey, Gwen
would stand on her head or, better still, do an impersonation
of Charlie Chaplin.[4]

This was incomprehensible to Lady Farrar. Gwen's attitude
smacked of gross ingratitude. It was a blinkered, self-defeating,
pig-headed rejection of the lifestyle that she, at Gwen's age,

had craved. She had made her childhood dreams into a reality, by great good fortune, and now her daughters had these opportunities on a plate. It was sheer stubbornness on Gwen's part to reject them. If she persisted and refused to conform, it would reflect badly on the whole family and damage her sisters' marriage prospects. Quite apart from that, how would Gwen herself get by without a husband? The arguments raged.

The conflict with Gwen was more than her mother could stand. Within two weeks of Gwen's return, Lady Farrar had booked herself and the younger children on the first available passage to South Africa. Gwen was left at Chicheley Hall without nannies, governesses or parents – just servants, grooms and horses.

In Radclyffe Hall's iconic novel, *The Well of Loneliness*, Stephen Gordon (who, despite her name, had been born a girl as far as the family were concerned, and was thus expected to conform to Edwardian notions of femininity) could almost be modelled on Gwen. Stephen Gordon comes into bitter conflict with her mother, Anna, but adores her father, Sir Philip. He takes her hunting astride her beloved horse, Raftery. Confiding her secrets to the horse and finding solace in riding, Stephen temporarily escapes her bewildering sense of social alienation.

Gwen's prize-winning pony, Harold, served a similar role. Gwen had brought some thirty silver riding trophies with her from South Africa and now put them on display in her room. She donned her breeches and rode out on Harold. If she felt she had been abandoned, she did not let it show.

One imagines the staff at Chicheley Hall were fond of Gwen and that the scenes she had with her mother were a cause of great entertainment below stairs. It must have been amusing to see their imperious employer wrong footed. There was nobody like Miss Gwen: she was her own person and they admired her for it; she had no airs and graces and she made them laugh.

Years later when Gwen hit the headlines for catching a runaway horse, one of Chicheley Hall's servants cut out the clip and kept it, writing, 'Well done, Miss Gwen!' proudly at the top.

Gwen rode out with her cousin Joey, now a second lieutenant in the Reserve Battalion of the Northamptonshire

Regiment. But when the news got back to their grandmother, Helen Howard Farrar, that Gwen was sitting astride her mount instead of riding side saddle, the wild child was summoned to stay in Crescent Lodge, Bedford, with both her grandmother and great-uncle. Frederick Howard, industrialist and founder of the Britannia Iron Works, was the man whose money had paid for Sir George's education, whose business had provided the opportunity for George and his brothers to go to South Africa. The two God-fearing family elders, dressed in black, with stern faces and strict Victorian morality, were not to be trifled with.

It was decided that, as soon as possible, Gwen should join Muriel at Heathfield Girls' Boarding School, located in a beautiful Italianate building, not far from the famous racecourse at Ascot, thirty miles from central London. The keen expectation was that going to school for the first time and mixing with refined, wealthy and aristocratic young English girls would swiftly bring Gwen to her senses.

Gwen stayed for less than two terms. Besides the cliquiness of the other girls, many of whom had been there together since they were eleven, the teachers were quick to point out, regularly, in front of the rest of Form 5A, the glaring gaps in Gwendoline's knowledge. Although she was witty and intelligent, days spent horse trekking, playing the cello and locked in stubborn conflict with Miss Berry had taken their toll on Gwen's formal education.

The end of term could not come soon enough. The only qualification she was interested in was the cello diploma she would take in a year's time. That could be done independently from school. And so, used to having the run of large houses and big ships, Gwen found the school delivery bay. It was a simple matter, on a dry summer's day, to pay the Harrod's man to take her and her cello to London in his van.

Sir George and Ella, back by this time at Chicheley Hall, wondered what on earth they could do with their wayward daughter. Heathfield did not want the runaway back.

Gwen, champing at the bit for independence and adventure, could not have known how soon her emotional and physical resources were going to be tested. But for now, it was summertime. Chicheley was beautiful. There were horses to ride, games of tennis to play, music to learn. Best of all, her father was there, spending time with his children. The tensions between Gwen and her mother were temporarily relieved, as Lady Farrar was busy matchmaking. On the latest sea crossing, an Australian lieutenant in the Royal Flying Corps had impressed her as good potential husband material for her eldest daughter, Helen. He was invited to stay.

Muriel could tell Helen was interested in handsome, tall Bruce Turner. 'Our yardstick was the English poets. To one admirer she read Longfellow, to another Tennyson and so on. If it was Swinburne, she wanted to marry him.'[5] To Basil Turner, Helen was reading Swinburne.

Sir George had acquired a particularly fine stable of hunters for the upcoming season and everyone was looking forward to riding out with the Oakley Hunt.

Then on 4 August 1914, Britain declared war on Germany. Immediately, Sir George left for London, to see Lord Kitchener, to offer the horses to the Government and to volunteer for service on Sir Ian Hamilton's staff. The horses were accepted, but Kitchener told Sir George that, instead of serving in Europe, he would be posted to South Africa.

Perhaps he gathered his daughters together as he had when they were young, with their newly acquired monogrammed prayer books. Or perhaps, in the rush to mobilise, his departure was just one of many leave-takings in the family. Gwen was sorry to see him go, especially as he was an ally in her own conflict – the war with her mother. He valued the traits that Lady Farrar seemed to want to eradicate: Gwen's individualism, her quirky sense of humour, her spontaneity.

And so he sailed, on 15 August, to take up the role of assistant quartermaster general in the campaign to conquer and occupy German South West Africa (now Namibia). Railway tracks needed to be laid and maintained across desert terrain to supply vital food and water to troops and horses. This would be a hugely demanding role for Sir George (now fifty-five), continuing into the southern hemisphere's hottest months. He had always rolled up his sleeves and led from the front, doing everything with total commitment. This campaign would be no exception.

Gwen yearned to be in London, a place she had passed through but never independently explored. The Yeomanry had four reserve cavalry divisions operating in the Rotten Row area of Hyde Park. Part of their role was to 'remount', or retrain, some of the thousands of horses that, like the ones from Chicheley, had been volunteered or requisitioned for the war effort. Girls who had experience with horses (and the right connections) were assisting with this work. Gwen had both and was accepted straight away. She was in her element. Like thousands of her contemporaries, for whom the war would bring the chance to nurse, drive ambulances, run farms, work in factories, she was allowed to make herself useful in a practical way.

Describing the mobilisation of women for the war effort and, in particular, the way it gave lesbians a degree of visibility for the first time, Radclyffe Hall wrote:

> They were part of the universal convulsion and were being accepted as such, on their merits. And although their Sam Browne belts remained swordless, their hats and their caps without regimental badges, a battalion was formed in those terrible years that would never again be completely disbanded. War and death had given them a right to life, and life tasted sweet, very sweet to their palates.[6]

The first years of the Great War were to take their toll on Gwen's family, both at home and abroad. In Bedford, the year 1915 began with the death of Gwen's great-uncle Frederick on 6 January. The matriarch Helen Howard now had good reason to wear black. She had lost her beloved and respected brother.

In April, the Yeomanry were posted to France and Gwen's stint in Hyde Park was over. In the months working with them, she had achieved her independence and shown she could be useful; circumstances were on her side in the battle against her mother.

Lady Farrar was busy organising funds for the many relief agencies which had now been set up in North Buckinghamshire. In aid of the Serbian Distress Fund, she held two concerts at Chicheley Hall, hosting, as the chief attraction, the famous Australian contralto, Ada Crossley. Gwen played the cello and the concerts raised £110.

In the last week of March 1915, Gwen's sister Muriel travelled to France to begin work for the Soldiers' Rest Homes. Then On 7 May, without any warning, the Cunard liner, the *Lusitania*, was torpedoed by a German U-boat with the loss of over a thousand lives. 'There but for the grace of God!' thought the Farrars. The whole country was shaken by the news and it was the one topic of conversation at Chicheley Hall, until a telegram from France arrived two days later.

Cousin Joey had been killed, leading his men in a dawn raid at Aubers Ridge. This was devastating. The younger Farrar girls, Marjorie, Kathleen and Ella, had grown to idolise their big cousin as much as their older sisters did. He had fought at Mons, Aisne and Ypres and survived those dreadful early battles unscathed, as if he had a charmed life. But on 9 May at 5.40 a.m., an enemy gunshot to the heart was immediately fatal. If it was any consolation, he had died instantly. He was twenty-seven and Percy and Mary's only child. Sir George wrote to his brother from South Africa, 'Always remember he played the game right through.'

Ten days later, Sir George was travelling along a railway line with two other men on a manually operated inspection trolley when they were hit by a train from the opposite direction. They were thrown clear of the track and Sir George insisted that the trolley driver's serious injuries be attended to before his own hip wound, which seemed trivial by comparison. In the event, by dawn the next day, both the driver and Sir George were dead. He had been working himself so hard in such hot and demanding conditions that his famous reserves of energy and fitness were depleted and his body could not deal with the shock of the accident. The epitaph he wrote for Joey could just as well have been his own.

This was an unspeakable blow for the family at Chicheley Hall. The campaign Sir George was fighting was easily won a few weeks later, in no small part due to the infrastructure he had put in place. Compared to other theatres of war there were very few fatalities. His death was unnecessary, a fluke accident, brought on by his unceasing work ethic.

Helen Howard, the matriarch in black, had lost her brother, her son and her only grandson in the space of six months.

Lady Farrar made immediate plans to leave Southampton for South Africa. The decision was taken that Helen and Muriel should go with her, but not the youngest girls... and not Gwen. Given Gwen's closeness to her father it is most surprising that she did not take this voyage. It suggests the relationship with her mother was very strained. But the experience of being left at Chicheley Hall to grieve with her younger sister Marjorie seems to have forged a bond between these two which would be of lasting value as their lives continued on parallel paths.

Sir George's funeral was held on 16 June 1915 in St Mary's Cathedral, Johannesburg. It was conducted by the Archbishop of Cape Town and attended by members of the South African Government.

Simultaneously, in England, Gwen and fourteen-year-old Marjorie led the mourners in the short walk from Chicheley Hall to St Lawrence's Parish Church, where a memorial service was held to coincide precisely with the funeral in Johannesburg.

In his address to the congregation at Chicheley, the Reverend GF Sams listed Sir George's many good qualities, adding:

> These are the very men who are now being cut off in their
> thousands, while the laggards and the degenerates are
> left behind to cumber the ground and to transmit their
> worthless characteristics to future generations.

This singularly un-Christian message was a poor substitute for the comforting words Gwen craved.

Soon after her mother and sisters returned, the news arrived that Rudyard Kipling's son John – Gwen's childhood friend – had been killed. Though he had originally been rejected by the

Army and the Navy on account of his short-sightedness, his father had used his influence to get him a commission in the Irish Guards. He was killed in action less than six weeks after arriving in France.

Christmas 1915 was a desperately sad occasion at Chicheley Hall. Adding to the family's misery, the whole country was under threat from Zeppelin raids, one of which had killed a mother and daughter only a few miles away in Northampton.

Food shortages were an issue and Lady Farrar became an advocate for the Women's Land Army. Sir George had been profoundly interested in agricultural matters in South Africa and his widow was determined to follow his example and play her part in keeping the nation fed.

To what extent Gwen was involved in the cultivation work we do not know. It seems she was mainly busy preparing to take her cello diploma. She was a private student of the distinguished cello teacher Herbert Walenn and the focus was on technique. A later student of Walenn's, Zara Nelsova, said, 'I had to bring in two memorised études per week, difficult ones... Needless to say, I worked many hours per day in order to keep up.'[7]

Gwen worked independently with Walenn, without being enrolled at a conservatoire. She visited the Royal Academy of Music only as an external candidate, to sit the Licentiate Examination in December 1916. When the results were published in March she was one of a handful of musicians to have qualified as both performer and teacher simultaneously, and the sole cellist.

Gwen had no need at all to work, but an absolute determination to do so. Sir George's fortune would provide plentifully for his widow and daughters, but Gwen was going to make sure that she had an income in her own right as well.

On the other hand Lady Farrar was still determined that all her daughters would eventually enter society and get married. Helen and Lieutenant Turner were now engaged. General Smuts himself was coming over from South Africa for the wedding. Lady Farrar thought Muriel and Gwen could be bridesmaids. How lovely it would be to see her three eldest girls in matching dresses as in the old days. How they all deserved a chance to look feminine again after all their agricultural toil. How important it was to carry on, in spite of the war. What a wonderful way to defy the Kaiser. How proud it would have made Sir George… Every sort of emotional blackmail was used to make Gwen agree.

The old arguments began again, overlaid with anger, sorrow and regret. Lady Farrar insisted, in the name of Sir George, that she should comply, while Gwen knew, equally strongly, that her father was on her side. He was not there to prove it, but for the sake of her sanity she held on to her belief. She remembered how he took her for picnics and taught her to barbecue chops on an open fire. How easy it had been that summer she turned sixteen at Bedford Court: games of croquet and tennis with him and his friends, sketching, playing the cello. The straightforward companionship and trust they shared; the acceptance and approval she always felt from him. He understood her, accepted her and praised her. But from her mother, it was only ever criticism and scorn.

Everywhere at Chicheley were things he had left behind: furniture, books, photographs, lists and plans for his intended return. Bottles of old Constantia wine lay in the cellar and brandies and spirits in half-filled decanters in his study. It was both a pain and a comfort to go in there. Gwen liked the leather and dark wood, the lingering tobacco smell, the sense of privacy and order in this masculine space. She had always loved to be here with her father. His study at Bedford Court was just the same. A room to think in and be still. A place to take oneself seriously. A sanctuary that Miss Berry, Nanny Elsden and Mother, with their conflicting demands, could not invade. How a room like this would make a person feel purposeful and grand. Perhaps she reached for the brandy and poured a glass. It was sweet under her nose, and warm on her tongue. She settled in her father's armchair with his brandy glass and a book by her favourite author – a man, like her father, born in the 1850s, a man who shared his name and, she felt, his wisdom – the Irish writer, George Moore.

PART II
PARTNERS AND PALS
1917–22

Norah and Gwen pictured in the Tatler, *1918*

~ 5 ~

DRINK TO ME ONLY

On 17 December 1916, Norah Blaney performed for the first time at the London Palladium. She was part of a concert for the National Sunday League, organised by the comedian George Robey, in aid of a Free Buffet for soldiers and sailors at Victoria Station.

A month later, her husband Albert Lyne, his military training now complete, set off with his regiment in a troop ship bound for Salonika. Their objective was to help maintain the relatively secure Allied presence on the Macedonian Front against the Bulgarian Army.

Possibly he and Norah had spent Christmas together at Digby Mansions, visiting Molly and Walter just over the river. Or perhaps they had been estranged from each other for years, their marriage simply one of mutual convenience or youthful folly. Norah appeared to take little, if any, account of him in her plans – and none at all in her later recollections.

She took time off at the start of 1917 to rest and to work on her repertoire. The weather was unusually severe from January to March with frequent snow, harsh frosts and icy conditions making travel difficult.

Norah was invited to do another tour of the French camps and hospitals. Lena Ashwell's concert parties were now expanding and, due to their enormous popularity, at last had the full support of the War Office. The distinguished tenor Gervase Elwes would be leading this next trip. He was well known in classical musical circles for his wonderful voice and ability to interpret lyrics.

Elwes was fifty years old and the father of several sons who were serving in the war. He and his wife Winefride had a home in Northamptonshire, at Billing Hall, making them neighbours of Lady Farrar, fifteen miles away at Chicheley. No sooner was Gwen qualified than Lady Farrar introduced her to Elwes, who was evidently impressed, for he included her in a concert he gave at the Electric Theatre, Newport Pagnell, on 1 May. The artistes were advertised as Mr Gervase Elwes, 'the squire of Billing,' a tenor of world repute, and Miss Gwendoline Farrar LRAM, cellist.

According to Norah, speaking years later, Lady Farrar was so exasperated with Gwen's behaviour that, hearing Elwes was bound for France, she implored him to take Gwen with him. She seemed perfectly happy to send her daughter out to a war zone, but never dreamed that her intervention would lead to the momentous (and in Lady Farrar's view, undesirable and dangerous) meeting between Gwen and the woman who would change her life.

Norah recalled Elwes briefing her about the trip, saying, 'There is one girl I am doubtful about. She has never been to France and she's rather a spoilt child. Her father is a millionaire and I don't know how she will turn out.'[1] He looked to Norah to take Gwen in hand. 'She'd have to behave herself because any sign of disobedience or bad behaviour, she would be sent straight back.'[2]

Gwen had a different story which left her mother out:

> When I finished at Hyde Park I looked around for
> something else to do. I met Miss Norah Blaney who was
> already a popular favourite with the Tommies. She had
> given up her concert work in order to entertain the men in
> training and in the hospitals. She discovered that I could
> play the 'cello a bit, and suggested that I should go in for
> concert work amongst the troops.[3]

Talking about her father's death, she added, 'It was in the hope of trying to forget my own sorrow that I first began entertaining the wounded and the Tommies in training.'[4]

Another version of their first meeting, pieced together with some imagination from Norah's private conversations with Derek Hunt, takes place on 8 June 1917 at Victoria Station, in a railway carriage. Gwen was smoking Turkish cigarettes. Norah's taste was for a milder brand. There was some sort of altercation between them; part of the process of sizing each other up. Perhaps Norah, the seasoned pro, was putting nineteen-year-old Gwen to the test. 'I could picture to myself what sort of a girl she would be – a spoilt darling who would put on a lot of side because of her father's millions.'[5] Norah was twenty-three, a married woman and worldly, with a huge amount of professional experience under her belt. She was vivacious, charming and good looking. Gwen was four years younger, plain and physically gauche. Her one professional engagement had been a result of nepotism. Apart from ocean liners and servants halls she had no experience of people outside her own class. Norah would need convincing that this girl had what it took to be an asset to this tour.

They had a carriage to themselves on the three-hour journey to Portsmouth. Gwen unlocked her cello from its case and eased it out. Norah was surprised to see she was going to play on the train and even more startled when she lodged the cello's maple back and spruce belly firmly between her thighs. When Norah was studying, women cellists played to one side.

Gwen explained she had sold her horse-riding trophies to buy this latest instrument, which she had found in a shop in Bond Street for five hundred guineas.[6]

As soon as she started to play Norah could see Gwen had a wonderful connection with her instrument. Her technique and artistry were superb. The train's movements and the sight and sound of this bold young cellist mixed with the powerful scent of her Turkish tobacco to produce in Norah, sitting on the velveteen banquette diagonally across from Gwen, the same visceral response she had experienced at Casals' feet – especially when Gwen played the Prelude from Bach's Suite

No. 1 that the great man had played. The rhythmic cadences, effortlessly executed, seemed to blend with the sound of the train on the tracks, the cello's baritone pitch always reminding Norah comfortingly of her father's bassoon playing.

She envied Gwen this beautiful, resonant, portable instrument; an intimate companion she could call into service anywhere. She privately marvelled at what it had cost and the risk she was taking to bring it with her to a war zone.

Gwen switched without pause from the Bach to an English song, ages old but hugely popular, 'Drink to Me Only with Thine Eyes'. Everyone knew the words, it was a Victorian parlour party standard, but academics and those with queer sensibilities knew of its roots in erotic Athenian verse.[7]

Gwen had been staring down at her instrument with intense concentration up to now. Norah admired her sleek black hair. She wondered if she should join in – the words were on her lips – 'Or leave a kiss within the cup and I'll not ask for wine.'

Then came the phrase, 'But might I of Jove's nectar sup,' and Gwen looked Norah directly in the eye.

It was subtle, but unmistakable. Norah was intoxicated by the girl's daring. It wasn't impertinence, it was spirit. Norah had enjoyed lingering looks in the limelight and snatched intimacies in dark passages backstage with girls in silky stockings and tight bodices. These moments thrilled her more than encounters with men.

Gwen finished the phrase with a solemn flourish of her bow. Then, to break the tension of the moment, she pulled a funny face, clicked her tongue and started to jazz the song up. She abandoned her bow to strum and pluck the strings and beat the cello's belly, syncopating the melancholy old tune in a wholly modern and exciting way that made it burst with joy.

Completely taken aback, Norah collapsed in peals of laughter. Gwen quickly restored her cello to its case, raised her eyebrows quizzically at Norah and let out a deep chuckle, at roughly the pitch of her cello.

Norah later recalled, 'Gwen and I took an immediate liking to one another and we chummed up from the moment we first met,' adding that she was, 'the girl with the most delicious sense of humour I have ever known...'[8]

Gwen's privilege and confidence, the devil-may-care approach that sprang from her grief, combined with her already forthright personality and some Dutch courage from her brandy flask, made her immediately interesting to Norah. Her musicianship made her fascinating. Her sense of humour made her irresistible. In Gwen, Norah had found a rare match: an exquisite musician who adored her craft but above all wanted to make people laugh and had the skills to do it.

At Portsmouth they met the other members of the concert party and sailed by ferry to Le Havre. Gwen recalled:

> Entertaining the troops in the camps wasn't always a
> picnic. It meant long journeys in crowded trains and very
> indifferent lodgings in out of the way places. But we both
> enjoyed ourselves.[9]

Norah immediately impressed Gervase Elwes, who wrote to his wife, 'Miss Norah Blaney is very amusing and a wonderful pianist.' He noted her ability to improvise when the audience included some French soldiers. 'During her "Songs at the Piano", she brought them into her gag, much to their amusement and delight. It was very funny.'[10]

Norah remembered teaching a verse of the hit song 'Broken Doll' to a French officer. The entire audience would chorus the words in brackets:

> You called me baby doll a year ago
> (Year ago, year ago, year ago)
> You told me I was very nice to know
> (Nice to know, nice to know, nice to know)
> You made me think you loved me in return
> (In return, in return, in return)
> Don't tell me you were fooling after all
> For if you turn away, you'll be sorry some day
> You left behind a broken doll.

Norah's old colleague from Margate, Clifford Grey, was now a household name, having written the huge hit 'If You Were the

Only Girl in the World' with composer Nat D Ayer.

Norah included the song on request:

> Sometimes when I feel bad
> And things look blue
> I wish a girl I had... say one like you.
> Someone within my heart to build her throne
> Someone who'd never part, to call my own.

There were plenty of opportunities to look across at Gwen as she sang.

These performances were, in Norah's words:

> ... not a bit like stiff, conventional concerts one often goes
> to over here where each artiste makes a careful exit after
> every song and only gives an encore after a tremendous
> amount of persuasion. It is such a long time since most
> of the soldiers have seen an English girl that they cannot
> bear to let you go out of their sight; so we all sit around the
> platform while the others are singing in the most informal
> way. The sea of khaki with eager faces turned towards you,
> watching your every movement, is a wonderful stimulus:
> you feel you must make them enjoy themselves. It makes
> you long to do your very best.[11]

Though they were the focus of a kind of attention that might have felt uncomfortable, in this sexually charged atmosphere, Gwen and Norah knew that professionally they were delivering exactly what was expected of them. Privately their emotional interest was focused on each other. They could perfectly avoid any accusation of the kind of impropriety which War Office officials were so alarmed might result from these visits. It was thrilling to have this secret which immunised them from suspicion of heterosexual dalliance. What was playing on Gwen and Norah's minds was beyond the imagination of the authorities.

They sensed in each other what poet Adrienne Rich would one day describe as 'the audacity to claim a stigmatised desire'[12] but the chemistry between them was something they had to disguise.

If they had been part of a women's ambulance or nursing unit, their growing closeness might have been observed with greater scrutiny and received the kind of critical warning meted out to Stephen Gordon in *The Well of Loneliness*:

> These are strenuous times, and such times are apt to breed many emotions... But I'm sure you'll agree with me, Miss Gordon, in thinking it our duty to discourage anything in the nature of an emotional friendship. It's quite natural of course, a kind of reaction, but not wise.[13]

Lena Ashwell (who was about to be awarded an OBE for her work on the many concert parties she now had running simultaneously) singled out this one as:

> A very brilliant party... Norah Blaney and Gwen Farrar began their friendship [and] Gwen Farrar played the cello with very real and exceptional talent.[14]

Ashwell made a personal appearance with the group on 17 June 1917 reciting patriotic verse and Elizabethan love lyrics. She was deeply moved when a sergeant took to the stage 'shaking from head to foot' and read out a letter of thanks from the men to the artistes:

> We confess that we would rather listen forever to their melodies than go back to the horrid orchestra of war, but they have helped us to realise again that we are fighting for Empire, Home and Beauty and for all they mean in the life of mankind.[15]

Elwes said he would never forget the experience of that particular concert and the appreciative letter as long as he lived. Ashwell said, 'The cheers which followed shook my heart and scattered my senses.'[16]

Gwen and Norah, thoroughly wrapped up in each other, left no record of their response. But this surely enhanced the feeling, very new to Gwen if not to Norah, of being in the right place at the right time, with the right person. On average they gave three concerts a day, providing them with ample opportunities to impress each other with their performances and, sitting side by side on the stage while others played and sang, to convey shared, secret understandings and responses through looks and smiles.

Elwes sang 'Sigh No More Ladies' as part of his set:

Sigh no more, ladies, sigh no more.
 Men were deceivers ever,
One foot in sea, and one on shore,
 To one thing constant never.
Then sigh not so, but let them go,
 And be you blithe and bonny,
Converting all your sounds of woe
 Into hey nonnie, nonnie.

Gwen and Norah were the embodiment of 'blithe and bonny', perfectly happy to take Shakespeare's advice to let men go. The song became a delightful in-joke between them, part of which they were soon obliged to share. Gwen nicknamed Elwes 'Uncle Nonnie'. When one of his sons, Guy, arrived for a few days, Elwes wrote delightedly to his wife telling her how Gwen had christened him 'Wee Nonnie', much to everyone's amusement.

The company travelled from one location to another by train or car. At night they slept in huts or other lodgings organised by the YMCA. After the evening show there was dinner in the officers' mess. This was a chance for the performers to let their hair down.

Elwes realised his reservations about Gwen had been unfounded and now fully appreciated her ability to make people laugh, even joining in the mimicry himself. He wrote to his wife:

Miss Farrar and Miss Blaney make up the young and giddy part of our company and, of course, have great fun with the young officers. We call them the 'bad girls of the family.' Miss Farrar and I have dogfights sometimes for the entertainment of the officers when we are dining at their mess. She can growl excellently and her 'wounded dog' is priceless, so that when we are both doing dogfights the noise is really quite lifelike and has more than once had a *succès fou!*[17]

One evening, on the way to one of these gatherings, something happened which would put Gwen's comedy antics centre stage and give her and Norah the chance to spend more time alone together. Wish Wynne, the comedienne of the party, injured herself. Norah later recalled:

> One night, we were going across a ploughed field to the officers' mess camp when Wish, having had a few drinks, fell down and sprained her ankle. It meant she was out of the show. Gervase said, 'What are we going to do without Wish?' So somebody said, 'Well Norah and Gwen are always having little, funny jokes and making fun of sentimental songs and that sort of thing.' (In a way we were sort of satirists, even in those days, you see. On our own.) 'They'll do something.' Well we had no rehearsal or anything. I sang my silly little songs and Gwen didn't know them, so she stood up at the piano and pulled faces at me and I don't know why, but the soldiers loved it. And that was the beginning of it. She made funny noises and if I mentioned the word 'dog' she did a dog yelping and all that sort of thing. But it was all unrehearsed, you see.[18]

There is a consistency about this story, whether Norah is speaking in 1981 or 1924:

> Gwen saved the situation and proved that she could not only play the cello but play the fool just as well! That was really the start of our turn for after that Gwen and I always played together.[19]

In her account, Gwen pinpoints how subverting of the seriousness of their classical repertoire by suddenly shifting the tone became a key feature of the act. 'Burlesquing', at that time, meant 'sending up'.

> Miss Wish Wynne was taken ill and Miss Blaney and myself went on without any rehearsal and started to sing ragtime songs as a duet. Together we found ourselves burlesquing them.
>
> We got such a reception for the first number that we emphasised burlesque in the second song, and made the

third 'rag' we sang a sheer travesty. Henceforward we made
this part of any entertainment in which we appeared.

We always started our turn with a little real music and
I think the contrast provides one of the reasons why the
audiences appreciate our burlesques.[20]

They were dazzled by each other's musicianship. Gwen loved
Norah's ability to improvise, change key, swap genre from
classical to ragtime in the space of a beat. Norah adored Gwen's
facility with the cello, how she teased out the tone, wringing
every last ounce of emotion from her classical pieces. Then she
would pick the thing up and sling it on her shoulder like a sack
of coals and walk off. It was so funny. In Gwen, Norah saw
someone, like herself, whose musical brilliance matched her
desire and ability to entertain.

Their audiences often numbered thousands. There was
no amplification, so performers relied on good technique to
project their voices. Gwen could sing in tune but Norah saw
there was scope for improving the way she produced her voice.
It would need to be properly supported to survive undamaged
in these demanding performance circumstances. Norah had
accompanied enough singers at the College and Academy to
know about the physiology of vocal technique. It required the
activation of muscles deep in the body's core. Gwen happily
consented to have lessons from her friend.

Elwes wrote home to describe an unexpectedly idyllic
summer evening:

> The third concert was given in the open, amongst pine
> trees, where they had erected a platform and hung over it
> strings of Chinese lanterns. When it got dark, towards the
> end of the concert, the effect was perfectly charming...
> with the lanterns, mostly red, with one occasionally falling
> blazing to the ground, the soldiers in a half circle in front
> of us in rising tiers, officers in front and behind groups
> of peasant children attracted to the spot and chattering
> amongst themselves. It was immensely picturesque. It was
> a goodish way off and we had a delicious motor drive home
> in the cool.[21]

It is inconceivable to imagine that Gwen and Norah did not enjoy the picturesque concert setting and the deliciousness of the motor drive that night. In the two weeks since that first train journey, their musical compatibility and rapport had resulted in a stage performance that put smiles back on the faces of their war-weary audiences and brought the warm approval of their colleagues. They had acquitted themselves admirably, with good humour and resilience in challenging circumstances, dispelling all doubts about their suitability for the task. Elwes, whose devout Catholicism did not prevent him having a marvellous sense of fun, was delighted with them.

None of the members of the concert party thought Gwen and Norah's closeness was anything more than youthful exuberance and girlish friendship of the kind that could be happily indulged. When the tour ended on 10 July, they returned to London and, in Norah's words, 'Gwen and I were such good pals by this time that the thought of parting from each other was almost unbearable.'[22]

It would have made perfect sense for them to take the short cab ride from the station to Norah's home at 5 Digby Mansions. She was fairly sure Albert would not be there. In fact he was on board the *Aragon* troop transport ship at that moment, sailing across the Mediterranean from Salonika to Alexandria. As Norah recalled in 1982, 'Gwen said she wasn't going home, she was coming to live with me. I had a little flat and we set up our little home, our little stall.'[23]

This was the same place where, four years earlier, Norah had started married life with Albert Lyne. Did Norah still think of herself as his wife? Probably not, for in later life she never mentioned him. She and Gwen immediately started working hard on their double act and the neighbours soon began to recognise the strains of a cello playing in delicious harmony with the piano they were so used to hearing.

Although Gwen was determined not to live at Chicheley Hall ever again, her little sisters wanted her to visit and Gwen felt sure Marjorie, Kathleen and Ella would like Norah. It was Gwen's twentieth birthday on 14 July and Lady Farrar, pleased with the reports she had heard from Elwes of Gwen's success, had ordered a motorcar from the Aston Clinton works ready for her daughter's arrival. Gwen could not wait to take Norah for a bracing spin in her new vehicle.

In her study of early women motorists, Georgine Clarsen points to the hero of the *The Well of Loneliness* and the significance of owning her first car:

> The aristocratic Stephen Gordon graduated from
> accomplished horsewoman to competent motorist at the
> same time as her inchoate sexual longings crystallised into
> a recognition of her same-sex desire... The car enabled the
> women to... travel to 'places where lovers might sit'.[24]

This new car had similar potential for Gwen and Norah, though owing to Gwen's recklessness behind the wheel, this first outing was far from a relaxing, romantic experience for Norah. She was very glad of some quiet time afterwards in the little parish church of St Lawrence.

With its family pews and brasses and statues of the Chester Family, the church was a reminder that, for all their grandeur and wealth, the Farrar family were only renting this ancestral estate. Norah had half hoped to see Farrar portraits and memorials stretching back to medieval times but the truth was the Farrars were self-made Victorian industrialists with no aristocratic lineage to speak of.

Nevertheless, Norah was amazed by the house: its tall ceilings, beautiful furniture, grand staircase and the stunning views of the grounds from every window. She and Gwen had been allocated connecting rooms on the second floor. Above that were the younger girls' bedrooms and the schoolroom on the top floor where Miss Berry still held court. She was less in demand for her piano playing now. The three younger girls preferred outdoor pursuits to music and recitations and the days of Lady Farrar showing her daughters off like prize poodles were long gone.

Marjorie, almost sixteen, had a friend staying called Peggy de Knoop, and the four young women played tennis. Then they walked about the grounds with ten-year-old Kathleen and six-year-old Ella, inspecting the rows of growing vegetables, playing hide-and-seek in the woods, kicking a football and watching the moorhens on the lake. Gwen drew cartoons to amuse the children. Norah watched her happily. She liked the feeling of being part of a big family of siblings.

Lady Farrar (we may imagine) spent the day wondering what this girl was doing here. Her parents lived in a semi-detached house and she could barely disguise her London accent. She couldn't ride a horse and knew next to nothing about the countryside. She had never travelled abroad further than Paris. She was a show-off at the piano and not a good influence on Gwen or the little girls. She would not be invited to Helen's wedding.

To secure a booking at the very fashionable St Luke's Church, Chelsea, Lady Farrar had purchased a house within the parish. Number 217 King's Road was a charming three-storey Georgian building on the corner of Glebe Place, which led to Cheyne Row and the Thames. Gwen's sisters Helen and Muriel, back from France, were up there now, using the house as a base for their committee work and planning the elder girl's nuptials. When Helen married and moved out, Gwen could live there instead. It would put a stop to this ludicrous situation of her sharing a flat in Hammersmith with this unknown girl.

Lady Farrar was even more alarmed by their plans to perform together in music halls. It was nonsense of course, but very disturbing. She would arrange with her brother-in-law, Percy, as soon as possible, that Gwen should have an allowance of at least £5,000 per year. Then she would have no need to work and these girls' ridiculous plans of entertaining in public would come to nothing.

After their nursery tea, Kathleen and little Ella were put to bed, but for Lady Farrar, Gwen, Norah, Marjorie and Peggy there was an evening meal of lamb and homegrown leeks, carrots and potatoes, washed down with '75 vintage Constantia.

Afterwards, Gwen and Norah solemnly said 'good night' and retired to their separate rooms. We can imagine that, seconds later, Gwen sprang open the connecting door and leapt on Norah's bed where they both had to stifle their delighted giggles.

In a room above them, Marjorie and Peggy were very likely also cuddled up. Like Gwen and Norah, they dreamed of spending their lives as a pair. The odds were stacked against them. The very idea condemned them to futures dulled and muted by discrimination, self-doubt and fear. So natural and harmless a dream, but regarded as so unpalatable, corrosive and depraved that it could not be discussed. It would take a hundred years to start to free their stories from silence and shame.

In January 1918, prompting a case that acted as a barometer of public opinion about female homosexuality, a proto-fascist Member of Parliament, Noel Pemberton Billing, published, under the heading, 'The Cult of the Clitoris', an attack on an actress in his journal, *Vigilante*. It led to a libel trial in which he claimed Maud Allan was 'a diseased mad girl' and that her performance, in Oscar Wilde's *Salome*, was 'calculated to do more harm... to all who see it... than the German army itself'. He was acquitted of libel, winning huge popular support, and was re-elected to Parliament. Allan was disgraced and ruined. The point was clearly made in the newspapers that lesbianism, or even the suspicion of it, was a filthy, contagious, treasonous practice.

Gwen adored the novels of George Moore[25] and devoured his 1918 book of short stories that contained 'The Life of Albert Nobbs'.[26] In this novella, a character named Hubert leaves an unhappy marriage and motherhood, to live and work as a man. Advocating the idea of queer marriage to the tortured eponymous hero, Hubert describes how, after meeting a girl, Polly, they 'arranged to live together, each paying our share. She had her work and I had mine, and between us we made a fair living, and... we haven't known an unhappy hour since.'[27] Moore's books were banned in public libraries for sensational themes such as this. Yet in this story Gwen and Norah saw a rare and welcome depiction of a domestic and working arrangement not unlike their own.

'We both take our work seriously – for burlesque is a serious business,'[28] said Gwen. And as the more established artist, Norah had solo bookings already in the diary:

> It so happened that I was engaged to sing at the Palladium, at one of the Sunday evening concerts, and I asked the manager if I could bring my friend along with me and do a double 'turn.'
>
> He didn't like the idea at first, but at last, I managed to win him over. So Gwen came along, almost as a 'bit of makeweight,' as she afterwards put it, and absolutely refused to share my fee, although I pressed her to take half.[29]

Norah had such confidence in Gwen that she was prepared to go into equal partnership. She was also humble enough to recognise that they needed advice. A ventriloquist called Arthur Prince thought their act had promise. He had been invalided out of the war and was breaking back in to working the halls with his puppet, Sailor Boy Jim. He had the right connections and bagged Gwen and Norah a trial week at one of the music halls, giving them advice after each performance. It was a baptism of fire, as Norah wrote:

> To put it tersely we 'got the bird!' The audience simply howled us down, but we stuck it gamely to the end. The next night the audience was less hostile, quite friendly, in fact, and by the end of the week we knew that we had won success.[30]

A playbill in Gwen's archive advertises Arthur Prince at the Birmingham Grand Theatre of Varieties from 24 to 29 June 1918 supported by (spectacularly misspelt) 'Nora Blayney and Gwen Farrah'.

Another story, which emerged later, is that an agent told Norah the double act would not succeed, urging her to drop Gwen if she wanted her own career to progress. In music hall terms, Gwen would be classified as a 'feminine grotesque' and Norah's career as a rising ingénue would be hampered by the association. His words to Norah (as reported later, self-effacingly, by Gwen in a newspaper article) were: 'You'll do, but you must drop your friend. She'll have things thrown at her and I've got a reputation to lose.'[31]

Of course Norah stuck with Gwen, but progress was initially slow. Then, 'Suddenly it went like fire you see and we never looked back.'[32] But Norah knew the importance of public relations. Speaking to the press in 1924 she was happy to make it sound as if success had come overnight. Referring to their first appearance at the Palladium, she claimed:

> We made a wonderful 'hit,' and the manager was delighted with us. After the show a music hall agent came round to see us and... booked us 'solid' for four years.[33]

Female double acts known as 'sister acts' were becoming fashionable at this time. Gwen and Norah were rarely on the same bill as a sister act because of the perceived similarity. The successful Trix Sisters – Helen and Josephine – had a parallel career in this period, performing in the same halls as Gwen and Norah, but never at the same time. With Helen on piano, they sang duets, harmonising musically – their voices almost identical to each other. In this respect they differed from Gwen and Norah whose voices contrasted very obviously, Norah having a range from mezzo to soprano and Gwen being a deep contralto and often mistaken for a man in the recordings they were to make later.

The Trix Sisters, who were American, 'established a reputation as a temperamental pair who were constantly at each other's throats'.[34] The Scottish Houston Sisters, too, were renowned for their backstage slanging matches. In their act, older sister Renée played the naughty girl while Billie – much more boyish in looks, vocal tone and personality – took the role of big brother, in flat cap, bow tie and sleeveless pullover. Their onstage dialogue consisted of one-upmanship and banter, while offstage Billie and Renée 'fought like cats... Our reputation for fighting and arguing preceded us'.[35]

Lorna and Toots Pounds were an Australian sister act who achieved some fame at this time; while the Duncan Sisters,

Rosetta and Vivian from California, were soon to visit London.

Beatie and Babs (the Samuels sisters) had started out in 1908 as child performers and were billed as juvenile comediennes. In 1912 they had performed at the first ever, one-off, Royal Command Performance in front of King George V. But their careers were soon to end when they both married and retired from the stage.

Elsie and Doris Waters, later to become the most famous UK 'sister act' of all, were still playing minor venues with their piano and violin act and closely observing rising artists they admired, Blaney and Farrar in particular.

With all these other female double acts on the circuit, it was crucial that Gwen and Norah distinguished themselves from the competition. As soon as they had regular bookings Gwen engaged a flamboyant young designer named Reginald de Veulle to create her stage costume. Reggie's creation was a stylish, tailored two-piece design, made of black satin and white cotton in the style of a seventeenth-century cavalier. There was a large white collar, cut close to the neck and spreading backwards, forwards and sideways across a shoulder piece, which was extended to cover the top of Gwen's chest. The sleeves were long and fitted tight over the arms, finishing with long white cotton cuffs. The bodice disguised Gwen's small bust with a flat panel at the front with parallel rows of military style buttons. Below the waist, black pantaloons gathered loosely at the calf, where more buttons completed the effect. The overall look was part Pierrot, part Harlequin, part Royalist soldier. It was entirely practical for playing the cello but still stagey and chic – the perfect outward expression of Gwen's eccentric style. With the addition of her horn-rimmed spectacles, variations on this outfit would form her stage 'look' for the rest of her career. Norah was able to coordinate with Gwen by wearing black or white, creating a magpie effect.

In July 1918 Gwen and Norah were featured in the society magazine *Tatler*, Gwen sporting her new costume and Norah in a rather less distinctive, off-the-shelf dress with full-length diaphanous sleeves. Two days later, Gwen spent her twenty-first birthday, 14 July, onstage with Norah and a host of stars in one of the capital's largest and most prestigious venues, the London Coliseum.

'Norah Blaney and Gwen Farrar are unconventional musicians, whose ragtime burlesque, with its youthful auxiliaries, is delightfully fresh,' said the critic from the *Financier*. [36]

Another wrote:

> Women steal a lot of men's thunder nowadays. The ragtime act with piano, usually done by energetic young men, has its feminine counterpart in the turn of Nora [sic] Blaney and Gwendoline Farrah [sic]. And very nice too. Courage is required from a young lady to climb on a piano, smoke a cigarette, do cat-calls and generally hold up the comedy corner of an act of this kind... Gwen manages it cleverly and throws in a bit of effective cello work as well. These two girls have grit and talent. As a combination they go very well and should have a future.[37]

The same agent who had advised Norah to go it alone was said to be 'running around us both in circles waving his date book in the air'.[38]

Caricature of Norah and Gwen in The Punch Bowl

~ 6 ~

A SWING OF THE PENDULUM

A s their stage act became fashionable, the duo acquired a home to match. When Gwen's eldest sister Helen married in Chelsea on 1 November 1917, she vacated the house on King's Road that their mother had purchased as a foothold in the fashionable borough. Gwen was allowed to move in. But to Lady Farrar's enormous disappointment, she insisted that Norah would be joining her.

After almost a year in Norah's small flat in Hammersmith, the move to Chelsea was a thrilling step for them both. They began packing boxes and making preparations, fitting the work in between rehearsals and almost nightly performances.

For Lady Farrar, Gwen's decision to perform in music halls was deeply shocking. As a young woman she had experienced a meteoric rise in her social status when she met and married George Farrar. Having achieved so much, through his wealth and honours and her own social networking, she was implacably opposed to anything which might undermine the family's somewhat fragile claim to be real aristocrats. A girl of Gwen's background and resources appearing on the music hall stage was simply 'not done'.

Gwen said in a newspaper interview:

> Until quite recently I always regarded myself as a very
> sedate and serious person. If it had been suggested, only
> a short time ago, that I should be amusing the music
> hall public, I'm afraid some of the people I know would

Gwen's drawings of their Chelsea home

have raised their lorgnettes and said, 'And, pray, what are
music halls?' When I declared that I intended to adopt
entertaining as my career [my friends] tried to argue me out
of this resolve, but the war had given me a new view of life.
I had seen it so clearly demonstrated that every girl, if need
be, should be able to earn her own living.[1]

In his book *The Sweet and Twenties,* Beverley Nichols humorously
echoed this theme:

> Disapproval of the music of the period was extended
> to some of its performers, in particular to a young lady
> with straight black hair, horn-rimmed glasses and square
> shoulders, who was called Gwen Farrar. Really, said the
> dowagers, there was no excuse for Gwen; after all she was a
> lady; she was quite rich, she had a delicious panelled house
> in Chelsea.[2]

The 'delicious panelled house' was the property which Gwen
now owned at 217 King's Road, on the corner of Glebe Place.
There was just one staircase – a beautiful square oak structure
– rising from the ground floor to the top of the house. Under
the eaves lived a cook and a maid, while on the first floor an
elegant drawing room at the front had views stretching north
up the length of Manresa Road towards Kensington. The only
other first-floor room was Gwen and Norah's bedroom, looking
out onto a small courtyard at the rear.

Next door lived the veteran theatre performer Ellen Terry,
aunt of beauteous Phyllis Neilson-Terry who had commissioned
Norah's Shakespeare compositions years earlier. Norah later
recalled a visit from the national treasure:

> Well, you know what moving's like. We were all sort of
> jammed up with tea chests, packed full of saucepans and
> goodness knows what. We'd only moved in a few days.
> There was a knock at the door and it was Ellen Terry, our
> next-door neighbour. We were so thrilled!
>
> And she said, 'Oh, I heard you'd come to live next door
> to me and I had to come and see you to tell you how
> delighted I was... I've always admired you so much!'

79

Gwen and I looked at each other in a strange sort of
way because we had only just *started*. Our feet were on the
bottom rung of the ladder.

She said, 'Now I must go. But I just wanted to tell
you how glad I am you've come to be my next-door
neighbours.' And she gave us a kiss and said, 'Dear, dear
Beatie and Babs.'[3]

The great lady had confused them with a rival 'sister act', but
how kind of her to call in!

Norah's account gives us a touching insight into their
moving day, a hands-on, joint effort. She crafted the story
to derive the utmost humour from the mistaken identity.
Expectations are subverted: Ellen Terry should have been
grand, but she was friendly; she thought the pair were famous,
but they were not. Good manners dictated that Gwen and
Norah must communicate their mirthful reactions through
looks and smiles. Suppressing their laughter made for an even
more ecstatic climax. In delivering these oft-repeated stories,
Norah continually focused on the non-verbal communication
she and Gwen shared, giving us clues about the nature of their
relationship, unconsciously making a connection between
their secret laughter and their clandestine sexual activity and
delighting herself by publicly recalling these occasions of great
personal happiness.

Ellen Terry's kindness to her new neighbours continued on
further acquaintance and she was alert to Gwen and Norah's
special bond. She introduced them to her daughter, the openly
lesbian director, producer, and costume designer, Edith Craig.
Edy, who lived in a sapphic *ménage à trois* in Kent, had founded
the Pioneer Players in 1911 to produce socially aware and
feminist plays. She was a generation older than Gwen and
Norah but they were to have many mutual friends and move in
overlapping circles all their lives.

Gwen made sketches of the interior and exterior of their
home and on the back Norah wrote, 'Drawings by Gwen of our
house at 217 King's Road, Chelsea.'

They made plans to refurbish the single-storey studio space

at the rear of the property as their music room and party venue. They were earning regularly now, and on top of that, Gwen's annual allowance of £5,000 meant they could afford to live in style.

By October 1918 the war was drawing to a close. The exciting developments of the past year had helped Gwen and Norah forget the reality of the conflict, barely giving them time to reflect on how they had each changed in the past four years. The war had deprived Gwen of her father, her cousin and her childhood friend; but in its later years, ironically, it had brought her satisfying work, independence and a wonderful new companion. Norah had come a long way since the Margate concert party, the unwanted attentions of Fred Wildon, and her hasty marriage to Albert Lyne. She wondered if her husband would make contact on his return to England and what the outcome would be. Gwen had a growing sense of unease about this unknown man who had the legal right to disrupt their blissful professional and personal partnership.

Albert was heading in a homeward direction, having seen action in Egypt and Palestine. Arriving in France, there was an optimistic rumour in his regiment that they had done their last turn in the line. In October, however, an order was suddenly issued forbidding the use of the word 'Armistice' and they were commanded to move forward to the attack, near the border with Belgium.

Albert was now geographically the closest he had been to England since his batallion was mobilised. So near and yet so far. The British line had pushed north-east and the Germans were in retreat, but their machine gunners still held out in pillboxes, strategically positioned across a terrain scarred by craters, wire and mud.

In what reads like an amalgam of all the horrors of the First World War combined, Albert's division went into action in an advance beset by confused and contradictory instructions, gas attacks, ceaseless rain, deep mud, miserable cold, night manoeuvres, low-flying enemy aircraft and supplies not getting through. The front line had advanced beyond the trenches and the only shelter was in hedges or in waterlogged shell holes. The *Regimental Gazette* described 'days and nights of hideous discomfort' from 11 to 14 October. There were long hours of waiting in ghastly conditions, followed by an advance, during which many German prisoners were captured but the gunners held out. Following an act of great bravery, Albert was seriously injured by machine-gun fire on 14 October. He was put on a hospital train bound for England, then hauled off the train at Calais and taken to the 30th General Hospital.

On 31 October 1918, Albert, still in Calais, died from his injuries, just eleven days before the end of hostilities. He was posthumously awarded the Military Medal.

We do not know when or how Norah was informed, but the records show that it was she who selected and paid for the inscription on Albert's headstone in the Military Cemetery at Sangatte. It reads: 'Mourned and Loved by his Wife and Parents.'

Her words were chosen with consideration and dignity. They formed a caring statement for the only audience who mattered in this instance – Albert's grieving mother and father. They were tactful words, free from sentimentality, that could be read in the past or the present tense. They were well chosen to avoid any insincere reference to eternity. They did all these things and they provided closure.

Gwen had the sensitivity to let Norah sadly remember Albert, barely admitting to herself the relief she felt that their partnership could no longer be challenged by a third party. Within two weeks they were back onstage at the London Palladium.

A sobering parcel arrived at the house, addressed to Mrs Albert Lyne. It contained Albert's few possessions, his final soldier's pay and a war gratuity of twelve pounds. Norah was entitled to a widow's pension but she did not apply.

The loss of Albert and so many of his contemporaries, on all sides, in the Great War, was traumatic. There was widespread recognition that this must be 'the war to end all wars'. Life had to go on and in a different vein.

On a personal level, the war had a profound psychological

impact on Norah and Gwen, as it did on their whole generation. They quietly grieved the friends they had lost and were conscious of having escaped combat and possible death by virtue of their gender. On top of this, their sexuality set them at odds with what they had been taught to believe. How could they reconcile their personal happiness with the guilt and shame they were supposed to be feeling?

The Church, in the past, had impressed its doctrines upon Gwen via Miss Berry's notions of original sin. In Norah's case, her parents' Catholicism and desire to conform were hugely influential. Gwen and Norah had been taught about the punitive fate that befell the inhabitants of Sodom and Gomorrah and knew the physical side of their relationship was an unspeakable transgression in the Church's terms. An all-powerful God saw within people's hearts and punished wrongdoers in the fires of hell.

On the other hand, they had just seen good men, like Sir George, Joey, John Kipling and Albert die in a hellish conflict, needlessly. The war, sanctioned by God and the Church, had made that happen. Their 'olders, wisers and betters' had failed, spectacularly, to prevent the greatest catastrophe of all time. Gwen and Norah sensed, along with many of their generation, that now was the time to challenge the outdated Victorian morality they had been brought up with.

Spanish-American writer and life-long lesbian Mercedes de Acosta said:

> The young – especially in England – kicked over the last
> vestiges of Victorian influence which had circumscribed
> and inhibited their lives… Now, at last, impulses concealed
> or suppressed were allowed to assert themselves, and young
> people of both sexes, thrilled with their new personal
> freedom, bounded out into the open.[4]

Celebrations to mark the Armistice were wild, ushering in a new era of hedonism for those who could afford it. On 27 November a Victory Ball Celebration Party took place at the Albert Hall. Extravagant fancy dress was worn. Famed society beauty Lady Diana Manners, dressed as Britannia, headed a great procession into the Hall, while an orchestra played Elgar's *Pomp and Circumstance March*.

The masculine-identifying artist Gluck went with a girlfriend. 'They made their costumes... Pierrot and Columbine [and] danced from ten at night until five in the morning.'[5] Gwen and Norah almost certainly attended the ball.

Another guest was the writer Alfred Noyes. His sense of the jarring disconnect between the celebrations and the reality of the conflict led him to write an anti-war poem called 'The Victory Ball'. It contained the lines:

> Shadows of dead men
> Stand by the wall,
> Watching the fun
> Of the Victory Ball.
> They do not reproach,
> Because they know,
> If they're forgotten
> It's better so.[6]

Even men who had survived the war felt forgotten. There was high unemployment and a rise, for the first time, in applications for divorce, as men returned home broken by the conflict and found that women's horizons had been broadened. On a political level there were calls for the establishment of a League of Nations to help maintain peace.

There was a flu pandemic and, in the street and at the theatre, some people wore gauze masks across their mouths and noses. Gwen drank liberal quantities of spirits before bed to ward off the virus. One of Norah's aunts by marriage died and her mother, Molly, rallied round to help with the children.

Norah's father, Walter, was a professor of the bassoon now and he and Molly still lived at 65 Lonsdale Road. They worried about Norah and the risk she was taking with the new act. What if it failed? Though they were impressed by the Farrar family pedigree, they were not at all sure about their daughter's cohabitation with Gwen. Like the parents in Sarah Waters' novel *The Paying Guests*, they worried, 'how would it look... people would suppose [them] fast, no man would ever want to marry [them].'[7]

Despite parental concerns, for the time being Gwen and Norah were managing their careers and their domestic lives perfectly well. Unlike a married couple starting out, they had no formal structure to refer to for organising their lives, resolving domestic issues or dealing with third parties. Nor did they have the protection, guarantees, respectability and social blessings that legal marriage conferred on a couple. In some ways this was liberating. They could make their own rules for coexistence, based on equality and personal autonomy. It worked, but against the odds, for, in spite of a growing recognition of women's capabilities, society continually undermined them with messages about female skittishness and unreliability. Even in granting the vote, Parliament had insisted only women over the age of thirty were eligible. So, when there was a general election on 14 December 1918, Gwen and Norah could not take part.

The first Christmas in their new home was a happy one. It was their second Christmas as a couple. Life was good. The growing success of their act reflected the harmony and strength of their relationship. The rapport they shared was obvious. The joy they derived from each other's musical expertise and comic imagination was contagious. Increasingly, audiences warmed to this clever pair who did not take themselves too seriously.

Touring provincial theatres was now an important part of Gwen and Norah's growing fame and success. They often travelled in Gwen's car, taking their life in their hands. Fortunately Norah had a sense of humour about being the passenger, claiming that Gwen described herself as, 'a girl in a leather motor coat, bending over the wheel, with big horn specs on her nose and an oily smudge down one cheek,' and adding, 'If you see a dark-haired girl sitting at her side with terror-filled eyes, you'll know it's me!'[8]

They saw in the New Year 1919 at the Bristol Hippodrome, followed swiftly by a trip to Leeds. Norah recalled: 'Gwen had never been into theatrical digs before and she was fascinated and horrified at the same time.'

Moving in for the week with a landlady, they ascertained from her that it would just be the three of them in the property: Gwen and Norah had the exclusive use of the front room and the first-floor rooms above it. 'That means the bathroom is all ours!' they rejoiced.

One night they were caught in a rainstorm on their way back after the theatre. They arrived drenched, took off their wet skirts and hung them on chairs in front of the fire while their landlady brought them baked beans on toast and cocoa. When they had finished eating, they picked up their skirts and made their way upstairs to bed – 'In our knickers!' recalled Norah. 'Gwen went up first and I was following in her footsteps, when suddenly I felt a grab at my bum and I shrieked. I looked round and there was a horrible man.'

The man disappeared, 'and we skedaddled up to our room. There was no key on the door so we pushed a chest of drawers up against it.'

The next day, a visitor came round to see Gwen after the show. He was a friend of the Farrar family, a senior judge, who happened to be in Leeds for work. He had noticed in the paper that Gwen was performing.

'How do you like being on the stage?' he asked them both.

'Well we haven't been at it very long.'

'Where are you living here?' he wanted to know.

'We're living in digs.'

'Oh, where?'

They told him the address and he invited himself to tea the next day. The landlady was busy making sandwiches down in the kitchen when the man arrived in his car, so Norah let him in. He had come to make sure he was correct about the property. Yes, the look on the landlady's face, when she saw him, confirmed it! He had been the presiding judge when she had been convicted of keeping a brothel.

Whether the story got back to Lady Farrar is unclear. It would no doubt have fuelled her disapproval. Gwen and Norah took these things in their stride. It was another funny story to relate. Things that would have been horribly unpleasant as a solo artist travelling alone, were bearable – even exciting – with a lover and friend to share the adventure.

Norah finished the anecdote, fifty years later, by adding that they accepted the judge's offer of a ride to more salubrious lodgings where they stayed for the rest of the week.[9]

Telling the story, Norah delighted in mimicking the judge's pompous concern over the girls' predicament. Her account was not unsympathetic to the unfortunate landlady. She mined the story for its entertainment value and, possibly, as with all her stories, embellished it at the expense of accuracy. One knows, though, that there was a strong kernel of truth in her words, because of the confidence of her narration and the delight she took in remembering Gwen's responses. In her accounts, Norah and Gwen's ability to laugh at themselves gives them agency and perspective. In her narration of the story, as in real life, the judge was not in charge of this situation, though he may have thought he was. Gwen and Norah were.

In the August sunshine they motored north to Newcastle and thence to Sheffield and Liverpool on a tour of Hippodrome theatres. Speaking thirty years later, Norah recalled:

> One day in Liverpool I made a desperate personal decision. I went into a hairdresser's and had my long hair cut off. When I got home my poor old Dad cried, it looked so revolting. The only thing was to go a bit further and have it shingled.[10]

The landlady at their Liverpool digs, perhaps because of Norah's new hair, was convinced that she looked like someone, but she couldn't remember who. Every day she'd look at Norah and shake her head, trying to remember who it was she resembled. The walls of the dining room were covered with framed, autographed photographs of previous theatrical guests. One day, as she was serving their breakfast, she suddenly exclaimed, 'I've got it!'

Pointing at a photo she declared, 'It's him!'

'He... looks like Miss Blaney?' queried Gwen.

'Spitting image.'

'That man?' said Gwen.

'Ooh, yes,' the landlady insisted. 'That's him – the Royal Sussex Dwarf!'[11]

The idea of being mistaken for a man was absurd to Norah, who prided herself on her femininity. If either of them was going to be taken for a man then it was Gwen. Like Ellen Terry thinking they were famous, it was topsy-turvy. It became another of Norah's favourite theatrical stories, almost all of which revolve around the looks and suppressed laughter she and Gwen shared.

Gwen had her own way of highlighting the humour of life on the road by drawing sketches of them both onstage, in the bath and in bed. It is hard to resist the charm and candour of these simple images showing the two women facing their audiences hand in hand and sharing the same room night after night. They were drawn for Norah's delight, humour being one of the key ways they communicated their love for each other. Norah's recollections and Gwen's sketches combine to give us a really happy picture of their partnership in this period.

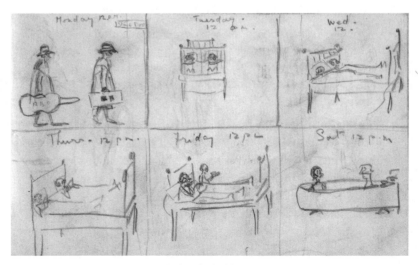

Gwen's sketches of life on tour

In March 1919 Norah and Gwen were at the Hackney Empire, where they met the song-writing duo, Robert Weston and Bert Lee. These prolific composers aimed to write a new song each day. They had scored a hit with 'Good-bye-ee' in 1917, and earlier still Weston had written 'When Father Papered the Parlour'. They would go on to compose several songs specifically for Gwen and Norah. Seeing Norah's new short hair they came up with 'Shall I Have It Bobbed or Shingled?', the first in a series of topical songs that marked an expansion of Gwen and Norah's repertoire.

> Sweet Susie Simpson had such lovely hair,
> It reached down to her waist;
> 'Til friends sweetly told her that around Mayfair
> Having hair was thought bad taste.
> 'Bob or shingled it must be, dear,'
> Said they, 'If you wish to wed,'
> Until in blank despair, in the fatal chair,
> At the hairdressers shop she said:
>
> 'Shall I have it bobbed or shingled?
> Shall I have it shingled or bobbed?
> Sister Cissy says, "Oh have it shorn short, Sue,
> Shingled, shorn and shaved like the swell set do."
> Shall I have it shingled shorter?'
> Said Sue as she sighed and sobbed;
> 'Sister Cissy says she'd sooner see it short and shingled,
> But both my brothers Bert and Bobby say it's better bobbed.'[12]

A further verse imagined Lady Godiva in the hairdresser's chair facing the same dilemma.

Weston and Lee's songs were quintessentially English and when Gwen and Norah started including them in their repertoire it added a new dimension to their turn that properly distinguished them from other 'sister acts'. In collaboration with Weston and Lee, Gwen and Norah became satirists of English manners, making comic topical observations on subjects like the fashion for men wearing plus fours, the craze for crossword puzzles and the growth of the London suburbs.

These songs helped them gain popularity fast and could be slotted into their act alongside the romantic songs they sang, in high camp fashion, to each other. But as quickly as topical material ignites the public imagination, it starts to burn out and seem dated as the moment passes. Being famous for topical material partly explains why they were later forgotten and definitely accounts for their exclusion from the classification 'highbrow' by snobbish critics and academics of the period. Gwen and Norah's act would most definitely have been dismissed as 'middlebrow'.

This comment from a twenty-first century reappraisal of women's fiction previously dismissed as 'middlebrow' is perhaps relevant to Gwen and Norah's topical writing and performing:

> Immediately responsive to shifts in public tastes... aware of the latest trends, both popular and intellectual – the 'middlebrow' was able to continually reinvent itself, incorporating highbrow experimentation, language, and attitudes almost as soon as they were formulated, and combining them with a mass accessibility and pleasurable appeal.[13]

It was hard work to stay on top of current events but Gwen and Norah kept this satirical element in their act for over a decade.

In the first few months of 1919 Gwen and Norah were able to consolidate their London fan base with a series of performances in and around the capital. They followed a run at the Victoria Palace Theatre in January with an exceptionally successful week at the Coliseum. A critic from the *Stage* reported that they:

> contrast very effectively the appeal of high-class pianoforte and 'cello solos with their enjoyable burlesques of ragtime melodies. The young lady who plays the 'cello now gives an excellent rendering of Saint-Saëns' *La Mort du Cygne*.[14]

In fact he focused more on Norah and Gwen than on the acts at the top of the bill – two names that still resonate today: the legendary male impersonator Vesta Tilley, who had been delighting audiences since 1870 and, by contrast, Sergei Diaghilev with his ultra-modern Ballets Russes.

Vesta Tilley, most famous for her man-about-town character, Burlington Bertie, swaggering about in top hat and tails, was the best known of several major female stars who performed dressed as men. Hetty King, with her signature song, 'All The Nice Girls Love a Sailor'; and Ella Shields, who sang 'Oh! It's a Lovely War!', were others. Of the three of them, Tilley was the most careful to deflect criticism of her masculine performance style by cultivating an ultra-feminine persona offstage and being seen in the latest fashions, jewellery and furs. At fifty-five, she was at the start of a year-long 'farewell tour', necessitated by her husband's desire to become a Conservative MP. Up to now Walter de Frece had been a producer, rivalling Oswald Stoll with his range of Hippodrome theatres around the UK. The couple's continuing association with the stage was thought to be incompatible with his political ambitions. He was awarded a knighthood in 1919 and Vesta Tilley became Lady de Frece.

Diaghilev had a genius for bringing together the most exciting avant-garde designers, composers and choreographers in short ballets that stunningly blended music, dance and visuals. They had taken Paris and America by storm. Diaghilev had left his native Russia, never to return – when the Revolution came Soviet leaders branded him the epitome of bourgeois decadence. He is famous for his tempestuous relationship with his sensationally talented male star Nijinsky.

The lineup at the Coliseum that week represents a historic juxtaposition of two remarkably famous acts: one old, one new; both clearly enjoying huge popular appeal; both destined to hold their place in cultural memory; and both, in their way, offering a look at the world through a queer lens. Norah and Gwen more than held their own alongside these cultural icons. Their act could be appreciated in a variety of ways by different sections of the audience, from gay sophisticates who understood the camp coding of their interactions, to more conventionally minded spectators who saw nothing out of the ordinary in their quirky comedy and sentimental ballads. For audience members enjoying the fantasy of a world in which Tilley was a man and the Ballets Russes dancers were fauns and puppets, Norah and

Gwen's witty lesbian camaraderie fitted right in. Their ability to send up high art by expertly rendering a classical piece then shifting, in a beat, to ragtime and clowning worked well with audiences who were there to see both artistry and comedy.

If Walter and Molly were still disappointed that Norah had deserted the concert platform, they must have been grudgingly impressed to see her and Gwen sharing the stages of London's biggest theatres with hugely established artists.

In April, Norah and Gwen appeared at the Southend Hippodrome with their mentor, Arthur Prince. This time their names were spelled correctly.

By now Norah had a bespoke stage costume to match Gwen's Pierrot outfit. Taking his inspiration from Pierrot's love interest, Columbine, in the traditional *Commedia dell'arte*, the French designer Jean Patou created an attractive sleeveless white muslin dress for her with a black satin sash at the waist. A black rosette adorned the right shoulder and similar circular black appliqués patterned the skirt, which fell around the calf with a handkerchief hem.

In the centuries' old stories, Columbine was coquettish and unfaithful to Pierrot, the buffoon, who pined with love and forgave her infidelities. In identifying themselves with these stock heterosexual characters, Gwen and Norah, consciously or unconsciously, were revealing something about the intimate nature of their relationship, but what they could not know was how close they would come to living out these roles in real life.

In a studio session they were photographed in these outfits, carefully posed, side on to the camera, Gwen's hand resting almost secretively on Norah's hip. Their right legs are bent at an identical angle, their right heels are raised and their pointed toes rest on the floor in camp fashion.

This studied theatricality was a reflection of their onstage interaction:

> There is something immensely attractive about Gwen
> Farrar's fierce humour. She takes the line of being
> quite obviously furious with Norah Blaney's perpetual
> 'enthusing,' and has a whimsical way with her that strikes a

new note. They are both excellent musicians – Norah at her piano and Gwen Farrar her cello. It is soothing and pleasant to hear the low notes of 'Drink to Me Only with Thine Eyes' peal from the strings of Gwen's great instrument.[15]

This was the verdict of a critic watching Norah and Gwen when they returned to the Palladium in November 1919, still performing that seductive song. Gwen's fury with Norah was an act. There are none of the tales of offstage rows and bickering that attach to the Trix Sisters or Billie and Renée Houston.

Norah said, 'Ah, Gwen was... well I can't describe Gwen. She was unique. I loved her more than anybody in the world. But she was... she was quite unique.'[16]

At the Palladium in 1919 they were sharing the bill with Ella Shields, who, like Vesta Tilley, appeared as a version of Burlington Bertie, supremely confident in top hat, tails and silver-topped cane. In this and other drag roles she delivered suggestive songs with titles like 'Why Did I Kiss that Girl?' and 'If You Knew Susie like I know Susie'. Watching these performances informed and emboldened Gwen and Norah's later masculine incarnations. What is more, Ella Shields and her dresser Minnie Goss had a discreet sapphic connection that Gwen and Norah recognised as distinctly familiar.

But the age when male impersonators were hugely popular was coming to an end. Since the war, seeing women in men's attire onstage was, for audiences, less of a novelty. Beatrice Lillie spent most of the war performing in drag as a 'girl hero' and made a huge success of it, but, by 1919, producer André Charlot had decided she should go back into skirts. It had something to do with the men returning from the Army and wanting to see traditional gender roles restored. There was a sense, for conservatives, that the world had gone mad and the idea of a return to normality became a priority.

Whatever 'normality' was, a return to it was impossible. Leslie Baily describes the behaviour of those who could afford it after the war as 'a pagan orgy of thanksgiving... a swing of the pendulum from horrors that young people knew they had so narrowly escaped.'[17]

Fashion was starting to favour an androgynous look for women, but that set alarm bells ringing amongst the old guard. Women were asserting themselves in the workplace, but the patriarchy was not ready to roll over. The Twenties was about to be a decade of experiment and freedom, but moral censors, bigots and chauvinists had not gone away.

Gwen and Norah were making their mark and mixing with the greatest artists of the day. For Norah, this was the culmination of many years of dedicated professional work. For Gwen it was more of a novelty, a distraction from the grief of losing her father, a madcap adventure, an opportunity to put her cello-playing experience to good use, a chance to defy her mother, a way to experiment with expressing her personality and sexuality onstage.

She was now incorporating into her comedy performance the full range of childhood influences: the rubbery facial expressions of Frank Rhodes; Kipling's po-faced delivery of nonsense language; quacks and barks and the engine cranking noises of the first family car. Because she showed such artistry on the cello and worked so musically with Norah, Gwen's comic additions and interruptions seemed even funnier. The silly noises and asides cleverly undercut the apparent seriousness of her playing. In André Charlot's revue, *Cheep*, Beatrice Lillie was deriving similar sorts of laughs, as part of 'The Dedleigh Dull Quartet', with sheet music perched on a chrysanthemum protruding from her bosom. Lillie went on to enjoy great acclaim in England and North America as 'the funniest woman in the world'. She was a dark-haired, mischievous, daring comedy performer who came to life in front of an audience. Her droll sophistication and camp double-entendres were adored by audiences, particularly those with an understanding of the queer nuance behind her wit. As a solo performer, Lillie was working with great style and panache in a similar vein to Gwen and Norah, and they became good friends.

Gertrude Lawrence was another rising star, a regular colleague of Lillie, who would go on to achieve fame on both sides of the Atlantic and, later in life, chalk up interesting queer form.

Charlot was soon to recognise and promote Gwen and Norah, and incorporate them in his revues, just as he had with Bea Lillie and Gertrude Lawrence.

On 9 May 1920 the British press competed with each other to be the first to 'out' Gwen as an aristocrat. The *Evening Star* headline read: MILLIONAIRE'S DAUGHTER ON LONDON STAGE. The *Sunday Post* claimed an exclusive: 'Very much surprised that her secret was out, Miss Farrar consented to unfold the story of her romance.'[18]

The 'romance' was, of course, not the truth of Gwen's devoted love affair with Norah, but the entertaining news that she had left behind the luxury of enormous family wealth to travel the country entertaining the general public.

Beverley Nichols satirically summed up the reaction of the moneyed classes to Gwen's career choice:

> She insisted on singing in public, on the music hall stage,
> with that young Norah Blaney at the piano. True they drew
> the town, but somehow when one remembered Gwen's
> dear father, who was a near millionaire, it all seemed a great
> pity.[19]

The newspapers celebrated Gwen, enjoying the way she had succeeded on merit rather than through wealthy connections. She was quoted at length:

> On a level with everybody else! That was my main idea.
> If I had gone on the Music Hall stage as the daughter
> of Sir George Farrar, backed up with a publicity boom, I
> might have been a nine days wonder and then possibly a
> complete fizzle.
>
> It's not easy for women to be really funny on the stage;
> but they tell us that we are, and that's our reward.
>
> To the unknown, untried performer, the audience, as
> a whole, shoves out its neck and looks as though it were
> saying, 'Now then, young woman, show us what you can
> do. Make us laugh in less than a couple of minutes or off
> you go.'
>
> On the halls we actually measure our success in minutes.

It is difficult to keep people tickled when they demand that you shall be either funny, clever or striking or all three at once.

One thing more I think ought to be said about the present day Music Hall audience. The women are sometimes quicker in picking up the fun than the men.[20]

The *Sunday Post* ran a large picture feature showing Chicheley Hall and the Farrar home in South Africa, Bedford Court, as well as interviewing Gwen about the experience of crossing the ocean so often as a child and her father's political and military honours.

The press frenzy was good publicity for their act, which especially pleased Norah. However, it was now her turn to be sensitive to Gwen's loss, for the article stirred painful memories. Bedford Court was lying empty. An inventory of items still left there reveals a family home frozen in time, stopped in its tracks by the single shattering blow of Sir George's death. In October 1920 Gwen's sisters, Muriel, Marjorie, Kathleen and Ella, set off for South Africa with their mother on their first visit since Sir George's funeral in 1915. Their task was to divide up or dispense with the items that held so many memories and put the house and land on the market.

Some items that could not be brought back were taken east to the family home eldest sister Helen was building with her husband, Basil Turner, in White River. There, in a blessed diversion from the arduous task at hand, Lady Farrar met her first grandchild, also called Helen.

Of the family, only Gwen was too busy to travel to take part in this necessary exercise.

Muriel was soon to be married. Her fiancé, Anthony Lowther, was a nephew of the 'Yellow' Earl of Lonsdale whose family seat in Cumbria was the immense Lowther Castle. Outlying members of the huge Lonsdale clan owned swathes of land, including Lonsdale Road, Barnes, site of the smart, Edwardian semi-detached house where Norah had spent her teens and Molly and Walter still lived. Norah revelled in regaling her parents with this coincidence. The Cordwells loved a brush with nobility. Taking advantage of her parents' snobbishness, Norah was able to use the Farrars' aristocratic connections to distract them from the truth of her domestic setup with Gwen. Women-only households, though not at all rare since the war, were regarded as a sad substitute for heterosexual marriage and family life. No one in Norah or Gwen's family imagined this would be a permanent arrangement.

Writing in the *New Statesman* in 1920, Virginia Woolf had urged women wanting professional lives to 'make a dash for it and disregard a species of torture more exquisitely painful, I believe, than any that man can imagine'.[21] Gwen and Norah sang a topical song on the same theme. Titled 'We Don't Want to Get Married', the lyrics went on:

> We're having too much fun,
> We don't want to be bothered with any certain one...
> Behind a husband love may lurk,
> But I'd much sooner look for work.[22]

They were secretly creating for themselves an admirable contemporary alternative to marriage which could flourish alongside their growing careers. They had 'made a dash for it' and now the task was to sustain their lifestyle with the same style and energy they had used to create it.

They had similar tastes in home decorations, sharing a fondness for antiques:

> These days the bachelor girl is just as keen on her house
> and her furniture as the matron and Gwen Farrar and her
> friend Norah Blaney... are keener than most. When you
> go and see them at their charming house in King's Road,
> Chelsea, you usually find that they have just picked up
> something for its adornment.[23]

They acquired a puppy called Flea, a white wire-haired terrier. When journalist Margaret Chute visited what she described as 'the delightful house where Norah Blaney lives with Gwen Farrar or vice versa or both', she was introduced to Flea in the music room. 'Isn't he divine? He hears all our songs and if he likes them, that's good enough,' they said. Chute described:

> ... sitting in a fascinating music room, watching Gwen
> Farrar perched on the grand piano singing seconds in her
> particularly penetrating voice, with Norah Blaney at the
> keyboard, playing like an artist and singing like an angel
> with a sense of humour.[24]

Now their newly laid-out music room was complete, Gwen and Norah began entertaining. Musical party games, quizzes and practical jokes characterised these occasions.

Noel Coward was a frequent guest. 'He knew all the answers to everything,'[25] Norah recalled. Coward, who would go on to be recognised at 'the Master' of brilliant, brittle social comedies and witty songs that satirised English behaviour, had a number of things in common with Norah. They both came from lower middle-class homes in the south-west suburbs of London, both had ambitious mothers who immersed them in music from an early age and both had prodigious talent and drive. Their lives would be linked by parallel enterprises and mutual friends for decades, but it would be forty years before Norah would join Noel on the same project.

Another visitor was Anthony Eden (later Prime Minister), whom Gwen knew well and loved to tease. One day, knowing he was coming, she went to an art gallery in the King's Road and picked up a couple of abstract oil paintings. 'Awful daubs,' Norah called them. Gwen deliberately hung them upside down in the studio and made a point of asking 'Tony' Eden what he thought of them. Putting in his eye glass, he had a good look and said, 'Very fine, very fine,' much to the girls' amusement.

Gwen and Norah were involved in a more serious art venture when, in February 1921, they helped set up a gallery at 91 King's Road. For the opening, the walls were hung with paintings by young hopefuls, as well as some by the distinguished war artist CRW Nevinson. After a great deal of initial publicity, there is no more trace, suggesting the gallery was not a long-term success.

Ivor Novello was another guest at their house at 217 King's Road. Like Coward he was a young gay actor/composer with a busy social life and an increasingly large fan base. Gwen and Norah went to his famous parties at Flat 4, The Aldwych, above the Strand Theatre, going up in the notoriously shaky lift, to do a turn alongside stars such as Gertrude Lawrence and Bea Lillie.

Teddie Gerard was also to become a regular visitor to Gwen and Norah's home. Before the war this Argentinian actress had innovated the backless dress, parading in front of a chorus of young men who sang, with double meaning, 'We're so glad to see you're back, dear lady!' The famous photographer Cecil Beaton described Gerard at a party: 'She was quite drunk... a perpetual tomboy. She hooted with foghorn laughter. She sat on someone's knee, tried to be a vampire and toppled over backwards on to the floor.'[26] Mercedes De Acosta said, 'Everyone loved her. She moved like a panther. She was gay, wild, beautiful, generous, full of fun, and a trifle mad.'[27]

The men of the British 'Establishment' were meanwhile becoming alarmed by what they saw as women's increasingly disturbing behaviour. On 4 August 1921 the House of Commons voted to amend the law to outlaw 'acts of indecency' between women. The idea was swiftly rejected by the House of Lords, who feared passing the bill would plant ideas in women's heads. The Earl of Malmesbury said:

> We all know that vice has been increasing partly owing
> to the nervous conditions following on the war, but I
> believe... that all these unfortunate specimens of humanity
> exterminate themselves by the usual process.[28]

Other epithets, such as 'unbalanced', 'neurotic' and 'decadent' were used to describe the perpetrators of an offence which none of the Lords could bring themselves to name and few believed was practised by any but a small, albeit growing minority. Lord Desart argued that the amendment would lead to cases of blackmail and that women 'would pay anything sooner than face being brought into a public court to meet a charge of that kind'.[29]

Though most of the speakers emphasised women's gullibility and innocence, none of those present could erase from their minds the case of Maud Allan three years earlier, and the implication that her alleged behaviour had endangered national security.

There were new rumours that suggested 'the taint of this noxious and horrible suspicion'[30] was on the increase: cases like that of Violet Keppel – daughter of Edward VII's mistress, Alice, who was working desperately hard to suppress rumours about Violet's passion for Vita Sackville-West (consummated in a Cornish cottage in July 1918).[31]

Radclyffe Hall was living openly with Lady Una Troubridge, and had been publicly labelled a 'grossly immoral woman' for allegedly wrecking Admiral Sir Ernest Troubridge's marriage. Their friend Toupie Lowther, whose brother Claude was Conservative MP for Lonsdale (another distantly connected member of the Lowther/Lonsdale clan) spent 1921 courting the lesbian painter Romaine Brooks, a key member of Natalie Clifford Barney's Parisian circle. An interconnecting network of wealthy British, French and American lesbians was growing, dining in smart restaurants, attending theatrical first nights and holidaying in Capri, Florence, and fashionable resorts in France. Oil heiress Joe Carstairs had just settled in London, with a healthy disregard for convention and a passion for women and fast motors.

The family behind the hugely successful Lyons tea rooms and Corner Houses were despairing of a young relative they perceived as female who dressed as a man, smoked a pipe, used the name 'Gluck' and was busy building up a portfolio of paintings in readiness to present 'a one man show'. They diagnosed 'a kink in the brain'.[32]

While men were getting hot under the collar in the Houses of Parliament, all over the country women were independently and discreetly settling down to life after the war, many of them in same-sex partnerships. There was a 'surplus' – as it was unkindly called – of about two million women. No doubt some were profoundly unhappy and frustrated by the lack of a husband, but many flourished, both professionally and personally, outside the confines of conventional marriage, in committed and loving female friendships.

There was no shared vocabulary, though, to openly discuss these lifestyles. Gwen and Norah had no established role models; instead they were serving as role models for others, like Marjorie and Peggy.

They knew, of course, of Edy Craig's unconventional *ménage à trois* in Kent. Their neighbour Ellen Terry was entirely accepting of her daughter's domestic arrangement, and spoke with great approval and support of Gwen and Norah too, unperturbed by their setup. When they played the Bristol Hippodrome in March 1921, the *Western Daily Press* quoted Miss Terry at length, in an article specifically 'recommending that uncommon pair of entertainers Miss Norah Blaney and Miss Gwen Farrar' and calling them 'her protégées'.[33]

Such an endorsement was another boost to their burgeoning careers. These girls seemed to be living charmed lives, even walking away without a scratch from a serious collision in which their car turned over.

In July 1921 they signed a contract to replace the American Duncan Sisters in a West End revue, *Pins and Needles* at the Gaiety Theatre. This was the iconic venue where Norah had been taken as a child to see her idol, Gertie Millar.

A week later Gwen and Norah turned, respectively, twenty-four and twenty-eight. They had much to celebrate. Their act was in tune with the zeitgeist and the events and trends of the 1920s would soon prove a rich source of material for their satirical songs.

As the decade got into its stride, Gwen and Norah were on the crest of a wave.

In Gwen's sketches she talks to the Prince of Wales while Norah sits on his lap in the taxi; Norah rings the bell for Kathleen as he lights Gwen's cigarette

~ 7 ~

SUITORS

As Gwen and Norah's fame grew, they received bookings to perform at private parties, arriving after they'd finished at the theatre.

Sir Philip Sassoon, one of the era's most extravagant hosts, was parliamentary private secretary to the Prime Minister, David Lloyd George. He invited the PM and Edward, Prince of Wales, to a lavish soirée at his Park Lane home, at which Gwen and Norah were to provide the entertainment. Prince Edward[1] (David to his friends) was passionate about the theatre, loved to party with Ivor Novello and his crowd, and was a fan of Gwen and Norah.

Norah takes up the story:

> When we got there after our show, the prince was sitting looking quite impatient in the hall. I think he had been rather bored and when we arrived he said, 'Ooh, thank goodness you've come.'[2]

After they had performed and the party was coming to an end, the prince and Lloyd George offered to see them home. They took a taxi. Norah sat on the prince's lap and when they arrived and she and Gwen got out, so did the men. The prince said, 'Come on, let's just come in and have a drink.' It was very late by then. Gwen whispered to Norah, 'We haven't got any drink in the house.'

The prince said to Norah, 'What are you two whispering about?'

'Well, I'm afraid we haven't got any drink.'

'Oh no!' he said.

So Gwen said, 'Ooh, I know. Kathleen' – the cook – 'has got a bottle of rum that a sailor gave her.'

'Well, let's have that,' said the prince.

When they reached the front door, Gwen found she did not have her key. The only thing for it was to ring the bell. They looked up to the top of the house and saw the light go on in the maid's bedroom. And a few minutes later, down came Kathleen, her flaming red hair in curlers. She put on the hall light, opened the door and nearly fainted when she saw the Prince of Wales and the Prime Minister. Norah ends the story by saying that the bottle of rum was brought down from Kathleen's bedroom and thoroughly quaffed.[3]

Gwen recorded a version of this story in her sketch book, but in her drawings there is no sign of Lloyd George and there is evident rivalry between herself and the prince, who seems to be laying claim to Norah in an entitled fashion as she sits on his lap.

Perhaps Norah embroidered her version of the story to include Lloyd George in order to detract from the impropriety of this triangular encounter. Norah's divided loyalties were laid bare, exposing the tension between, on the one hand, her desire to kowtow and conform and, on the other hand, her love for Gwen. This tension was to resurface again and again throughout their relationship.

Norah even hinted to Derek Hunt, in later years, that her relationship with the heir to the throne had extended, briefly, to an unofficial two-week-long engagement. No evidence for this exists but in making such a claim perhaps Norah was weaving a romantic cloak to simultaneously shield her relationship with Gwen and place herself centre stage in the ultimate princess fantasy. How much more glamorous would such a liaison have seemed to the outside world (in 1976, just as in 1921) than the secret of her forbidden love for Gwen, around which romantic dreams could not be publicly constructed.

Both women knew that Norah's flirtation with the prince

was little more than a passing excitement and, in sketching these royal encounters, Gwen seems to delight in portraying herself as equal, if not superior, to him in the rivalry for Norah's affections. Her sense of humour about the situation is evident. This was not a relationship that would threaten her and Norah's bond. Nor would it do any harm to their careers.

On 26 November 1921 crowds thronged Leicester Square and Charing Cross Road, pressing as close as they could to the Hippodrome Theatre.[4] Gwen and Norah were appearing second on the bill at the first of the regular Royal Variety Shows. However, the crowds were there to see the newly engaged Princess Mary, only sister of David, Bertie and George. All the publicity went to her and her fiancé, Viscount Lascelles, so we know little about the performance. Our only eye-witness account comes from Lady Farrar, who had consented, perhaps for the first time, to see her daughter onstage with Norah. She wrote to her eldest, Helen: '[Gwen] was very good and the Royal Party seemed pleased,' adding, 'She is very thin and rather sad. I don't suppose for a moment she is, as she has chosen the life she leads.'[5]

The final sentence betrays a real distaste in Lady Farrar for Gwen's choices and a conviction that her way of life was perversely unhealthy. Although she was an inveterate snob, Lady Farrar could not take pride in the sight of her daughter appearing by royal command. Showing an alarming failure of the imagination, she seems to have interpreted Gwen's hangdog, laconic, camp, faux-depressed performance style (rolling her eyes in comic exasperation) literally as sadness. Lady Farrar wanted to see gaiety, elegance and demure charm. What Gwen delivered was the exact opposite. It was, of course, very original and funny, but Lady Farrar was too ashamed of Gwen to be able to relax and enjoy her performance. She deplored Gwen's lack of femininity and dreaded to think what kind of life she would lead in the future.

A few months earlier, in August, Gwen and Norah appeared at the Sheffield Hippodrome alongside the queer entertainer Fred Barnes. In 1907 he had written the song that made him a star, 'The Black Sheep of the Family'. Audiences were excited by his self-awareness in a performance that as good as declared his homosexuality. He acquired thousands of women fans, who, with Fred as the object of their affections, could indulge in passionate, but entirely safe, romantic fantasies. By 1921 he was a wealthy star. But bouts of heavy drinking masked the grief he felt about his father's suicide, which allegedly resulted from profound embarrassment about his son's stage persona.

Gwen began adding to her repertoire a large number of self-deprecating songs, along the lines of Barnes' lyrics:

> I'm the black sheep of the family
> Everybody runs me down
> People shake their heads at me
> Say I'm a disgrace to society.[6]

The titles of the songs Gwen performed over the next few years give a sense of their content: 'I'm Always Just a Little Bit Not Right', for instance, or 'I Can't Get the One I Want', 'Somebody's Wrong', 'I'm Following You', 'Sitting Around', 'What About Me?', 'You Flew Away from the Nest', and 'I May Be Wrong but I Think You're Wonderful'.

Countless comics cite the need to draw attention to their own perceived shortcomings as a way of anticipating and defusing audience sneers or hostility. It is a well-known strategy. But there were dangers in making herself the butt of the joke. The risk was that not only the public, but she herself, would grow to believe in the inadequate, buffoon version of Gwen.

Theatrically, these tragi-comic songs benefitted the double act by building empathy with the audience. They helped differentiate Gwen's onstage character from Norah's, adding another dimension to their dynamic.

Their star was rising. 'Gwen Farrar and Norah Blaney are of course the premier British double turn at the piano,'[7] said the critic from the *Sunday Post* in November.

In 1921 new, relaxed licensing laws permitted alcohol to be served until past midnight if ordered with food. The Metropole Hotel in Brighton began the idea of dinner cabarets to take advantage of this change. Gwen and Norah were frequent Sunday visitors to Brighton, often taking the Southern Belle steam train which left Victoria at midnight. The return fare was twelve shillings – more than half the average weekly wage.

> It was practically packed with theatrical people all rushing down to Brighton to get their noses full of a bit of ozone before they went back to the show on Monday night (those of us who could afford it). We always used to sit together, our little gathering... The waiter would look after us every week.[8]

It is likely that Gwen and Norah also visited mid-week to perform at the Brighton Metropole. By the start of 1922, these cabarets had proved such a success that the *Midnight Follies* were launched at London's Hotel Metropole, then in Northumberland Avenue between Whitehall and the Strand. The producer André Charlot was involved in this venture and he put in his established star, Gertrude Lawrence, as the main attraction, while appointing a twenty-three-year-old ex-Guards officer and old Etonian, Philip Durham, to manage the nightly show. Six nights a week audiences arrived at 9.30 for dinner and dancing, before the show began at 11.30. The idea was a novelty and felt appealingly decadent after the privations of the war. It was a huge success.

Gwen and Norah were hired by Charlot to join the twelve-strong lineup of performers, and so began their association with the man they called the 'Guv'.

A snippet of footage exists of Gwen and Norah in the *Midnight Follies*,[9] which is interesting not only because it was shown in cinemas as part of Pathé's new weekly content for women, *Eve's Film Review*. It was also extremely quirky.

A grand piano stands on the dance floor which is surrounded on three sides by people at tables, cabaret-style. Gwen and Norah are caught on camera at the end of their act, right at the front of the performance space, turning to make their exit. Gwen takes hold of Norah's hand and suddenly squats and waddles across the dance floor, very much like a duck. They let go of hands in order to get past the piano. Then Gwen stands and races Norah up a flight of stairs. At the top she performs a very formal bow, her upper body bent forward as her feet and legs move to the left. She straightens herself to stride off, casting a business-like glance back at her partner. Norah's bow and general demeanour are as graceful and demure as Gwen's are forthright and assertive. The audience are seen applauding them delightedly. Unlike the cinema viewers, the live audience has been treated to a performance of their songs.

According to Norah, when André Charlot was asked, 'Why do you have Norah Blaney and Gwen Farrar in your shows?' he said, 'Norah fills the stalls with all the young men, and Gwen has all the lesbians in London to see her. I've got the best of both worlds!'[10] If his use of the 'L' word sounds anachronistic, let's remember Charlot was born and raised in Belle Époque Paris, a city as frank and accepting of alternative sexualities as London was embarrassed by them.

While Gwen and Norah were still performing at the Metropole, Charlot put them in *Pot Luck*, his latest revue at the Vaudeville Theatre on the Strand. It also starred Beatrice Lillie, a kindred spirit, unconventional, witty, playful and camp.

Gwen and Norah had arrived. Their professional lives now matched the chic sophistication of their Chelsea lifestyle. However, Gwen and Norah's 'bachelor girl' ménage was about to be disrupted, if only on the surface.

As far as the newspapers were concerned, what Gertrude Lawrence and Bea Lillie had in 1922 that Norah lacked was a handsome Guards officer admirer. Lillie had already married hers and through him would become Lady Peel. She wrote:

> [He] was a firm favourite with Mumsie who kept busy pasting in yet another scrapbook whole pages from the society magazines with such scrumptious headlines as 'A Wedding Bell and Its Peel.'[11]

Gertrude Lawrence was dating the well-connected Captain Philip Astley, who was 'everything a knight in armour should be, as dreamed of by a young romantic girl'.[12] Weddings were in the air. With all the fanfare and excitement of a modern royal wedding, Princess Mary and Henry Lascelles (who had wowed the crowds weeks earlier outside the Hippodrome) married in Westminster Abbey in February. Three weeks earlier, Gwen's sister Muriel had tied the knot with Anthony Lowther.

It is hard to overstate the role parents played in arranging and staging these nuptials. Lady Farrar's success in finding good matches for her eldest daughters, Helen and Muriel, had given her a real taste for the role of marriage broker, which she saw as her raison d'être. With so many men lost in the war it was a difficult task, made even more problematic by the fact that her next eldest girls, Gwen and Marjorie, showed no interest at all in complying. It was a matter we can imagine she would have discussed openly with Muriel's new father-in-law, Lancelot Lowther, a widower, with whom she had become close and in whom she confided, in the absence of Sir George. It was obvious to them both that Gwen's career and partnership with Norah were a major barrier to finding a suitable husband for her. The solution, they decided, was that Norah should be given every encouragement to marry first. This would isolate Gwen and force her to capitulate.

With a mother's instinct for doing what she was thought was right by her daughter, Lady Farrar was very interested in any eligible man inhabiting Gwen's world, and old Etonian Philip Durham was effectively acting as Gwen and Norah's manager in the *Midnight Follies*.

As Muriel and Anthony's wedding had taken place in South Africa, with Gwen unable to attend, Lady Farrar suggested throwing a party for the couple in the Chelsea house. To Gwen's surprise her mother encouraged her to invite not just family but theatrical friends too. It seemed a miracle that she was suddenly so accepting of her new career and partnership.

The party was held on Sunday 23 April 1922.[13] As part of Gwen and Norah's gregarious world of young, aspiring theatrical people and as someone they saw nightly at the cabaret, dashing young Durham was now a friend. One can imagine Norah asking him along as a theatrical 'mate' who would help

The wedding party: Captain Ellis, Gwen, Philip Durham, Norah

to stop her feeling outnumbered by the intimidating Farrar/
Lonsdale clan. It is not hard to picture vivacious Norah sharing
laughs and smiles with him or even making a public display of
affection.

Lady Farrar saw her chance and nudged her co-conspirator,
who rose to his feet. After proposing a toast to his son and his
new wife, Lowther then 'startled them all by making public the
romance of Miss Blaney and Mr Durham only eight weeks after
their first meeting'.[14]

Short of spoiling the event by flatly denying it, what
could Norah or Philip do? Gwen recognised her mother's
role in the scheme with disappointment but not surprise. An
announcement of the engagement somehow appeared the very
next day in the *Pall Mall Gazette*. Other newspapers spread the
news, inventing a story about Durham rescuing Norah when
Gwen's car broke down.

At the end of the week Norah made a statement that the
date of her marriage was not yet fixed: 'I have a contract to
fulfil.'[15] But her parents, Molly and Walter, were thrilled by the
news. The pressure and expectation grew.

Some of this story is conjecture, but how else to explain
the recorded fact that it was Lancelot Lowther (no relation to
either of the supposedly happy couple) who announced the
engagement?

'In August... the gossips were intrigued by the postponement of the wedding.'[16]

Was Norah to have a reprieve? Eventually – perhaps inevitably – she, Gwen and Philip agreed that the only way to avoid embarrassment would be to go through with it. So, 'The marriage took place secretly in the following month on 7th September 1922 at the Catholic Church of the Holy Redeemer, Chelsea.'[17] Norah's father Walter gave her away. There were expensive wedding presents as endorsements from the elders.

The wedding party, if the photograph is anything to go by, did not take it too seriously. Gwen, acting as both witness and bridesmaid, is smiling, dominating the picture, her arms linked loosely with the men on either side: Philip Durham, the groom, and his best man, Captain Ellis. Durham gave his address as the Hotel Metropole. He was certainly not looking for a conventional marriage that would tie him down to monogamy and domestic life, any more than Norah was.

It was always made clear that she would continue on the stage. The fact that Philip Durham was, currently, her and Gwen's manager seemed, at least to newspaper editors, a suitable excuse for her to carry on working. In reality, she would soon find herself financially supporting her husband, just as Bea Lillie and Gertrude Lawrence were supporting theirs.

Lady Farrar's plot had failed. No sooner was the ceremony over than Norah was back onstage with Gwen. 'The bride and Miss Farrar left for the Coliseum Theatre, where they are now appearing.'[18]

Lady Farrar would never again arrange a match. Two months later Muriel had a baby son, James, and, thrilled at the arrival of a longed-for boy in the family, Lady Farrar diverted her attention to the role of grandmother. Single-handedly preparing to host a children's party – an annual treat for the Sunday school – just before Christmas, she injured herself. Wanting, typically, to be in control, she had been moving furniture herself rather than relying on the Chicheley Hall servants. The damage was internal, necessitating an operation. She seemed to recover, but then relapsed and unexpectedly died on the afternoon of 29

December. She was fifty-two years old.

The woman whose thwarted ambition had been to raise a boy missed her grandson James' baptism by just ten days. Her youngest daughter Ella was only eleven. Resilient Marjorie, then twenty-two, with her companion Peggy's support, took over responsibility for both Ella and Kathleen, and for Chicheley Hall with its grounds and staff.

The funeral, at St Lawrence's Church, was held on 3 January 1923. Gwen attended and the Blaney/Farrar performing diary was cleared for several weeks. Sometimes the loss of a parent with whom one has not seen eye to eye can be as painful as mourning an adored one. It dawned slowly on Gwen that there was now no hope of an improved relationship with her mother, for she was suddenly and finally gone.

Long ago Gwen and Norah had accepted that their job required them to be funny, even in the midst of personal pain. Having to be on top form every night was sometimes a great tonic to Gwen's spirits, but inevitably there were times for both her and Norah when going onstage was a considerable strain. Gwen's self-deprecating songs, now an established part of their repertoire, sometimes came from a place of real sadness. In the period following her mother's death, she began to rely more and more on brandy and other spirits to help her prepare to perform, and afterwards to relax.

Norah worked harder than ever to keep their career on track. She knew the cello was a great source of comfort to Gwen and that its presence helped set them apart from other 'sister acts'. Drawing on her conservatoire training she had composed a ballad, 'My Cello Man', essentially a love song to Gwen and her instrument. The lyrics were probably a collaboration between the pair as no one else is credited. They were invited into a recording studio by HMV in November 1922, following earlier visits in the spring.

Norah displays all her vocal tricks to evoke maximum emotion and serves up the piece as a coded hymn to their private passion. The masculinity of the cello 'man' acts, on one level, as a nod to convention, but on another level it plays

IN "POT LUCK," AT THE VAUDEVILLE.

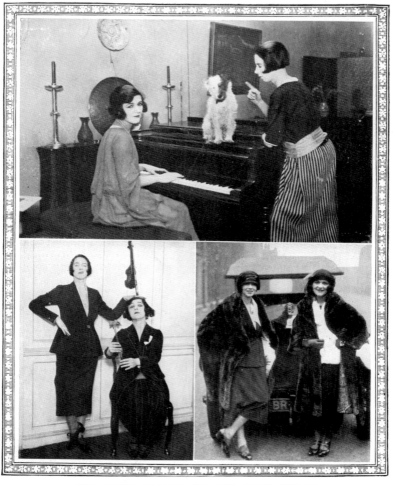

MISS NORAH BLANEY AND MISS GWEN FARRAR

At home at 217 King's Rd, Tatler, 3 May 1922

Gwen and Norah as cover stars, 8 March 1924, and (above) the original photograph

Gwen and Norah (photographed by Dorothy Wilding in 1924), sheet music

A Musical Comedian at Home: Miss Gwen Farrar.

A MOMENT'S REPOSE : MISS GWEN FARRAR ON HER BED, WITH ITS FIVE CANDLES.

A KEEN MOTORIST : THE WELL-KNOWN COMEDIAN AND 'CELLIST WITH HER BIG CAR.

ONE OF THE ARTISTS OF "THE PUNCH BOWL" : MISS GWEN FARRAR AND HER 'CELLO.

AT HER WRITING-TABLE : A CHARMING STUDY OF MISS GWEN FARRAR.

A CORNER OF THE DRAWING-ROOM : MISS GWEN FARRAR AT HOME.

Gwen photographed alone in Chelsea for a feature in the Sketch, *12 August 1925*

Caricatures of the cast of The Vagabond King *with Norah as Huguette
in the* Stage, *1927*

An audience of stars for Charlot's Revue, Illustrated Sporting and Dramatic News, 11 April 1925

There were two performances on the first night last week of the new version of "Charlot's Revue," at the Prince of Wales Theatre, one at 8 p.m. and one at midnight. At the latter show friends trooped in from other theatres, "not single spies but in battalions," to see the performance, and our picture shows some of this audience of celebrities. (L. to R.) (Back Row) : Andre Charlot, Joseph Coyne, Herbert Mundin, Peter Haddon, Jack Hulbert, Leslie Henson, George Grossmith, Noel Coward, Laddie Cliff, Henry Kendal, Jack Buchanan, and Morris Harvey. (3rd Row) : Fay Compton, Phyllis Dare, Phyllis Monkman, Maisie Gay, Lilian Braithwaite, Violet Loraine, and Zena Dare. (2nd Row) : Cecily Courtneidge, Gwen Farrar, Norah Blaney, Isabel Jeans, June, Heather Thatcher, and Ivy St. Helier. (1st Row) : Rosaline Courtneidge, Irene Browne, Tallulah Bankhead, Beatrice Lillie, Gertrude Lawrence, and Dorothy Dickson.

Gwen and the chorus of *Shake Your Feet*, 31 August 1927, Bystander

Bubble and Squeak.

A MAN was passing a shop which sold fishing accessories, and noticed in the window a card bearing the words, "Splendid Fishing Tickle." He entered the shop and pointed out the spelling mistake to the proprietor. "Hasn't anyone drawn your attention to it before?" he inquired. "Hundreds of people," replied the proprietor. "But whenever they drop in to tell me, I can nearly always get them to buy something."

* *

The late Sir W. S. Gilbert once received a letter from an amateur composer suggesting that they should collaborate. "My score," wrote the amateur, "will be satisfactory, for, through being educated as a chemist, I am a born composer." Gilbert wrote back regretting that he could not comply with the request. "I should have preferred," said he, "a born chemist who had been educated as a musician."

MISS JOYCE BARBOUR, MR. BILLY MERSON, AND MISS GWEN FARRAR

Three of the big guns in Mr. Laddie Cliff's winner at the Hippodrome, "Shake Your Feet." The more the public sees of Miss Joyce Barbour the more is it persuaded that there is a part waiting for her somewhere in straight comedy. Mr. Billy Merson, as usual, holds his end up, and of Miss Gwen Farrar more below

An English tourist was climbing to the top of a Scottish mountain with his guide. When he reached the summit he gazed around at the glorious view and then exclaimed: "After climbing all this way to see the view, I've forgotten the glasses!" "That's a' right, sir," said the guide, "there's naebody aboot; we can just drink oot o' the bottle."

*

The old salt was telling a long and thrilling yarn of an adventure he once had off Arijaba. His audience imagined coral reefs and waving palm trees. "By the way, where is Arijaba, isn't it?" "South Seas!" cried the astonished mariner. "Why it ain't twenty miles from Clacton. Don't you know "'Arwich 'Arbour'?"

* * *

The following amusing story is going the rounds. An omnibus recently had stopped at a fare stage, and the conductor, who happened to be on top, imagined that all the passengers were aboard, and rang the bell for the vehicle to proceed. Instantly a shrill female voice called out, "Hey, wait a minute till I get my clothes on." The passengers, craning their necks, saw a woman struggling aboard with a laundry basket.

L ittle Joan was put in an upper berth of a Pullman sleeping-car for the first time. The novelty of the position was rather too much for her, and she cried until her mother, to comfort her, told her not to be afraid because God would watch over her. After a short silence Joan

MISS GWEN FARRAR

Her own humorous and entertaining self in "Shake Your Feet," and is here seen shaking hers in her own droll fashion

called out, "Mother, are you there?" "Yes, dear," came the reply. Another silence. "Father, are you there?" "Yes," A fellow-passenger lost all patience at this point and shouted, "We're all here. Your father and mother and brothers and sisters and aunts and uncles and cousins. Now go to sleep!" There was a long pause, then, very softly, "Mummy, was that God?"

S ir J. C. Percy tells the following:—

An illiterate person who always volunteered to "go round with the hat," but was suspected of sparing his own pocket, overhearing once a hint to that effect, replied: "Other gentlemen puts down what they thinks proper, and so do I. Charity's a private concern, and what I give is nothing to nobody."

MISS JANETTE GILMORE

Who is also shaking her feet in the Hippodrome success. She dances delightfully all through this excellent show

Gwen throwing a shape to publicise Shake Your Feet *in a page from the* Tatler, *17 August 1927, also featuring Joyce Barbour, Billy Merson and Janette Gilmore*

out as queer fantasy. Norah's words, 'And as he played his tune so sweet he simply swept me off my feet,' are Gwen's cue to enter with an exquisite instrumental harmony. Norah liltingly responds, 'That dreamy cello, so soft and mellow... brings back memories of love's young dream again... Oh how it haunts me... I go to pieces when I hear that tune. It makes me shake and shiver...'

After Gwen's rubato-laden obligato played across the full range of her instrument, in perfect synchrony with Norah's piano, they climax:

> Oh that tantalising tone!
> How it thrills me to the bone!
> Aaaahh! Aaah!
> Come back and play me one more tune again.

They recorded the song a few weeks after Norah's 'marriage' but do not seem to have made it a regular part of their live act, perhaps because it touched too closely on the reality of their private lives for audiences to know quite how to respond. The public loved to see Gwen and Norah sending themselves up, but here they were in earnest.

The song was in stark contrast to one they had recorded in January. Weston and Lee had written 'The Queen of the Oojah Isles' to showcase Gwen's comedy techniques. To modern ears it is a culturally insensitive piece. Though the target of the comedy is an evangelical Christian missionary plucked from the cannibals' casserole pot by a bold and assertive Pacific Island Queen, the song is an example of 'primitive modernism' – the prevailing fascination with things African and Oriental in the period, which was, too often, an excuse (conscious or unconscious) for the racist assertion of colonial power structures.

This is evident in Weston and Lee's song where the missionary marries the Queen. She and her new husband share a strong mutual attraction to which Gwen and Norah give gleeful voice in their vigorous (and suggestive) evocation of rhythmic lovemaking:

When I saw you, oh you fairy
I forgot I was a missionary
Oh you Boojah, Queen of the Oojah
When I saw your smiles
I pursued ya and I wooed ya
And I chew'd-jah, chew'd-jah, chew'd-jah
Down in the Oojah Oojah Oojah
Down in the Oojah Isles.

In her uninhibited delivery, Gwen delights in highlighting the comic euphemism, together with the loss of the clergyman's previously high-minded ideals.

These gramophone records sold well and received high praise:

> They both have excellent diction, the first requisite in
> the kind of stuff they perform, they are both extremely
> versatile [and] have an apparently inexhaustible fund of
> 'stunts'... but the burlesque is never so exaggerated as to
> be ludicrous... High spirits and creative imitation are the
> hallmark of these extraordinarily clever young music hall
> artists.[19]

André Charlot put them in his new revue, *Rats!*, at the Vaudeville Theatre. Gertrude Lawrence starred. Alfred Lester, a kindly, well-known character actor, played several roles, among them a grumpy stationmaster.[20] The revue got its title from a 'Pied Piper' reference but that didn't stop Gwen performing a wholly unrelated topical song about Howard Carter and Lord Carnarvon's recent discovery of Tutankhamun's tomb. It brought the house down. She, Norah and Lester worked an extra gag into the applause:

> When Miss Blaney led [Gwen] on to bow her thanks for
> about the umpteenth time, we discovered that the Pierrot
> was not the lady at all, but Mr Lester cunningly disguised
> as Miss Farrar, in the hope that he might collect some of
> her applause. At least so he says; and he appears quite
> pained that his deception should have been so quickly
> found out... his backchat with the two ladies is one of the

funniest things in the show. I have not heard so much joyous laughter for years. *Rats!* is one of the most laughter provoking shows in Town.[21]

The Egyptian number had to be hastily scrapped on the grounds of good taste when in April the curse of the pharoahs supposedly struck and Lord Carnarvon was killed by a deadly mosquito bite. In Charlot's next revue, *Yes!*, a respectable six months later, the Egyptian theme was back, complete with set, props and costume to complement Gwen's physical comedy.

This was a show of quick changes, for Gwen and Norah also appeared in gorgeous eighteenth-century costume as puppets in a sketch described by the *Stage* critic as 'a capital little love story'. Norah wore a shepherdess outfit, once again identifying with Columbine. This time Gwen, looking very much the romantic hero, was dressed not as Pierrot but as his successful love rival, Harlequin, perhaps reflecting a growth in Gwen's personal confidence and self-esteem.

In *Yes!*, the *Stage* reported, 'Miss Farrar is able to display her skill as a cellist... as a character comedienne... and in a skit, "But is it Art?"'[22] This skit featured Gwen as a street painter, peddling abstract art, recalling her trick on Anthony Eden.

But it was not only Gwen who shone in this latest revue. Under the heading, 'Yes, We Have No Dull Numbers!' the *Pall Mall Gazette* declared:

> Another remarkable advance in *Yes!* is that of Miss Norah Blaney, whom we have hitherto thought of as little else but a lively accompanist of Gwen Farrar in their famous turn at the piano. This happens in *Yes!* as elsewhere and a capital pair it remains... but besides this, Miss Blaney now composes a large part of the music for the revue and proves herself amazingly versatile and entirely charming as a singer and dancer quite on her own account.[23]

It is clear that Norah made an impact in the vastly male-dominated field of composition and might have gone on to do more. Perhaps her versatility was her enemy, as it left her little space for the time-consuming activity of composition.

Producers were looking for other things from her, as were the men who interviewed her later in life, who failed to focus on her song writing.

Instead, when discussing her work for André Charlot, she modestly and laughingly remembered him calling her a 'clumsy cow' in a dance rehearsal. She knew dancing was the weakest skill in her performance armoury and she responded to his insult with a very loud raspberry and a V sign which got her promptly sent to her dressing room. There she sulked, until she wanted a cup of tea and so had to apologise.

Charlot could be impatient and rude. He was famously furious when Gertrude Lawrence brought an unknown Noel Coward along to audition for him unannounced. Somehow, though, he managed to inspire artists' loyalty. Along with Charles Cochran and Gerald du Maurier, he was one of the great producers of his day.

His production of *Yes!* was doing well at the Vaudeville, but there was big competition from a show half a mile away at Wyndham's Theatre, where Gerald du Maurier's production of *The Dancers* was attracting crowds of 'gallery girls' swooning over their idol, the new arrival from the United States, Tallulah Bankhead.

Caricature of Norah and Gwen by Nerman

PART III
FÊTE AND FLATTERY
1922–26

(Above) Una Troubridge and Radclyffe Hall, 1935 and (below) Joe Carstairs (centre) on board her yacht Vergemere II with Teddie Gerard (right) and an unknown woman, 1924

~ 8 ~

FRIENDS

Orphaned and with a large allowance from the trustees of the Farrar millions, Gwen entered what her obituary writer would later describe as 'a period of theatrical and social triumphs, of fête and flattery, of hectic parties'.[1]

She was an instantly recognisable figure in the theatre world. The West End was alive with restaurants, hotels and clubs: the Savoy, the Ritz, the Berkeley, the Eiffel Tower restaurant, the Hambone Club, full of new friends and admirers – and new people to admire.

She and Norah now usually ended the evening apart. Norah wanted her beauty sleep, while Gwen stayed out late and dug deep into her Farrar allowance when her theatre pay ran out.

She became friendly with the stars of Gerald du Maurier's hit play, *The Dancers*, which was causing such a stir. Its leading ladies were two awe-inspiring actresses: a RADA graduate named Audry Carten, who was to become a significant figure in Gwen and Norah's story and, from the Deep South of the USA, the legendary Tallulah Bankhead.

A huge amount has been written about Bankhead's arrival in London in February 1923 and her eight-year stay in the West End. She came direct from New York, where she and fellow actors Estelle Winwood, Eva Le Gallienne and Blyth Daly had been dubbed 'The Four Riders of the Algonquin', from their association with the Algonquin Hotel literary 'round table' and the lesbian fellowship they enjoyed there.

Tallulah wasted no time surrounding herself with lesbian and bisexual women in London. Gwen and, to a slightly lesser extent Norah, were very much part of her scene and would remain so throughout the 1920s.

Dancer Anton Dolin recalled performing on a variety bill at the London Coliseum and noticing a very beautiful young woman sitting in the first row of the orchestra every week on a certain matinee day. It was Tallulah, there to see her friends, Gwen and Norah. He met her afterwards in their dressing room. 'Despite all her flamboyant "I am, I am" she listened too.'[2]

According to Norah, Noel Coward thought 'Tallu' was a crashing bore, desperately self-centred and demanding. 'I can't think why you bother about her,' he told Norah, who replied by telling him that she thought Tallulah was very attractive to look at. She had fantastic cheekbones and great big eyes. Soon after arriving in London she cut her long hair short, making Gerald du Maurier cry with rage. Long hair was essential for her part in the show, he said. When she went onstage with her new bob, the gallery girls began spontaneously chopping off their locks and throwing the tresses onto the stage.

In New York, Tallulah's initiation into the joys of lesbian sex had come at the hands of the British-born stage artist Eva Le Gallienne. Afterwards Tallulah was supposed to have introduced herself to strangers at parties by saying, 'I'm a lesbian. What do you do?' She later quipped, 'My father warned me about men and booze, but he never mentioned a word about women and cocaine.'

According to Norah, Tallulah could be fun. She was quick and intelligent. She could make people feel that she was really interested in them, though she also loved to be the centre of attention.

Tallulah was the name on everyone's lips. She was a sensation, a phenomenon – in theatrical terms, a true star. No one in London had ever met anyone quite like her. Dolin remembered being at her house one night when the mournful strains of a cello were heard outside the window. It was Gwen, in a midnight serenade, playing and singing, 'I want my Tallulah baby.'[3]

Norah's relaxed attitude to Gwen's infatuation with Tallulah is illustrated in this story she told Derek Hunt in 1976:

> When Lady Farrar died, she left a lot of very beautiful pearls and, as she had six daughters, the pearls were to be made into six separate necklaces. When Gwen got hers, of course, she was very pleased with them. It was a single row of very nice pearls.
>
> For some reason or other Tallulah was a bit narked about these pearls and she said, 'Ooh you with your ugly neck and me with all my glamour and I haven't got any pearls!'
>
> It must have been a bad day! So Gwen, with her usual generosity, trotted off to Cartier… and she chose a necklace of single pearls for Tallulah and gave it to her. Of course, she didn't have to pay because she had an account. I was a bit worried about this. No, it wasn't jealousy. I just knew that Gwen couldn't afford them because she was overdrawn. I used to look after her affairs to a certain extent and I knew she was very badly overdrawn with her allowance. So, I thought, those pearls had better go back to Cartier. So, a friend of mine – a friend of Gwen's too – she was an adventuress, with a lovely turn of mind – she and I put our heads together.
>
> Previously I had said to Mrs Locke, who was Tallulah's dresser, 'What does Miss Bankhead do about her jewellery when she's at the theatre, Mrs Locke? Does she take it with her?'
>
> 'Ooh no. You know those pearls that Miss Farrar's just given her? She keeps those in a teapot in the kitchen!'
>
> Well, with this friend of mine – who was called Joe [Carstairs] – we got painters' overalls and a stepladder and we climbed up the back of the house. Got through the window that was left unlatched. Teapot. Kitchen. Pearls.
>
> The next day off I toddled to Cartier's and told a story with tears in my voice. They said, 'Certainly Miss Blaney, we quite understand. We will take them back and the bill will not be sent to Miss Farrar.'
>
> And Tallulah never said anything. It could have been that she thought she'd lost them and didn't have the heart to tell Gwen. But Gwen never knew.[4]

Norah was less tolerant of Gwen's closeness to Tallulah's co-star, the young actress Audry Carten, whom Angela du Maurier, a lifelong lesbian, described as 'not only... an exceptionally clever actress, but... the most perfect companion; funny, witty, the most appalling tease'.[5]

Charles Duff, whose mother Caroline Paget eventually became Audry's long-term partner, said:

> Audry was iconoclastic, wild, rebellious, insecure and wonderful fun... bursting with artistry, with a long face like a foal's, fluffed-up brown hair and pale blue, understanding eyes behind thick horn-rimmed spectacles... She was no beauty but her face was vivid and her features mobile, her expressions reflecting her good nature and kindness.[6]

The children's author Noel Streatfeild, also a lesbian, had 'watched [Audry] with awe' when they were at RADA together, 'a brilliant and beautiful girl... the most gifted member of her class.'[7]

Norah could see that Gwen and Audry were, in a way, kindred spirits – and she grew wary of her. She started to believe that Audry wanted to spilt Blaney and Farrar up.[8] Time would tell if her suspicions were warranted.

This was the first serious threat to their personal and professional partnership and it came at a time when they were making a breakthrough in the West End and much was at stake. They were now starring in a revue called *The Punch Bowl* and its enormous success had turned Gwen and Norah into stars. Before the days of topical TV or radio comedy, it was to their set at the Duke of York's Theatre that the public flocked for the latest funny references to politicians, stars and news events. Gwen kept on top of writing these lines and they both had to learn them at short notice. The pressure was intense. This was in addition to Gwen's very full social life. Something would have to give.

After six years together Gwen was still only twenty-seven, while Norah was into her thirties. Their chemistry was still strong and they had developed a high level of trust and mutual understanding. Norah knew that Gwen loved her and relied on her onstage as well as off, but she also saw that it would be wrong to try to repress Gwen's puppy-dog enthusiasm for pranks, parties and people who were bold and exciting.

She knew from experience that when Gwen got an idea in her head for a practical joke, there was no stopping her. Years earlier, while Lady Farrar was still alive, Gwen said to Norah one night in the dressing room that her mother was going to Lady Londonderry's exclusive reception to mark the opening of Parliament. She added, 'I'm going.'

'You haven't had an invitation.'

'No,' she said, 'but I'm going.'

Norah recalls:

> I thought she was joking. But she wasn't! She had already been to Willy Clarkson – the costumier of the time – and got herself rigged out with king's robes, false ermine, cloak, cardboard gold crown, crepe hair beard, wig, the lot... looked exactly like King George V. She then hired a white horse... and rode on this horse into Londonderry House, up the steps and up the staircase into the ballroom, where the horse left his card on the ballroom floor. Then she turned round and rode out. She didn't do it for publicity – she didn't need to. She did it for kicks.[9]

Gwen found a fellow prankster in the shape of the openly lesbian oil heiress and adventurer Joe Carstairs. She was in London having just established the X Garage – a taxi firm consisting of a fleet of Daimlers. All the drivers and mechanics were women, recruited from friends she had met as a girl driving ambulances in France.

Carstairs was to become one of the great British sportswomen of the 1920s as a powerboat racer. She would break the world water-speed record in 1926 and eventually win more than three dozen trophies and receive the International Motorboat Union Medal of Honour for Sport.

Writing a profile in 1930, the American journalist Lilian Sabine described Carstairs:

Rollicking boyishness, good looks, fine brown eyes, short cropped brown hair, wit, snappy modernity, up-to-the-minute sparkle, courtesy and charm... She has a straightforward manner, unaffected and sincere. She is fearlessly honest in the modern spirit. More than anyone I have ever met Marion Carstairs seemed to me a product of her generation... As you look at her you wonder what she's really thinking way down under that boyish hair. And you speculate as to how she'd be in a filmy evening gown – all beady and earringy. She has more than good looks... and talks easily with the beautiful diction of cultured England.[10]

Gwen and Joe would continue to be friends until well into the 1930s. In a great public tribute to Gwen, Joe named an expensive racing speedboat after her in 1924. When it capsized in trials she rechristened it *Newg* – Gwen backwards. In it Joe would go on to win the prestigious Duke of York Trophy on the Thames.

When Gwen and Norah first met Joe, she had a string of ex-lovers, notably Dolly Wilde, niece of Oscar. Dolly worked sporadically for British *Vogue*, which from 1922 to '26 was in the control of a remarkable lesbian power couple – Dorothy Todd and Madge Garland, very much at the forefront of modernism in writing and design. Like Gwen and Norah, they lived in Chelsea, the party borough of choice for the famous names and Bright Young Things of the decade: Cecil Beaton, Rex Whistler, Frederick Ashton, Evelyn Waugh, Allanah Harper, the Sitwells, the Mitfords, Nancy Cunard, the Jungman sisters and the photographer and socialite Olivia Wyndham.

Other women in the growing circle of friendship that centred on Tallulah were performers Teddie Gerard, Cathleen Nesbitt, Elsa Lanchester and Betty Pollock. A rich young couple of siblings, Guy and Joan Laking, were frequently on the scene and so too, for a period in the early Twenties, were a well-known older lesbian couple – novelist Radclyffe Hall (known to her friends as John) and her partner, Una, Lady Troubridge. They were, in turn, friends with Romaine Brooks, the American painter who was a lover and compatriot of the formidably self-assured heiress and poet Natalie Clifford Barney. Barney's remarkable salon of artists and intellectuals in Paris included Colette, Gertrude Stein, Djuna Barnes, Janet Flanner and many more.

Bloomsbury Group writers Virginia Woolf and Vita Sackville-West remained aloof from this theatrical Chelsea set, but the children's author Pamela Travers (of *Mary Poppins* fame) greatly admired Gwen, and so did Angela and Daphne du Maurier, the eldest daughters of Sir Gerald du Maurier. Both would go on to be authors, Daphne becoming world famous for novels including *Rebecca* and *Frenchman's Creek*.

It is worth pausing in this dizzying list of Gwen and Norah's friends and admirers to tell the story of the du Maurier sisters' adolescent crushes on the pair.

Angela and Daphne were taken to see the first night of *The Punch Bowl*. Angela was immediately smitten and made no secret of it, telling her diary: 'Dreadful scene with Daddy over X and Z. He stormed like a madman.'[11] It was Gwen whom the twenty-year-old Angela adored most – and she wanted to see her socially, not just onstage. Her parents were implacably opposed. 'They are adamant about her. Oh God, help something to happen to get them to change their minds.'[12]

The du Maurier girls' biographer, Jane Dunn, has observed that Angela's younger sister was infatuated too:

> Daphne's eye had also been caught by the unconventional attractions of the crop-haired Gwen when she saw the revue and she wrote a fan letter to the actress. She admitted this to Tod [an old friend] and begged her discretion. 'I adored Gwen Farrar! I wrote to her last night (not a word of this!) saying, "Dear Gwen, I think you are quite perfect!" Shall I be drawn into the net too? I wonder. I hope she won't show the letter to anyone, or I shall be tarred with the same brush! Life's no fun unless there's a spark of danger in it!'[13]

Looking back in 1965, Angela recalled her adolescent infatuations: 'My loves were enthroned on sky high pedestals... all I ever aspired to in my thoughts were lovely, marvellous, rapturous kisses... I was very, *very* romantic.'[14]

Sir Gerald was so alarmed by Angela's crush that, thinking she needed a distraction, he arranged for her to be cast as Wendy in *Peter Pan*.

Gwen supported her young admirer's theatrical debut and on opening night Angela wrote in her diary that she had received 'marvellous flowers from the Greek' – by which she means 'the sapphist'.[15]

Later, looking back, she wrote of Gwen:

> In all the weeks and months I knew her, I never met anyone kinder, more generous, more amusing and so utterly un-contaminating in influencing the impressionable girl I was. She had every opportunity under the sun and never said a word on any subject that could not have been shouted from the house tops.[16]

Sir Gerald was obsessively protective of his daughters and regularly protested (too much, one is tempted to think) his disapproval of homosexuals. Gwen and Audry Carten found a way to tease Sir Gerald by serving him a dose of his own controlling tactics, in a wonderfully condescending rebuke to his chauvinism.

More than once they waited for him in Gwen's car outside the Garrick (the historic members' club for actors from which they were excluded on account of their sex). When du Maurier emerged from playing poker in the small hours they followed him home. He would stop his car, get out and tell them not to be so silly, they might have an accident.

'We won't,' they retorted. 'We know what we're doing. Carry on – we're seeing you home.'[17]

By the summer of 1924 Norah was tired of waiting alone in bed for Gwen to come home from late night jaunts with Audry and her friends. Six weeks after the opening night of *The Punch Bowl* a critic reported that Norah was ill. He went along to see the girl who was her understudy in the sketches and songs that preceded her set with Gwen. At the climax of the show he was astonished when:

knowing that Ms Blaney was suffering from nervous hysteria... suddenly, I saw her appear on the stage, looking charming... a perfect artist, singing quite calmly... You would not have believed such a transformation possible... Knowing there was no one who could appear with her partner [she] braced herself together and insisted on going on in the syncopated duets.[18]

This 'show must go on' mentality was typical of Norah, whose ambition and professionalism had always been paramount. There were no other reports of 'nervous hysteria' but it seems entirely plausible that this anxiety attack was one of several brought on by the stress of dealing with Gwen.

Life at 217 King's Rd was becoming chaotic. It was not Norah's job to manage the bills and placate the servants, but Gwen took no interest in domestic life any more. Norah was having to shoulder more than her fair share of the mental load as well as worrying about Gwen being out late, driving under the influence or, worse still, failing to come home at all.

It seems clear that at around this time Norah told Gwen she was going to move out. She was paying the rent on a flat in Carrington Court (in Shepherd Market, Mayfair), which was supposedly her marital home. Her husband Philip Durham was living there. Norah would move in there with him.

One can imagine a scene in which Gwen implored Norah to reconsider, using all the techniques in her repertoire: tears, doleful expressions, jokes and endearments. Norah found it impossible to be angry with Gwen for long.

In the end a compromise was reached where Norah took over one of the two rooms at Carrington Court for herself but remained a frequent visitor to the King's Road. And, of course, she and Gwen also saw each other at the theatre every night.

It is disappointing to think of Gwen and Norah's 'little stall' being partially dismantled and their happy 'bachelor girl' existence coming to an end. Perhaps this can be explained, in part, by the pervasive influence of a 'Bright Young Thing' mentality which was dedicated to the belief that the morality of the previous generation must be turned on its head and that behaviour must be entirely separate from the masses of 'ordinary' people. This led to a blasé attitude to love and faithfulness amongst the young and wealthy and an outlook characterised by Noel Coward as 'jagged with sophistication'.[19] Romance and coupledom were unfashionable in a world where everything was a pose and a party. While this had the beneficial effect of creating a space for greater sexual experimentation and freedom, it flew in the face of monogamy. Beverley Nichols wrote the story of a (thinly disguised) gay relationship temporarily disrupted by the superficial appeal of this hedonistic world in *Crazy Pavements*. The sleek, dark-haired, socially successful central character, Julia, writes, 'This life we're all leading... is killing us... If only we could stop dancing and drinking and being amusing and let ourselves be plain and bored and real.'[20]

As we have already established there was, in any case, no satisfactory template that Gwen and Norah knew of, against which to compare their relationship when external distractions and temptations arose. In writing his novel, Nichols had to frame the homosexual relationship between Walter and Brian as a hearty platonic friendship. The two men fight and Walter moves out of the house they share when Brian becomes infatuated with Julia, but eventually the loyal friends are reunited and sharing a room.

Similarly Norah's departure from the King's Road house was not to be the end of her intimacy with Gwen. Their emotional lives and their double act were still to encounter highs and lows aplenty.

At Carrington Court, Norah lived uneasily under the same roof as her husband who, it seems, had found an unlikely drinking mate in Joe Carstairs. The latter recalled in 1989:

> I went around with Philip Durham. We drank an awful lot. I got sick a lot, but the next day we'd do it again. It was just crazy. He was the manager of the Follies in London and had access to girls. He married Norah Blaney who had a sister act with Gwen Farrar – very famous at the time. When poor old Philip would get tight, he kept clothes at my place for when he was locked out of his own house.[21]

Perhaps Norah was taking out on Philip the frustrations she had felt when living with Gwen. She could not, of course, have locked Gwen out of her own house (and was far too fond of her to do so), but, as the person paying the rent at Carrington Court, she felt entitled to punish Philip Durham in this way.

More evidence that he and Joe Carstairs were friends and that Norah and Gwen were living apart appears in this newspaper article:

> Once [Carstairs] and Mr Philip Durham dressed up in
> workmen's overalls and wigs and, after insisting on going
> all over Miss Norah Blaney's flat examining the electric
> lights, arrived at Miss Gwen Farrar's house with a ladder
> and bucket of paste and plastered it with very inappropriate
> posters.[22]

There is certainly scope for this as 217 is on the end of a row. The side wall of the house presents a blank canvas. This jape of course has similarities to Norah's story about breaking in to reclaim Tallulah's pearls.

Joe Carstairs' biographer Kate Summerscale tells us that she 'took particular pleasure in beating actresses at their own game, outwitting them with her own disguises and impersonations'.[23] She may well have been the 'actress' mentioned in this episode:

> Shortly after eleven o'clock at night there was a ring at
> the front door bell of Miss Farrar's house in King's Road,
> Chelsea, London, and the servant girl on opening the door
> was aghast to find herself looking into the muzzle of a
> pistol pointed at her by a man who had 'burglar' stamped
> on every inch of his face and clothes. The burglar with the
> pistol ordered the servant back into the house. Back and
> back she was forced until she reached the stairs leading
> to the kitchen below. There the other servant was waiting
> startled and frightened... After a while they escaped by
> smashing a window in the scullery and climbing through...
> An actress friend of Miss Farrar's called at the house the
> next day, and, with great glee, explained that it was all a
> practical joke. She herself, she said, was the burglar with

the pistol. [She] waited for Miss Farrar to laugh, but she found that the joke had misfired. The servants had not recovered from the shock of their terrifying experience, and [had] placed the matter in the hands of a solicitor... unless settlement is arrived at the action will come to the courts.[24]

One hopes Gwen's staff were amply compensated. No legal procdings ensued.

For those who could afford it, thumbing a nose at the law was becoming a pastime, but, for those not in on the joke, the effect could be alarming.

A young Russian fashion model entered the London scene around this time. Natalia Mamontova had escaped from the Bolshevik Revolution and, once in England, like Gwen, had run away from boarding school. She was friends with Joe Carstairs and writes in her memoir that she 'spent a hilarious weekend in her yacht in Southwick'.[25] She met Gwen and Norah at the 'chronically Bohemian'[26] Hambone Club in Ham Yard, Soho – introduced to them by the female pianist 'Dickie' Dixon. Natalia says Gwen took her to a party thrown by (the famously drug-addicted) Princess Violette Murat. Gwen may have had designs on Natalia, but the latter proved to be eminently distractible. She flirted with the hugely talented, middle-aged, womanising painter Augustus John who whisked her off into a new social set, centred on the Eiffel Tower restaurant. Gwen came across her lunching there, drinking vast amounts of champagne with a boyfriend, and (allegedly) found her hat on a peg and destroyed it in a fit of jealousy. It was a red hat that Natalia particularly cherished, but when challenged about it, Gwen laughed in her face.

This is one of a very few (unauthenticated) stories that show Gwen in a less than good light. Another is a fleeting derogatory reference in Evelyn Waugh's diaries: 'All the usual people were there, including Tallulah Bankhead and the foul Gwen Farrar.'[27]

Coincidentally Waugh had also called Mamontova 'foul' when he met her a month earlier. She was briefly married to Val Gielgud, brother of the actor John, and he referred to her by her married name:

We were joined by the foul Tasha Gielgud and, in her company, a pert young woman dressed almost wholly as a man. They had many drinks with us and attracted a great deal of attention. We managed in the end to get rid of them only by leaving the restaurant ourselves and putting them to lesbianize in a taxi.[28]

Like Waugh, Augustus John was disconcerted by signs of female masculinity:

Gwen Farrar's voice, when first she turned it on in my hearing, gave me an enormous shock. I hesitated between laughter and dismay... what could she have been drinking? ... She had a voice like a coal-heaver. I have never cultivated coal-heavers; not that I have anything against them morally, but I find their make-up repellent; it is affected without being witty.[29]

Gwen did not defer to men for approval and this unnerved John, who saw his status as a bohemian sexual adventurer undermined by a woman who gave the impression she would rather compete with him than become his prey. Despite his prejudices, he and Gwen seem to have engaged in banter rather than outright hostility, for he had warm and insightful things to say after her death. She called him Augustus Jack. Looking back Norah was sure he had painted Gwen's portrait – as he famously painted Tallulah – but no trace of this exists.

It was on Thursday 28 August 1924 that Pathé released the clip (mentioned earlier, in the Foreword) of Gwen and Norah larking about on a golf course. It was shot on 35mm cellulose nitrate film with a hand-cranked camera that relied on the rhythmic abilities of the operator. It was almost certainly shot one day that summer, possibly at the London Country Club at Hendon. Here is part of Pathé's detailed description of the action:

Gwen has her arm around Norah's shoulder and they both smile at the camera. Gwen curls her lip. She is a bit of a strange character! The two girls laugh. Gwen continues to pull faces.

Close-up of the two standing very close together seen
from the side. Norah puts her finger on the end of Gwen's
nose and pushes it up. Gwen tries to push it down. She
then puts her open hand up to the side of her face...

They lark around on the golf course. Gwen tries to put
Norah off her stroke. Norah grabs her by the hair and
marches her off, putting her behind a net and shoving
her with a golf club. She takes a shot. Gwen hams it up
pretending to be stuck behind the fence. She pretends to be
a monkey! She eventually goes around the side of the fence
then runs along the ground like a monkey. Funny.[30]

Like the *Midnight Follies* clip it was shown as part of *Eve's Film
Review*. Jenny Hammerton has studied and catalogued fifteen
hundred items in this collection:

There is obviously great potential in these films for lesbian
spectators... *Eve's Film Review* is a space where women can
actively express their sexuality... There are many examples
of women looking at other women... The series provided an
opportunity for the vicarious enjoyment of expressions of
female sexuality for many different kinds of women in the
cinema audience.[31]

Given the intimacy and connection on show in this film, it
seems that Norah and Gwen were still lovers in the summer
of 1924, despite all the tension Gwen's behaviour had caused.

Infuriatingly for researchers there is no hard evidence of
where Norah was living during her puzzling marriage to Philip
Durham. Between them she and her husband had addresses at
Carrington Court and at 160 Earls Court Road. It is tempting
to assume that Philip Durham was also gay and the entire
marriage was nothing but convenience, yet Joe Carstairs'
comments suggest he was a drinker and womaniser and that
the 'convenience' for him was Norah's money.

What is certain is that by February 1925 Gwen was living
alone at the King's Road house. Pamela (PL) Travers, then
working as a journalist, visited to research a lengthy article she
was writing about Gwen.

She loves books and her precious house is stocked with them. Racine is there in all his curled and silken glory and he is very often taken down from the shelf. And George Moore in a very old and excellent edition – the whole of him... You cannot trip Gwen Farrar up anywhere in George Moore, she has him by heart. All the old books she loves, she has ploughed along strange, old, unknown-by-many byways in literature, wandered down wild lanes of rare poetry. Her bookshelves are veritable gold mines.[32]

Travers' detailed profile of Gwen includes a mention of her racier side:

There is the intrepid Gwen Farrar who drives her own car, and who, by the way, had certain differences with a policeman some months ago as to the proper speed to assume on a certain road, and who had her licence suspended for three months. But that did not damp her ardour, and I'll wager that when she gets out of sound and out of sight of those pillars of the law the speedometer runs up to fifty and sixty and that Gwen Farrar's smile widens at the adventure of it as she flies along.[33]

Travers glosses over the fact that the star had flown straight into a taxi cab.[34]

Photographs of Gwen 'at home' in the *Sketch* in August 1925 contrast with the ones taken at the house when Norah lived there with her. Three years on, Gwen has more trappings of success, but seems solitary and sadder. She lies on her double bed alone or, in another shot, gazes soulfully out of the window.

A month before these photographs were taken Gwen had been involved in an incident which had strained her relationship with Norah to breaking point.

On the night of 16 July 1925 (Norah's thirty-second birthday, as it so happened) Audry and Gwen were arrested outside the Savoy Hotel. Gwen had been asked by a police constable to move her illegally parked car. She complied, but then told him off for eating a toffee and disrespecting her. In the ensuing argument she tapped him on the chest, or, as Beverley Nichols put it, 'She gave him a brisk blow in the navel and was promptly carted off to Bow Street.'[35] She hired a famous barrister, Sir Henry Curtis-Bennett, to defend her against the charge of assaulting a police officer.

One can imagine that Norah was furious and spent the day wondering if there was a future for their act as she paced the floor, uncertain whether Gwen would be acquitted and blaming Audry for her bad influence.

The court was packed with press for the hearing. Curtis-Bennett spoke persuasively in Gwen and Audry's favour and the charges were dropped. Gwen telephoned Norah to apologise unreservedly, telling her she had a plan to make everything all right. As satirists of the news they could not shy away from an allusion to this brush with the law.[36] Gwen made her stage entrance that night dressed as a convict, complete with ball and chain, and brought the house down.

Luckily it turned out well. Norah would have been less forgiving if the incident had kept Gwen from performing or resulted in bad publicity for their act. Norah was always very money-conscious. Any loss of earnings as a result of Gwen's pranks would have made her furious.

Like a naughty puppy, it seems that Gwen never set out to make Norah angry and always went to great lengths to apologise, spending the ensuing days pleading for assurances that she was no longer cross. It would be another five years before Gwen recorded a song that would put into words exactly what she wanted to be told, 'Tell Me I'm Forgiven'.

This chapter on friends would not be complete without including the numerous appearances Gwen makes in the diaries of Una Troubridge.[37] She was the long-term partner of the novelist Radclyffe Hall, the most famous twentieth-century literary lesbian. Hall was known to her friends as John and it is by that name that she appears in the diaries.

Attracted to the West End world of theatrical first nights, for a while, in 1923–24, John and Una cultivated a friendship with rising star Gwen. This is documented in Una's diary, alongside accounts of their domestic lives, dog shows, and John's work as a writer, which was central to their existence.

More annotated appointment diaries than actual journals, the pages show up at least a dozen references to Gwen. On Thursday 21 June 1923, for instance, John had her hair waved in preparation for a party in the evening thrown by Gwen at 217 King's Road. On 21 September, Una and Johnnie ran into Gwen at the Berkeley and had lunch; a month later, they went to see her in *Yes!*

The friendship continued into the New Year. Gwen threw another party on 8 February 1924 and Una and Johnnie came straight on to it from Augustus John's *thé dansant*. The next day there was a party at Princess Murat's. 'Gwen came and was very depressed and quiet, but nice,' said Una to her diary. (This was the party where Gwen was given the slip by Natalia Mamontova.) On Sunday 10 February Una and John went to Teddie Gerard's. 'Gwen said she was coming but didn't turn up.' But two days later Gwen and Tallulah had tea with John and Una at home at 10 Sterling Street.

On Monday 21 April Una and John happened to meet Gwen, Tallulah and her 'witty, malicious' friend, Francis Laking,[38] at the Berkeley at lunchtime, and so joined them for tea at Tallulah's. Wednesday 7 May was Tallulah's first night in *Conchita* at the Comedy Theatre. Afterwards at Brett's, Una, John, Tallulah and Gwen danced till four o'clock in the morning. Two weeks later, the 21st, Una and Johnnie were at Gwen and Norah's first night in *The Punch Bowl*. Gwen dined with them the following Monday and off they went to see her turn in the same show again. Ten days later Una and Johnnie had dinner with Gwen and drove her to the theatre (she was still banned from driving).

Una was sitting for a portrait with Romaine Brooks. Writing to her lover, Natalie Clifford Barney, Brooks provided an update on the sittings, which had become very tense. Romaine was sick of Una's constant chatter about her new friends, many of whom she had met through Romaine.

> This lady has actually formed a gay set for herself out of
> my many introductions. I don't think much of the set in

question, but it has evidently suited her. She gave me a lurid description of Gwen Farrar who is her great friend now, telling me about her various abscesses in the throat and drink habits and then, after thoroughly disgusting me, proposing that I should paint a large portrait of her, adding that G. would surely fall in love with me. A pleasant prospect. Hell, I'm sick of them both for the time being.[39]

Romaine's account of Gwen, rather like her actual portrait of Una, was none too flattering. Gwen is described as easily love-struck but physically off-putting. Here too is a surprising first mention of Gwen's relationship with alcohol. There had been nothing in her house to drink at all (save Kathleen's rum) when the Prince of Wales called, but now Gwen appeared to have a habit.

Romaine Brooks' account should be viewed with some caution. Natalie Barney, though supremely confident at the head of her famous Paris salon, nevertheless elicited frequent written assurances from her lovers – Romaine on this occasion, and later Dolly Wilde – that their lives apart from her and the women they were seeing were dreary by comparison with the stimuli she offered. Letters to her from them played down London attractions in a way that makes it hard to know what they really thought.

For example, Romaine dined with Gwen, Una, John and Francis two days after writing that letter, and they all went to *The Punch Bowl* – a third time for Una and John.

A few months later, on 5 August, back from paying a visit to Natalie Barney on a trip to Europe, Una and John called in at 217 King's Road on the off-chance. They were disappointed to find Gwen out and only Joe Carstairs in her house. They had met Joe before and did not like her. They evidently dropped off an invitation; according to Una's diary, Gwen was their one and only guest for dinner to celebrate John's forty-fourth birthday on 12 August 1924.

Una and Johnnie were clearly interested in Gwen, as a performer, as a friend and perhaps as a case study. No doubt Hall discussed with Gwen her ideas about 'congenital inverts' (the least offensive term from a limited range of vocabulary available for them, meaning queer people). The term was coined by the 'sexologist' Henry Havelock-Ellis. His work was already beginning to influence Hall and would surface emotionally in the plea she made at the end of *The Well of Loneliness*: 'Acknowledge us, oh God, before the whole world. Give us the right to our existence!'[40]

John had plenty of opportunity to talk to Gwen during the fifteen months they were socialising regularly, plenty of time to hear about Gwen's childhood, the family's regret that she was not a boy, her love of horses and hunting, the closeness to her father and the shock of his tragic death following an accident when she was seventeen, the conflict with her mother over gender conformity, her romantic time at the Front, her mother's refusal to acknowledge her lover, and the subsequent experience of seeing the woman she had set up home with, get married to a man. It is not exactly the plot of the novel that would make Radclyffe Hall famous, but it is not far off.

We know that Radclyffe Hall took inspiration from those around her. Her biographer Diana Souhami writes, 'She did not invent in her novels. They were storehouses of her experiences and preoccupations.'[41] Noel Coward appeared in *The Well of Loneliness*, thinly disguised as Brockett; Natalie Clifford Barney was there as Valérie. An ambulance unit, just like the one Toupie Lowther set up in the war, was where Stephen met her lover, Mary. Some of Stephen's story is John's own, but much of it parallels Gwen's, right down to her Turkish cigarettes. Mr Pringle is there as Old Williams the groom, Harold her horse as Raftery, Sir George and Lady Ella as Sir Philip and Lady Anna, and Chicheley Hall as Morton. Like Gwen, Stephen found motoring 'the most tremendous fun'. The only major elements missing are South Africa and the cello.

Inspiration or not, the close friendship with John and Una did not last. Perhaps Gwen felt awkward being the only guest at John's birthday dinner. Perhaps Una's obvious dislike of Joe Carstairs was a problem. Three weeks later, Una says Gwen 'came but would not stay to dinner' and after that she is mentioned no more in Una's diary.

Norah, clearly, was not as closely involved in this friendship as Gwen, probably because John and Una were class snobs and found her less interesting. She, however, told Derek Hunt a funny story about their visits to see *The Punch Bowl*. John famously wore masculine attire and a large opera cloak on outings to the theatre. When Norah said to the stage door keeper, 'That was Radclyffe Hall,' expecting him to be impressed, he coolly replied, 'Oh, right you are, Miss Blaney. I thought it was Arthur Roberts.'[42]

Separated at birth? Arthur Roberts (right) and Radclyffe Hall

~ 9 ~

DRESSING-ROOM DIALOGUES

By 1925 the centre of Gwen and Norah's shared life was no longer the beautiful Queen Anne house at 217 King's Road, Chelsea. Now the place they spent most time together was their dressing room at the Duke of York's Theatre. Then, as now, the stage door was accessed down a dark alley off St Martin's Lane, leading to dressing rooms at the rear of the building. Here they added last-minute topical references to their act, prepared to go onstage and received guests.

The Punch Bowl cast also included a seventeen-year-old actress, Hermione Baddeley, who described the scene in her autobiography:

> I shared a dressing room with the two headliners, the stars of the show, Gwen Farrar and Norah Blaney. They sang naughty songs, did witty repartee that was sometimes risqué but never downright rude. To my eyes they were ladies of a certain age, frankly middle-aged, but they had a huge following... We didn't get in each other's way, for Gwen and Norah got into evening dresses for their act and had a sip of brandy or gin while they waited to go on... While they waited, a special friend would sometimes come in and have a drink and a chat with them. When this happened I would erect a screen in the corner and do my rapid changes behind it. One evening I dashed in, saw a male figure sitting in the corner, so I hurried behind my

screen. While I was changing I took a peep over the top of the screen. There sat the heir to the throne, David, Prince of Wales – golden hair, tip-tilted nose and shy smile. He caught my round-eyed, astonished gaze and smiled. He didn't wink, but he looked as if he might. He used to come round quite a lot – something about Gwen and Norah must have appealed to him, made him feel relaxed and at ease. I suppose it could have been because of his liking for older, bossy women.[1]

There was no love lost there, it seems. For her part, Norah said to Derek Hunt (off the record) that when Baddeley arrived at the start of the run, her hair was full of head lice which Norah combed out in a motherly fashion.

One evening the Prince of Wales arranged to bring 'Bertie and Betty' (his brother and his new bride, Elizabeth, Duchess of York) backstage to meet Norah. The prince had seen the show many times and was content to miss the long 'Punch and Judy Ballet' section that, by this stage of the run, included Gwen as Joey the Clown. So Norah was alone in the dressing room when the royal party arrived, and the duchess stayed with her while David and Bertie went to meet Alfred Lester. To Norah's great surprise, her visitor asked to try on the grey wig she wore as the showman's wife.

The duchess took off her tiara and put on the wig. It looked like a tea cosy.

'If you don't mind me saying so, you haven't got it quite right,' said Norah.

'You help me!' said the duchess. So Norah pulled back her thick, dark brown hair to help her position the wig. The duchess sat there for a long time looking at herself, before saying, 'You can take it off now.'

Norah took the wig and lent her a comb.

'Do you know why I wanted to do that?' asked the duchess. 'You see, one day I shall go grey and I shan't be allowed to dye my hair, and I just wanted to see what I shall look like.'

Norah thought it was rather touching and always remembered this 'enchanting time with this most delightful person'.[2] Within a couple of years this delightful person would give birth to the future Queen Elizabeth II, going on to live to a great age as the silver-haired Queen Mother.

Another visitor to their dressing room was Pamela Travers.

> There was a rush and bustle... as I entered. 'Blaney and Farrar,' as they call themselves, were busy changing for the next act. 'Blaney and Farrar.' Once those two words would not have conveyed much to the public at large, but now they conjure up sounds of a 'cello that sings divinely even when it's playing rag-time and ridiculous mirth-catching topical songs that swing up to tumultuous applause. They have got their public these two – got it tightly in their hands.[3]

Gwen and Norah were becoming household names, famed for their musicality and wit, 'a tower of strength in any show'.[4]

> But success has not spoilt them. Rather has it mellowed them until they are absolutely unconscious of success at all. They just do their turn, and, if it pleases the audiences, well and good, if not, but there is never a 'not'.[5]

From this account and the sections quoted earlier where she described Gwen's love for books and her motoring exploits, Pamela Travers seemed to find her fascinating. Is it fanciful to see in her description of Gwen the seeds of the unflappable, compelling Mary Poppins character she would go on to create?

> One feels that Gwen Farrar would not care much either way – that she would go her own serene way if the world were falling to bits around her. She sat in the lighted dressing-room and drank tea and ran a comb through her sleek, brown hair nonchalantly. She will do everything nonchalantly, this young South African. She is very much monarch of all she surveys.[6]

The Punch Bowl reunited Gwen and Norah with their friend Alfred Lester. He had dressed up as Gwen in *Yes!* and now he appeared as a fabulous *señorita* in drag – a send-up of Tallulah in her latest show, *Conchita*. He also played the old showman, opposite Norah in the grey wig as his wife.

Alfred Lester in an earlier role as Gwen in Yes!

> Mr Lester and Miss Blaney are very fine actors. Miss Blaney's
> jaded showman's wife, with her careworn air and exquisite
> show of feeling at the end, and the new monologue she
> gives as the Flower Girl lamenting over her Piccadilly 'Eros'
> were pieces of very good acting.[7]

Sadly, Alfred Lester died suddenly on a trip to Spain. The
intention was to improve his health and give him a short break
from the show, but it seems he was so horrified by attending a
gory bullfight that his bronchial condition suddenly worsened
and he died very soon afterwards.[8] Norah recalled receiving the
telegram with the news in her dressing room, then having to go
on, heartbroken, and perform with his understudy.[9]

Another co-performer was the camp comic Billy Leonard.
In a rare break from London, he and Norah had a day out on
Joe Carstairs' yacht, *Vergemere II*. This was the boat on which

Gwen as Joey the Clown

Carstairs had entertained Natalia Mamontova, along with many other women friends who enjoyed Joe's special attentions on deck and below. Whether Norah was one of Joe's lovers we cannot know. They were certainly good friends and Joe was fantastically promiscuous.

Back at the Duke of York's, Norah was scoring an enormous hit in *The Punch Bowl* with Irving Berlin's 'What'll I Do?' It was an enduring favourite, to which was swiftly added another Berlin hit, 'All Alone', at the request of the Prince of Wales, who had heard it on his tour of America. The producers secured the exclusive UK rights for Norah to sing 'All Alone' for the enormous sum of £2,000. It became her signature song.

The 1924 recording for the Columbia label shows Gwen had a significant role in the performance of this piece. Her cello obligato, without any gimmicks, is the perfect accompaniment to the piano octaves Norah plays as she effectively addresses the yearning lyrics to her partner. 'All alone by the telephone, waiting for a ring, a ting-a-ling.' Berlin recognised that the phone's potential for instant connection could (like subsequent technologies) increase anxiety and social isolation, by failing to bring the longed-for communication. In Gwen and Norah's arrangement, faultless harmonies – requiring acute tuning and teamwork – set the words at odds with the delivery. This poignantly highlights the tension between their love for each other, its taboo status, and the difficulties they were experiencing in their relationship.

Norah's mournful declarations – 'I can't live without you... there is no one else but you' – express the recurring contradictions of their queer past, present and future. They close this eloquent lilting waltz by climaxing in superbly judged harmony, their togetherness a miracle of mutual understanding and conscious irony: 'Wondering where you are and how you are and if you are all alone too.'

Songs and sketches were liable to be cut and replaced during the run of a revue, to encourage audiences to come back and to keep the material fresh and topical (*The Punch Bowl* publicists called it a 'new mixture') but these songs survived.

Gwen was keeping her end up too.

> Most women can 'play the man' when the occasion offers; but few of them can do it so effectively that they are asked to go on doing it. That is what Miss Gwen Farrar, the clever artist appearing in *The Punch Bowl*, is going to do. She took over the part played by Mr Sonnie Hale who was away with a fractured instep on Monday night, and did it so well that she shall continue to do it. When she heard that Mr Hale would be unable to play on Monday night she promptly rang up the producer at his flat and asked him whether she might go on in his place. She was at the theatre early in order to have a hurried rehearsal before she went on. 'I'm going to enjoy it immensely,' said Miss Farrar.[10]

She was pictured in her new role: Joey the Clown.

When it came to their act together, Gwen and Norah still

had the support of Robert Weston and Bert Lee in augmenting their topical comedy repertoire. Their song, 'In Our Little Garden Subbub' became popular.

> When you're tired of the club-bub, tired of the pub-bub
> Take a little house in our Garden Sub-bub
> There you can grow stewed rhub-bub
> Bath in the old rain tub-bub
> So leave all the hub-bub and the pub-bub and the club-bub
> And grow your own grub-bub in the sub-bub.

Another Weston and Lee number took a dig at the latest male fashion. Norah recalled:

> The odd thing was that while women were as angular as
> a choice piece of Picasso, men became more and more
> rotund. D'you remember a new dazzling fashion when men
> suddenly appeared in what looked like bloomers reaching
> almost down to their ankles? Gwen and I sang a song about
> it.[11]

That was 'Percy's Posh Plus Fours Are Priceless':

> They're round on the end and high in the middle
> And they take up half the Strand
> Although he's never, well hardly
> Ever, had a golf stick in his hand.[12]

Once they had warmed up their audience with some topical patter Gwen and Norah would sing a love song – to each other. 'Come Back' was remarkable for having both a woman lyricist and composer, Daisy Fisher and Hero de Rance.

The photograph on the front of the sheet music suggests they performed this 'straight' as a sincere love duet. Given the vicissitudes of their personal lives at this time it is intriguing to speculate what they were thinking and to imagine the irony with which some of the lyrics they sang might have resonated. Whatever the truth of this, their reputation for professional harmony was continuously maintained and audiences increasingly enjoyed the attractive rapport they generated.

'Their appearance together provided as faithful a replication of a heterosexual dyad as their audiences would accept from a same sex couple,'[13] notes Joel Lobenthal, Tallulah's biographer, going on to mention that the young Quentin Crisp was one of their fans.

In another song, anticipating the frank physicality of some of their later recordings, they sang together in syncopated harmony:

I miss you in the morning and at night-time I'm blue
I hug and squeeze the pillow and I dream about you.
Lookin' out the window, wearin' out the carpet
Watching and waiting for you.[14]

The work continued unabated. It was not just the shows six days a week. They had other engagements. In July 1924 Gwen and Norah were hired, for the impressive sum of a hundred and fifty guineas, to perform for Queen Ena of Spain at Polesden Lacey, the expansive Surrey home of Scottish heiress and socialite Maggie Greville. Comedian Will Fyffe, of 'I Belong to Glasgow' fame, was on before them.

'Oh girls, I wish you luck,' he said, as he came off. 'I sang my guts out to them, but I never got so much as a titter.'[15]

Norah judged a fashion show at the department store, Selfridges, and afterwards could choose a free gift.

Gordon Selfridge was the most interesting personality.
He was so sweet – very picturesque, with long white hair
and glasses with long black ribbon – *pince-nez*. So after the
judging we – the other actress was very often Evelyn Laye –
and the editress of *Vogue*[16] – we were taken round the store
by Gordon Selfridge. In those days it was very grand to
have real silk stockings, so sometimes I would get a dozen
pairs, which was very nice. Once I got a typewriter.[17]

Norah and Gwen ceremonially signed the store's famous window of celebrity autographs[18] all done with diamond paint. According to a biographer of the retail magnate, it was the duo who granted him 'the acceptance he so desperately craved... when he was memorialised in a little ditty performed in *The Punch Bowl*'.[19] They referred to him as 'The Earl of

Oxford Street' in a song specially included to allow for up-to-the minute topical references.

They recorded it in November and it became *the* hit song of 1924/25: 'It Ain't Gonna Rain No More'.[20] Gwen rewrote the choruses each week and adapted it after the 1924 general election when Labour Prime Minister Ramsay MacDonald left office:

> Since Ramsay Mac
> Has got the sack
> He ain't gonna reign no more.

Composer Wendell Hall produced another weather-related number that Gwen and Norah sang with great success, 'We're Gonna Have Weather':

> The English summer's mighty queer
> They say we had one here last year.
> I didn't see it, strange to say
> I overslept myself that day.

A third song on the same theme, 'It Don't Do Nothing but Rain', gave them the chance to sing together, very pally: 'It's hard to smile when the skies are black, And the rain keeps trickling down our backs.'[21]

The last forty seconds of their recording of this song consist of Gwen doing vocal percussion sounds, almost like beatboxing.

During 1925 Gwen and Norah, along with fellow performers from *The Punch Bowl,* broadcast on the radio for the first time. This involved visiting the 2LO studio just behind the Savoy on the Strand. According to Norah, Gwen thought the experience was degrading and she swore she would never do radio again, though they were always being asked.

Fortunately she had no such objection to making records and together they recorded more than twenty songs between 1923 and 1925.

While Gwen and Norah were the talk of London, Gertrude Lawrence and Bea Lillie were fast becoming the toast of New York. *Charlot's Revue* of 1924 was the great producer's attempt to make it on Broadway, using elements from his previous hits.

The gamble paid off spectacularly. Originally booked for six weeks, the show ran to packed houses for nine months at the Times Square Theatre.

When the hit revue returned from America and settled in for a run in the West End, a special 'midnight matinee' performance was arranged – in a blaze of publicity and attended by a host of stars. A photograph was taken after the show to mark the occasion, with Gwen and Norah seated prominently in the second row. Gwen sat between Norah and Cicely Courtneidge. Immediately in front of Norah was Tallulah, with Bea Lillie on her left, next to Gertrude Lawrence. This was a historic event featuring the thirty-two top musical comedy performers of the London stage.

Gwen and Norah were confirmed as top-flight celebrities, 'the coupling of their names as natural as the coupling of Swan and Edgar, whiskey and soda, ham and eggs'.[22]

When the legendary American producer Florenz Ziegfeld came to London in August 1925, word quickly spread that he might also be casting chorus girls.

> The heart of London became so clogged with crowds of young women seeking auditions that the police finally gave up on unsnarling the mess.[23]

In fact, Ziegfeld was on the hunt, not for dancers, but for leading artists to include in a show which could rival the Charlot revue. He needed English girls with star quality to match Lawrence and Lillie. He chose Blaney and Farrar. The *Tatler* announced:

> Whilst America gains two of our brightest stars of the revue firmament in Miss Norah Blaney and Miss Gwen Farrar, England gets back that delightful American dancer Miss Adele Astaire. [24]

It proudly reported that there were more British stars working in America than American artists onstage in London.

Philip Durham, in his capacity as their agent as well as Norah's husband, travelled with his wife by train from Waterloo to Southampton. Gwen drove down in her car. Norah, Philip and Gwen boarded the *Aquitania* liner on 31 October 1925.

Gwen wrote her occupation down as 'Cellist', Norah put 'Actress'.

A large majority of the *Aquitania*'s passengers were American and the ship's concert would be a good test of Gwen and Norah's appeal to a US audience. Naturally there was some anxiety about this, given the very English nature of their act. As it turned out, they went down very well indeed.[25]

Gwen was familiar with ships and ships' concerts, having been practically brought up on them. For Norah the voyage was a wholly new experience.

Though they both posed for photographs on arrival at Chelsea Piers on Manhattan's West Side on 6 November, it was Norah who gave the first press interview. Reporting from the ultra-modern Shelton Hotel, the theatre correspondent of the *World* described Norah's astonishment at being in a building twenty-six storeys high. The Shelton[26] had been built two years earlier by one of the architects later responsible for the Empire State Building.

The reporter was impressed by Norah's preparedness for the visit. When he asked for her initial impressions of the United States, she said, 'I was told the first question I would be asked when I arrived in New York will be, "How do you like America?" And so it was. The first stranger I met at the swimming party asked me that the moment we were introduced.'

'What did you answer?' asked the reporter.

'Gwen had the presence of mind to push me in the tank before I could reply.'[27]

Ziegfeld put Gwen and Norah into *Louie XIV*, a show which had been running successfully for several months at the Cosmopolitan Theatre in Columbus Circus. He billed their first appearance, on Monday 16 November, as a Gala Night, and placed large advertisements in the newspapers proclaiming Gwen Farrar and 'Nora' (*sic*) Blaney to be 'England's Greatest Entertainers'.

Although their act interrupted the dramatic action of the operetta, New York's critics praised the new arrivals, who were warmly applauded by the entire company as well as the

Misspelt advert for the duo's New York debut

audience. 'That these clever girls made a hit is unmistakable.'[28]

> A warm hand greeted Norah Blaney and Gwen Farrar...
> They did a short turn in the second act, especially pleasing
> their first American audience with a song called 'Those
> Henhouse Blues'. This team is reminiscent of Beatrice Lillie
> and Gertrude Lawrence of the Charlot revue, the one being
> comic the other wistful.[29]

This comparison was just what Ziegfeld had intended. He was
pleased with his new investment and offered Gwen and Norah
the chance of performing at Palm Beach, Florida, where the
most prominent members of American high society spent the
winter. It was not just the people but the warmer weather which
attracted Gwen and Norah to this proposition. They had both
succumbed to colds and Gwen was particularly unwell.

There was a gap of some weeks before they would travel
south. After the excellent publicity surrounding their gala
night at the Cosmopolitan, Ziegfeld lent them out for a fee

of $1,250 per week to the famous Keith-Albee management. Gwen and Norah were to perform twice nightly in two different venues: early evening in Brooklyn, then later at the immensely prestigious Palace Theatre in Times Square where African-American star Florence Mills had caused a sensation the previous year.

On the first day of their engagement, Gwen had a temperature of a hundred and three. Different newspapers variously described her illness as bronchitis, influenza, jaundice and indigestion. The women managed to extricate themselves from the Brooklyn bill, but no replacement could be found for them at the Palace. They were obliged to go onstage for the Monday matinee performance. To add to Gwen's misery, a fly buzzed repeatedly round her face. In good health this would have been a comedy boon, but she was too sick to improvise and almost collapsed at the end. She spent the next two weeks in bed, all performances cancelled. Norah was very worried about her.

Curiously Norah did not fill the breach by performing solo. She had plenty of experience of doing so in the years before she met Gwen. Perhaps Philip Durham was against the idea, or it was not something the American managements would consider. For them, Gwen and Norah's appeal was as a double act – the interplay between the two of them being its entire selling point and charm.

Gradually Gwen rallied, allowing them to appear at the Palace Theatre over Christmas. Topping the bill was the great American star Elsie Janis, a lesbian whose close friend Eva Le Gallienne was concurrently giving 'a transcendent performance, pulsing with emotion'[30] in Ibsen's *The Master Builder* at the Civic – a theatre she also managed.

Norah would have seen many familiar names and faces from her past – and some who would be part of her future – as she looked at the Broadway listings that Christmas. The celebrated pianist Jan Paderewski, who had granted thirteen-year-old Norah her piano scholarship, was performing at the Brooklyn Music Academy. Ruth Draper, the great monologue artist, at whose sister-in-law's salon Norah had met Pablo Casals, was performing her famous original character sketches at the Times Square Theatre. Noel Coward was starring in his own play, *The Vortex*. Meanwhile, the Marx Brothers were performing at the Lyric and a musical called *The Vagabond King* was pulling in crowds at the Casino Theatre. The Broadhurst was home to *The Green Hat*, the same sensational play that was keeping Tallulah busy in the West End. Norah met Michael Arlen, on whose novel it was based, and thought him a brilliant conversationalist. She met Charlie Chaplin too:

> He is the kind of man who prefers to sit in a corner by himself and say nothing. But when you do get him talking, he is delightful. His face is sad, but he has the most winning smile.[31]

She was introduced to a lesbian icon:

> One of the noblest-looking women I have ever met is [Alla] Nazimova. She was a real tragedy queen. She had a wonderful skin and she told me that the secret of it was that she massaged her face with ice every day.[32]

Cicely Courtneidge and Jack Hulbert were in town performing their revue, *By the Way*, at the Gaiety. Norah went, more than once, with the two of them to late-night blues clubs in Harlem. It was at the height of the famous Harlem Renaissance, with black singers such as Gladys Bentley, Ma Rainey and Bessie Smith challenging gender norms with their bold lyrics and fearless personal presentation. At the Clam House on 133rd Street, the writer Langston Hughes watched the young Gladys Bentley:

> [She] sat and played a big piano all night long, literally all night, without stopping... Miss Bentley was an amazing exhibition of musical energy – a large, dark, masculine lady, whose feet pounded the floor while her fingers pounded the keyboard.[33]

Gwen and Norah narrowly missed the sensational dancer and singer, Josephine Baker, for as they arrived in New York, she was taking Paris by storm.

Norah recalled that Hulbert, eager to learn the dance steps of a certain black dancer he admired, observed him closely on several occasions, then went back to practise in the hotel at night, much to the consternation of the Shelton's manager.[34]

Ziegfeld relied on a format that was altogether more conventional and conservative than the ground-breaking performances of these African-American artists. His *Follies* was chiefly famous for homogenous lines of fair-skinned, high-kicking chorus girls. Indeed to some sections of the press, looks were the only thing that counted in his productions. One journalist said of Norah and Gwen, 'They are pretty enough to fit appropriately into a Ziegfeld production – which is a certificate of pulchritude.'[35] *Variety* described Gwen and Norah as 'Ziegfeld's Imported $1,500 Beauties.'[36] Fortunately, looks aside, Gwen and Norah had been hired to carry on doing what they did best in this new show when it opened in Palm Beach.

While future stars Louise Brooks, Lucille Ball and Paulette Goddard paraded anonymously past them in the chorus, Gwen and Norah sang:

> Beautiful shop girl, who nobody knows,
> Would be the top girl in beautiful shows
> If she were dressed in her best
> From her head right down to her toes
> Beautiful faces need beautiful clothes.

The strapline for the show was 'Glorifying the American Girl'.

For this production (the only Ziegfeld show to be created in Florida rather than New York), the great producer converted a barn-like dance hall into a spectacular theatre, the Club de Montmartre. A backdrop depicted a moonlit Palm Beach night and the roof was a dome painted in varying shades of black to give patrons the feeling they were sitting under a starry sky.

The sewing-machine heir and long-term Palm Beach entrepreneur, Paris Singer, financed the conversion. His sister, Winnaretta Singer, came over from Paris with her companion Violet Trefusis, formerly the passionate lover of Vita Sackville-West. A fresh young designer, John Harkrider, was allowed to spend a staggering $90,000 on costumes and a further $40,000 on sets. On opening night, 12 January 1926, ticket prices started at $200.

Vogue magazine picked out:

> two wonderful girls who were down on the program as coming from London, England, called Norah Blaney and Gwen Farrar, who sang several amusing songs, with one about the Prince of Wales, whom they had asked to dine, but couldn't come, because if he brought his horse he would carry tales.[37]

The journalist went on to give a detailed account of all the society figures in attendance and exactly what they were wearing, before describing other fixtures in the Palm Beach season. Wednesday, he declared, was the fashionable night to go to the Ziegfeld show, implying that just one visit was not sufficient.

Another reporter described audience members returning on account of Gwen and Norah's songs:

> One of them is quite risqué, so much so that the words thereof cannot be had. The artists invented it themselves and keep it for their own use. The smart set is shocked, but also highly entertained and makes strenuous efforts to learn the complete song, merely from hearing it again and again.[38]

This piece continued:

> Although the two young women are very popular there are no significant love affairs looming up through the tropic night, as Norah Blaney has a perfectly good husband and Gwen Farrar thinks more of her career than of any gay young thing in a tuxedo.

The same paper picked up on another aspect of Gwen and Norah's appeal to their elite audience:

> Two of the *Follies* girls are daughters of English society with the many titles in their families, and an ancestral baronial hall and all the other things that a certain class of American women would give their back teeth to have.[39]

News of Gwen and Norah's success reached the London papers which identified yet another reason for their popularity:

> The fact that Miss Blaney is a gifted pianist has not gone undiscovered in the United States and a few nights ago she played the pianoforte quintet of César Franck with a famous New York string quartet at a private concert given by Mr Paris Singer, the millionaire pioneer of Palm Beach, at his magnificent house there. Mr Singer's hobby is music, and he engages the quartet for a fortnight every year during the winter season at Palm Beach to play every evening to him and his friends... At a concert next week at Mr Singer's house Miss Blaney is to play in a Brahms quintet and Miss Farrar will play the cello in a Schubert quintet.[40]

Gwen and Norah ought to have been in their element, especially on 31 January, when Singer hosted a dinner in their honour at his exclusive newly built club, the Everglades.

Yet the America trip barely features in Norah's reminisces. Her scrapbook contains just a few snapshots in which Gwen and Norah are together on the beach, well wrapped up, doing a crossword puzzle, in the company of a dog and a third, unidentified, young woman. Another photograph with the caption 'Taken by Philip outside our villa' shows where they stayed.

Three of them under the same roof was awkward. And as the weeks wore on it became clear that Norah and Gwen wanted different things out of this American stay.

There is frustratingly little evidence for precisely what happened in February and March 1926. We know that Norah was keen to stay in America and build their career. We know that a telegram arrived from the William Morris Agency asking them to name their fee to perform in a special nightclub engagement that Jack Hulbert was producing in New York and that Ziegfeld was keen to sign them for the Palm Beach show's Broadway transfer (under the title *No Foolin'*) which would happen in June. They were a hot property. But Gwen must have been restless. From her angle, she had made another sea crossing, then been seriously ill on her arrival in a country she did not really appreciate and where she felt uprooted. And perhaps her heart was elsewhere. She was a party animal, missing the London set she had come to rely on: Tallulah, Audry and Joe. She was away with Norah, her lover (or one of her lovers), but may have felt she was playing gooseberry while that lover's prankster husband was ever-present. Perhaps she had to say a chaste 'good night' and go to bed alone.

What we know for sure is that on 26 March 1926, Gwen arrived back at Southampton, alone, on board the *Aquitania*.

Norah was very hurt. Gwen had told her the trip home would just be for a week but when it became clear she had deserted them, Mr and Mrs Philip Durham sailed back aboard the returned *Aquitania* nearly three weeks later. This time Norah wrote down her profession as 'Housewife'.

Over fifty years later, in a tape-recorded conversation, Norah knew who to blame for Gwen's defection:

> There was a woman called Audry Carten and she said, 'If it's the last thing I do I'll break Blaney and Farrar up.' She hated me you see. She and Gwen were lesbian friends and she hated me.[41]

Only time would tell if Gwen could ever be forgiven.

PART IV
SOLO CAREERS
1926–30

Matching solo ads in the Stage, 1926

~ 10 ~

IF YOU HADN'T GONE AWAY

It was on all the playbills: BLANEY AND FARRAR SPLIT UP, BLANEY AND FARRAR BROKEN UP. Audiences and critics were reeling. Impresarios rushed to find a way to spin the news to their advantage. Sir Oswald Stoll thought it would be a clever stunt for the former duo to share the top of the bill at the Coliseum as two separate acts. Decades later Norah recalled her response:

> No, I thought it would be awful. Wouldn't do it.
> 'Well,' he said, 'in that case I'll have Blaney.'
> So I went on my own to the Coliseum and he put me top of the bill. He had Margaret Cooper's dressing room decorated for me… I went there for a week and he kept me there for six weeks. When I go to the Coliseum now I think, well, how on earth did I do it? Got people to join in with the chorus and all that. No band. Just my Steinway concert grand which Steinway's used to send.[1]

Norah's account is not strictly true and it ushers in a period when she and Gwen were each prepared to exaggerate in order to feel better about themselves. In classic breakup fashion they were each on a mission, fuelled by personal passion and pride, to outdo the other.

Norah's choice of opening song was designed to make a point. She sang the funny, upbeat foxtrot *If You Hadn't Gone Away* with feeling:

I wouldn't be where I am
Feeling like I am
Doing what I am
If you hadn't gone away.
Wherever I go
Whatever I do
I want you to know
I blame it on you![2]

The next song hammered the message home:

Like a birdy you flew away from the nest
You never said Goodbye to me
You went and left me up a tree.[3]

Despite the glum words, these were both jaunty songs and in choosing them Norah sent a message to her public that, though the split was Gwen's fault, she was going to make the best of it. Fundamentally of course it was also a message for Gwen, with whom she was no longer on speaking terms.

Oswald Stoll did engage Norah at the Coliseum, but not for a six-week run. He hired Gwen too – not at the same time as Norah, as he had wished, but the week immediately following. When Gwen's solo act debuted, Norah contrived to be performing as far away as she could, at the Liverpool Pavilion.

Under the heading 'Chatty Gossip of the Day', the *Sunday Post* informed its readers:

Two famous revue stars... have decided to twinkle apart. Their friends are laying odds as to which of the two will twinkle the most. They will have the opportunity of deciding the point pretty quickly, for Norah Blaney appears at the Coliseum this week and Gwen Farrar the following week.[4]

Like Norah, Gwen had given the launch of her solo career much thought. She spared no expense in engaging the services of a small jazz band, consisting of piano, banjo and drums, to play the *William Tell* Overture to announce her arrival onstage. There were other novelties:

> At first glance there would appear to be five young men
> assisting Miss Gwen Farrar in her new entertainment at
> the Coliseum. Two of them, however, quickly prove to be
> realistic dummies dancing with Miss Farrar in a laughable
> satire.[5]

The ticket agents and music publishers Keith Prowse were advertising Gwen's new comedy song, 'In My Gondola', alongside Norah's latest hit.

This latest number offered Gwen plenty of scope for her vocal tricks, as she posed as a love-struck Italian boatman, operatically serenading his girlfriend. It was full of sexual innuendo and wordplay.

> Beneath the moona we'll sit and spoona
> To you I'll croona
> My love inside
> And when I'm strumming on my sweet guitar
> You can funiculi and I'll funicula.[6]

Gwen was also appearing at an intimate dinner club, in Wardour Street, Soho, next door to Willy Clarkson's, the costumiers. The billing was hyperbolic: 'Gwen Farrar, one of the greatest humorists of this or any other time... is at the present time appearing at the Coliseum and Chez Victor's.'[7]

The consensus of critical opinion was that while each of them was perfectly capable of performing an entertaining act in her own right, it was a pity they had split, because they used to be so good together.

There was no reconciling them, however. Being ex-lovers who had shared a profound respect and reliance on each other's musicality, comic timing and talent, they knew how hard they had to work to compete.

Not to be outdone, soon Norah also had the backing of a band. On 4 November she and The Gilt Edged Four recorded the delightfully sexy, 'Yes Sir, I Prefer Brunettes', written for her by Weston and Lee in response to Anita Loos' bestselling novel, *Gentlemen Prefer Blondes*.

Yes sir I prefer the pretty little dark brunettes
Yes sir I prefer the dainty little dark coquettes
You'll never keep a blonde and pay your debts. Why no!
For when her hair goes dark at the roots
It's bang goes another five shillings at Boots.
Yes sir I prefer brunettes.[8]

Norah delighted in sending up the chauvinistic male character she played in this song, in a performance that owed much to the male impersonators, Ella Shields and Vesta Tilley, whom she had watched many times from the wings. There is no evidence that she ever performed it outside of the recording studio.

Gwen and Norah's rivalry extended to their social lives. Norah spent several months making sure she was as visible on the social scene as Gwen had always been. She went to first-night parties with the du Maurier girls. (She became lifelong friends with Angela and Daphne.) After seeing *Lady Be Good* she was soon 'quite a mate' of Fred Astaire's bisexual sister, Adele. She saw Tallulah open in her fourth West End play, *They Knew What They Wanted*.

In August 1927, she could not resist attending a fancy-dress party where the instruction was to come as a living celebrity. She went as Gwen. In horn-rimmed glasses, classic black and white Pierrot outfit and black wig, she was the unmistakable image of her former partner. Whether she did it in a spirit of celebration or provocation, she was certainly unafraid of being photographed taking her place among the other Bright Young People disguised as prime ministers, nuns and titled aristocrats.

It was a star-studded and queer occasion. Her friend Billy Leonard went as a turbaned potentate. Actor Ernest Thesiger dressed as actress Violet Vanbrugh and other guests included the Sitwells, Cecil Beaton and Stephen Tennant. Allanah Harper paraded as a guardsman in full uniform. This was Gwen's social scene, but on that night it was Norah who partied in her place.

Try as she might though to compete with Gwen as a party goer, Norah's behaviour in public was still influenced, to a large extent, by the continued presence of her adoring parents, Molly and Walter, still living at 65 Lonsdale Road, Barnes.

Norah (right) dressed as Gwen at a party of Bright Young Things with Billy Leonard and Isla Fink, Tatler, 1927

In their lifetimes she never fully broke free from the need to conform to their loving expectations of her. Consciously or unconsciously, Norah also stayed true to her lower middle-class background. Money was never far from her thoughts and she was always overly impressed by rank and social status. This tendency to socially climb ironically meant that she was looked down on by the snobbish people she sought to impress. All the more remarkable then that she and Gwen had bonded in the first place. A testament to their mutual desire and musical compatibility.

For the time being, however, there was no reconciling them to each other.

Unlike Norah, Gwen had no parents left to answer to, only the trustees of her father's estate, one of whom was the Bishop of St Albans. It seems that he and his fellow administrators had long since given up trying to manage her wayward behaviour.

In July 1926 Gwen turned twenty-nine and, with greater maturity, she found increased determination. She had to work very hard – both women did, for so much of their appeal to audiences, and their material, in recent years, had been based around their charismatic interaction in the double act.

Up to now they had been defined in the public eye by their contrasting stage personalities: Gwen always the dominant eccentric, Norah providing the feminine, submissive charm.

This binary interpretation disguised the truth. Norah was much more feisty, decisive and 'in control' than Gwen. The dynamics of the stage act also inclined those curious about their sexuality to assume that, of the pair, Gwen was 'the lesbian'. But Norah, too, was a dedicated lover of women.

When Derek Hunt interviewed Norah in 1976, he compiled, as his starting point, an alphabetical list of well-known 1920s stars, most of them men. When he went down the list and asked her if she knew each one, Norah was wont to reply, 'No, but I knew his sister!' Those words, knowingly spoken, prefaced her stories about Ethel Barrymore (who gave her a fob watch as a token of esteem), Adele Astaire (a great pal, with whom she shared a dresser), Binnie Hale (whose ability with Cockney rhyming slang she envied) and other women she admired.

Norah got on well with most of her male colleagues, but it was women who interested her most. It was not unusual for her to have conversations about women in which she appropriated the male gaze. After seeing the very beautiful star Dorothy Dickson in the first night of her play *The Ringers*, Norah and *Co-Optimists* star Melville Gideon, 'who couldn't resist a pretty girl', shared their opinions:

> [We] got talking about who we thought was pretty and who wasn't and we both agreed that Dorothy Dickson was quite one of the most lovely people we'd seen. She'd look smart in the bath![9]

Norah's conversation abounds with similarly appreciative descriptions of women's form: Edith Day was 'enchantingly pretty and young'; Alice Delysia 'the girl with the most lovely pair of legs in the world'. Apart from disparaging remarks about men's 'nasties', their bad breath or general lifting skills, she never referred to the physicality of any man in hours of recorded conversations.

Professionally, Norah now needed a role she could make her

own, and she found one in the West End production of a show that had been running on Broadway while she was there the previous winter, Rudolf Friml's *The Vagabond King*.

As Huguette she had two songs, 'Love for Sale' and 'Huguette's Waltz'. It was a romantic lead role, but one with a queer twist. The operetta was set in medieval France and Norah played a woman who disguised herself as a boy, in order to follow and protect the man she loved.

The show opened at the Winter Garden Theatre[10] on 19 April 1927 to enthusiastic reviews. The critic from *Sporting Life* said Norah made 'a highly creditable debut in a straight part' while the *Sunday Pictorial*'s reviewer thought her 'thoroughly effective in boy's clothes as Huguette de Hamel'.

'It would be impossible to omit praise for Miss Norah Blaney,' said the *Lady* magazine, 'who gives a curiously wistful and imaginative touch to her acting and singing.'

A mishap occurred on Saturday 2 July at a performance attended by 'Bertie and Betty', the Duke and Duchess of York. Norah's death scene that night was more than usually gruesome. A stage prop dagger failed to retract, slicing through the top of one of her fingers. She put her hand to her neck and blood flowed copiously down her tunic. This was a particularly alarming injury for a pianist, but Norah carried on and sought assistance only when the curtain fell. She was very grateful to the theatre doctor, who applied several stitches. The duke and duchess sent a telegram, wishing her a speedy recovery.

In September Norah chartered a plane from Imperial Airways and hosted what the newspapers called an 'At Home in the Air', amused by the idea of 'high' tea at two thousand feet. Nineteen friends were invited, but not Gwen.

For Norah, *The Vagabond King* was an enduring success but, during the long run, it was only to be expected that some minor annoyances would occur. Leading actor Derek Oldham played opposite his real-life wife Winnie Melville, while Norah played her love rival. She reckoned Winnie gave Derek spring onions for his tea before the show to make sure that when he kissed Norah it was a horribly off-putting experience. Norah said the onion fumes made her death scene all the more realistic – she went out like a light.

As Huguette, Norah sang the lyrics:

> Never try to bind me
> Never hope to know
> Take me as you find me
> Love and let me go.[11]

She was delighted when her friend, the genial comic actor Leslie Henson, sent up her performance at an annual dinner at the Green Room Club. She recalled with great hilarity:

> I got permission from the management to lend him my gear – he had my tights, my tunic, my wig. On the great night, I of course was in the audience. He came on, looking ghastly – you can imagine – and he sang words to this effect:
>
> > Never try to bind me
> > I am very loose
> > Constipation grinds me
> > Eno's is no use.

Inspired by this impersonation, Norah marked the operetta's two hundredth performance in October by borrowing a large flat to stage a spoof of the whole show. Entitled *The Rag and Bone King*, it saw members of the cast cross-dressing, including Norah herself as Guy Tabarie, the portly comic courtier. Willy Clarkson, who had supplied Gwen's regal fancy dress, appeared resplendent and hilarious as King Louis XI of France. Amongst the guests, sitting on floor cushions, was Gertrude Lawrence, at the time starring in George Gershwin's musical, *Oh Kay!*

A week later, on 9 November, Norah's finger injury flared up and became very painful in the afternoon. She managed to see the distinguished surgeon Sir Alfred Fripp, who diagnosed septic poisoning. It was not until after the show that he was able to operate and save her finger, further increasing Norah's awe and gratitude for surgeons.

She went to stay with her parents in Barnes shortly after

this. Ever aware of the need to appeal to different sections of her audience, Norah sought to reassure her more conservative fans that her life was not all high-flying plane trips, society parties and medical close shaves. Instead she presented a very cosy image in an article in the *Crystal* magazine.

> Miss Blaney's guiding love in life is for her mother, from whom she has inherited most of her brilliancy. They live together in a beautiful house in Barnes which has a still more beautiful garden to which both ladies are devoted.[12]

No mention is made of the fact that she is still married to Philip Durham. However the journalist refers to the 'dissolution' of Norah's partnership with Gwen and the 'fresh reputation' Norah has built up as a soloist. The choice of vocabulary is significant. 'Dissolution' means 'dissolving', of course, but also carries, in its alternative definition, a sense of debauched living. Did Norah deliberately choose to distance herself from Gwen or was that the writer's decision?

Norah had certainly not moved back home permanently. She still kept her flat, close to the West End, in Shepherd Market; and another, further out of town, at 160 Earl's Court Road.

The Shepherd Market area is the setting for an anecdote Norah told frequently. It concerned her (by now longstanding) friendship with Tallulah Bankhead.

> She was quite a mate. I knew her very well. Well, we were neighbours. She lived at 1 Farm Street, Berkeley Square, Bankhead House (well, that was just fun) and I lived in Shepherd Market, which was round the corner.
>
> She had a dreadful habit... when I was tucked up in bed with cold cream all over my face and Ovaltine and everything, she would ring me up at three o'clock in the morning and say, 'Darling, I can't sleep, darling.'
>
> 'Well. So what?'
>
> 'Well if you come round and tickle my feet it'll help me go to sleep.'
>
> I said, 'I'm not coming out to tickle your blasted feet!'
>
> She said, 'Oh yes you are! Because if you don't, I shall

send a very noisy young man with a very noisy car outside your house with a klaxon horn and he'll blow his horn and all the chauffeurs' wives who live in the mews will stick their heads out of the windows and shout, "Disgusting noise! I'll send for the police!"'

So there was nothing for it, but I had to get up. I thought, 'Well I'm not going to come smart. I'm going to put on a tweed suit and I've got no make-up on my face and I look like death.'

So she sent this car round – one of her boyfriends – and I went round. One of her parties had died, it had gone dead and she got so bored with all her guests that she went and had a bath. And sitting on the edge of the bath was Prince George, afterwards Duke of Kent, talking to her while she was in the bath. And I was there with my tweed suit and I had to amuse the guests. Who was there? Ivor Novello... oh, everybody. Not Noel! He couldn't bear her, he thought she was a bore.[13]

Meanwhile, Gwen had run into an up-and-coming jazz pianist and composer called Billy Mayerl who had contributed a couple of numbers to *The Punch Bowl*. Mayerl had a cult following amongst early adopters of the wireless craze for his broadcasts with the Savoy Havana Band. In the summer of 1926 he had just completed a live tour of music hall venues to consolidate his growing fame. He was an exceptionally good pianist. Gwen had despaired of finding a more accomplished accompanist than Norah. Imagine her satisfaction when, in Billy, she found a genius, one of very few individuals in the world of light entertainment who could rival Norah's pedigree. He had been the soloist for the first British performance of Gershwin's *Rhapsody in Blue* in October 1925.

> He is, perhaps, the foremost syncopated pianist in this country... an all-round brilliant pianist, and in performing the classics of the greatest composers his execution and technique are just as wonderful as when he is rendering the popular syncopated music.[14]

Billy and Gwen joined forces, with Gwen encouraging Billy to

Gwen and Billy Mayerl

sing, which he had never done publicly before. They tried out at the Exeter Hippodrome on 29 July 1926, where the act was a great success. Word spread. Soon they were topping the bill at the London Coliseum. Numerous bookings followed. Billy even managed to persuade Gwen to broadcast with him on the wireless on several occasions and they were among the first artists to be seen and simultaneously heard on film when they featured on a Lee De Forest Phonofilm in the autumn of 1926 with a song Billy wrote in collaboration with Kenneth Western, 'I've Got a Sweetie on the Radio'. Gwen was her irrepressible self in the studio and remarkably relaxed. Film writer Tony Fletcher has commented, 'This is one of my favourite phonofilms and the performance of Gwen Farrar taking off an early wireless works as well today as it did then.'[15]

Together Billy and Gwen made sixteen records: eight for Vocalion, two for Columbia and six for Decca, but it was onstage that they impressed the most. Much of the humour of Gwen's performance was visual and Billy's virtuoso piano playing tricks had to be seen to be fully appreciated.

> Mr Mayerl plays the piano with great skill: holding a
> thriller book in his right hand, he illustrated the dramatic
> development with his left; a telephone in his right hand, he

took his share of the conversation playing familiar airs with his left hand. He played two pianos simultaneously; and wove an interesting musical jigsaw with tunes suggested by the audience.[16]

Gwen now toured all over England with Billy.

> Gwen Farrar and Billy Mayerl top the bill, and they are a host in themselves. An artiste of rare distinction is Gwen Farrar, who plays the piano, plays the 'cello, and also sings. The pair had a great ovation on Monday night.[17]

Billy was married to his childhood sweetheart, Jill, also a pianist. They had met when they both worked accompanying silent films at the Imperial Cinema, Clapham, and were exceedingly happy together. Jill later remembered Gwen as 'a very clever person, very intelligent and always very nice to me'.[18]

Considering that, as a child, Gwen had been so reluctant to take piano lessons from Miss Berry, she must have learned some good technique from somewhere and followed it up with diligent practice, for she could hold her own as a pianist alongside Billy, who was so extraordinarily skilled.

In this period of rivalry with Norah, Gwen was keener than she had ever been before to promote herself. Here is part of the billing from the *Radio Times* for a broadcast she and Billy gave on 28 October 1926:

> Miss Gwen Farrar is known to all frequenters of variety and revue as one of the most piquant and original comedy singers of recent years. She was, quite recently, a student at the Royal Academy of Music, where she won three gold medals. After finishing her course there, she formed a partnership with Miss Norah Blaney.[19]

This suggestion that she studied at the Academy, when she was only an external student, and that she won gold medals, is untrue. Gwen clearly wanted to embellish her credentials in an effort to match Norah's remarkable record of conservatoire trophies. Likewise there is no evidence for the 'Paris salon' claim in this newspaper report:

> It is not generally known that Gwen Farrar is as good
> a painter and black-and-white sketcher as she is a
> comedienne. She has had many of her paintings exhibited
> at the Paris Salon and in London and she often sells her
> sketches for charitable objects. She particularly loves to
> draw comical caricatures of herself.[20]

Perhaps the article, published in a Sunday paper under the heading 'Gwen Farrar's Sketches', was designed to catch Norah's eye, with its salon boast a private joke and the mention of the sketches expressly delivered as a nostalgic reminder for Norah of the way Gwen's funny pictures had once animated their shared lives together.

Of course, in order to compete with Norah, what Gwen now very much wanted was a West End vehicle of her own, in the shape of a revue, as opposed to random variety bookings. The dancer Anton Dolin devotes a whole chapter of his autobiography to the venture that emerged from her idea:

> It was at Gwen Farrar's house in Chelsea that the first
> discussions for this production took place. Everard Gates, a
> young wealthy Yorkshireman, was interested in financing
> a revue and he wanted to produce something different,
> something out of the ordinary. It was to be highbrow revue
> and the Chelsea Palace... was discussed as a suitable theatre.
> Originally the cast suggested was to include Jeanne de
> Casalis, Ernest Thesiger, Gwen Farrar who, if not actually
> appearing on the stage, was to have some part in the
> production, and myself. It was hoped that... Viola Tree and
> Sir Gerald du Maurier would either write or produce some
> of the sketches; Augustus John and Frank Dobson were to
> be asked to do the scenery... It all seemed very feasible and
> full of promise.[21]

Billy's version of events concurs with this:

> Gwen's advice to Gates, which I backed up, was to make
> a start with a small, intimate revue which would risk not
> more than £5,000 and might make a lot of money. At first
> he accepted our advice. I made a start on the music, and

Gwen did some sketches and some of her friends helped to write songs and prepare scenes. And then Gates dropped a bombshell with the news that he had engaged Lew Leslie of *Blackbirds* fame to produce the show. Gwen and I had to take a back seat.[22]

Lew Leslie had previously worked with producer Charles Cochran to bring African-American artists to London in the highly successful revue *Blackbirds*. The Prince of Wales went twenty times to see New York's first female black musical theatre star Florence Mills wow audiences at the London Pavilion (now the Trocadero). Gwen and Billy had made their own recording of Mills' hit song from the show, 'I'm a Little Blackbird Looking for a Bluebird', which suited Gwen's self-deprecating style ('Never had no happiness, never felt no one's caress, just a lonesome bit of humanity, born on a Friday I guess')[23] as well as giving her scope to make some bird clucking noises.

Though Gwen recorded the song, Florence Mills never did, which is an enormous pity. She caused a sensation with her singing talent in New York, Paris and London. In June 1927 the cast of *Blackbirds* set off on a British tour. Mills became exhausted and ill and, returning to New York, died there in November aged just thirty-one. Thousands of people attended her funeral.

Before this sad event, the new revue, which was supposed to rival *Blackbirds* and was now titled *White Birds*, opened with a fanfare of publicity. The idea was deeply flawed – and to modern eyes highly problematic and racist, starting (but not stopping) with the title. None of this was Gwen's doing, as it was Lew Leslie who had taken the show off on this particular tangent. He had the grotesque idea of Gwen appearing dressed as Florence Mills in brown tights, which she furiously and flatly refused, even invoking her lawyer.

Opening night was postponed twice before finally happening on 10 June.

> There could be no two opinions about *White Birds*... It was bad. It was very bad indeed. And it went on being very bad indeed for so long (four dreary hours of it) that by the

end of the evening most of us in the stalls were complete wrecks, while even the galleryites, who began booing the show at half-past nine, had tired of this brutal sport by twenty minutes past twelve.[24]

In the drive to impress Norah with her ability to thrive independently, this was a humiliating defeat for Gwen.

After *White Birds* folded its wings, Gwen and Billy were immediately cast in another revue, *Shake Your Feet* at the London Hippodrome. Gwen set about promoting it with great vigour, appearing in a variety of guises and poses in the press.

Also in the company was Jack Hylton, 'The British King of Jazz', who, with his dance band, was a big attraction. The title of the show promised an excellent display of choreography to match the music.

In the *Tatler* the picture editor set a photo of Gwen throwing a shape, side by side with a shot of a trained dancer performing a coquettish high kick. The images were positioned in a way that focused the attention of the dancer, Janette Gilmore, onto Gwen, who seemed to answer the flirtatious display with a cartoon-like, clownish, wide-open physical pose and a smiling 'take', directed straight at the viewer. The caption highlighted Gwen's individuality. She is 'her own humorous and entertaining self... seen... in her own droll fashion'.[25]

When she stands, with perfect symmetry, in the centre of a chorus line of boys in waistcoats and slacks, and girls in floppy hats and short dresses, Gwen is the striking amalgam of the two extremes, in her silk striped trouser suit, fitted jacket with dandy trimmings and a dark, piratical version of the girls' headgear. The eight chorus members form a frame around her as they stand with pointed toes gazing indulgently at the androgynous merry-maker in their midst.

> Oh, we don't know what's coming tomorrow
> Maybe it's trouble and sorrow
> But we'll travel the road
> Sharing our load
> Side by side.[26]

So sang Gwen and Billy in pally fashion in the show. The truth was that tomorrow mattered very much. The verdict of the critics would decide the fate of *Shake Your Feet* and Gwen's pride was at stake. As she celebrated her thirtieth birthday on 14 July, Gwen wished for nothing more fervently than a West End hit vehicle like the one Norah had in *The Vagabond King*.

Sadly, despite the promise of the advance publicity, *Shake Your Feet* was not a success. The *Stage* critic deplored 'the generally mediocre and indifferent material which has taxed the brains of three librettists, several lyric writers and around half a dozen and more composers'.[27]

The reviewer for the *Illustrated London News* agreed:

> In *Shake Your Feet* are to be found first-class comedians like Mr Milton Hayes, Miss Gwen Farrar, and Mr Billy Merson, who only need suitable material in order to show their quality. But even they cannot make bricks without straw. The new show, then, at present, at any rate, is not very amusing.[28]

Surprisingly, the production survived a few months at the London Hippodrome and even transferred to the Palladium. But by November it was reported that Gwen was temporarily out of the show due to an ankle injury. She recuperated at home in Chelsea. The King's Road was bustling with artistic activity as usual. Two doors down from Gwen's house, at number 213, Syrie Maugham was creating a style revolution with her interior decoration based on the white room. Though Gwen may not have been a regular guest, she was certainly familiar to her neighbour's high-profile visitors, among them Cecil Beaton, the floral arranger Constance Spry (one-time partner of the cross-dressing painter Gluck) and Elsie de Wolfe, half of a lesbian power couple with American theatre producer Elizabeth Marbury. Next door to Maugham, at Argyll House, Sibyl Colefax hosted dinners and parties for famous guests and set up her own, rival interior design business.

On the end of this row, Gwen's house – with its eighteenth-century interior and dark wood panelling; its tall, narrow sash windows set in a dark brick facade – retained its outward respectability while servants came and went without any direction, planning or management from Gwen. The cook never knew who or how many to cater for and had to shop and prepare meals by guesswork. The maid had no idea when to light fires or heat water. Their bedrooms were right on top of Gwen's quarters, so their nights were frequently interrupted by loud women drinking, singing and debauching in a permanent haze of tobacco smoke. Though Gwen was never imperious or demanding, working for her required a broad mind and a high tolerance for periods of boredom and chaos. It is perhaps not surprising that some of Gwen's staff took advantage of her by misappropriating money.

Gwen was inclined to drink to excess when she had no work to distract her. The reviews of her recent shows had struck home. She knew she needed better material. As well as drinking with her great friend Audry, something positive happened: they started writing together. Success came when their sketch full of puns, 'Give Me a Ring', was included in the *Clowns in Clover* revue at the Adelphi. Her old friend Jack Hulbert was the producer and Cicely Courtneidge played the telephone operator receiving a proposal of marriage. 'As her share of the dialogue was in the familiar telephone language, the result was exceedingly funny... the best sketch in the first half.'[29]

Norah's run in *The Vagabond King* was coming to an end when, on Saturday 10 December 1927, she returned alone, late at night after the show, to the flat at 160 Earl's Court Road. The apartment was on the first floor, over a dressmaker's business. On reaching the landing she saw signs of disorder and suspected a break-in. She was terrified, thinking the intruders might still be on the premises. She ran to a telephone box and tried to get hold of her husband, Philip Durham. He was nowhere to be found. She called the police. And then, shivering in the freezing kiosk, Norah asked the operator for a number she knew by heart: Flaxman 9292.

Gwen came at once and comforted Norah as the police arrived to ascertain that the thieves were gone. They found the intruders had smashed a fanlight and ransacked the place.

Among the articles missing were pearl necklaces, rings, bracelets and watches.

The incident was in the press the next day, with Gwen and Norah giving a joint interview. 'I went to her immediately,' said Gwen. 'We had not met for a long time.'[30] They were not photographed together but several papers ran pictures of Norah, holding her West Highland terrier, Sam, in the doorway of her apartment.

Gwen offered a slightly implausible account of what they did together after the police had left the scene.

> When Miss Blaney had recovered from her shock, we just naturally sat down at the piano and sang again the numbers we had made popular when we appeared together.[31]

Does their musical act present a euphemistic cover, as it had done in the past, for a physical act of lovemaking, this time one of passionate reconciliation? Or was this neither the time nor the place for singing or sex?

Norah told the *Daily Herald*, 'We have been parted since we had a little difference in America. Now we have made it up.'[32]

Whether or not they consummated their reunion, Gwen's act of desertion seems, at least for public relations purposes, to have been forgiven.

Journalists were eager to know if the pair would get back together onstage, but Norah confirmed that their own separate professional commitments would prevent a reunion in the foreseeable future. It seems they did not get back together as a couple at this point but, to the relief of both, professional rivalries were put on hold.

A few days after the break-in at Norah's flat, Gwen underwent a throat operation. This was evidently successful – by 2 January 1928 she was back onstage with Billy at the enormous London Coliseum. There followed a week at the Brighton Hippodrome.

Norah might have felt cautious about renewing the professional partnership while Gwen had vocal difficulties, but the reason she had given to the journalists was also true: both their diaries were full with other bookings.

Norah was soon contracted to start rehearsals for a new play, *The Snare of the Fowler*, but it got off to a poor start and was rewritten and relaunched a few weeks later with a new title, *Out of the Blue*. John Laurie, famous years later as Private Frazer in *Dad's Army*, was also in the cast. Even with rewrites, the piece was badly structured and poorly reviewed, with critics feeling Norah was too classy for the part she played.

Despite this setback Norah was still well known enough to be paid to advertise cigarettes and be pictured on the side of buses. She made frequent radio broadcasts. Here is her billing in the *Radio Times* for Thursday 21 June 1928:

> Some years ago a partnership known as Norah Blaney
> and Gwen Farrar was dissolved. It was like the splitting of
> a star, and where there had been one light in the theatrical
> firmament there now twinkled two, one of whom will come
> to the microphone for a quarter of an hour tonight. Norah
> Blaney is a pianist and a composer as well as an actress and
> singer, although it was in the last capacities that she played
> so charmingly in *The Vagabond King*, and since then she has
> been playing a straight part in *Out of the Blue*. But with all
> these talents she is obviously capable of putting up a really
> first-rate one-man show when she visits the Studio tonight.[33]

It was two years since Gwen and Norah had split up so suddenly in America. The shock of the burglary had brought about a rapprochement, ending a period of intense professional rivalry. Their careers apart had been fuelled by the desire to outdo the other in fame. They had been more or less equally successful and neither seemed ready to abandon the career trajectories they were on. Gwen was still living the kind of party lifestyle that seemed incompatible with Norah's ambitious plans for her solo career. Though Norah was touched and grateful for Gwen's support in the crisis of the burglary and seemed to be playing down the significance of their earlier split, only time would tell if she had truly forgiven her – or what the future might hold for them as a pair.

MISS AUDRY CARTEN, MISS TALLULAH BANKHEAD
MISS GWEN FARRAR, AND MISS ELSA LANCHESTER

Gwen in 1929: Before her charity matinee at the Lyric (Tatler) *and at
Olivia Wyndham's 'Beer Vs Cocktails' party* (Sketch)

~ 11 ~

A Rendezvous of the Fast and Smart Set

It is a sign of Gwen's fame that she was the subject of one of the very earliest television broadcasts. Some time in 1928, John Logie Baird staged a demonstration of his new invention for the Prince of Wales. He arranged for Gwen to play her cello in a studio in Long Acre. A receiver was set up two miles away in a reception room at the Caledonian Club where the prince and other members could see a 'little flickering image'. The prince identified Gwen immediately, much to Baird's relief, by 'her large cowslick wisp of hair, which helped recognition'[1] and he stayed watching for longer than expected, almost causing the apparatus to overheat and break down.

Gwen's partnership with Billy Mayerl was approaching its second anniversary. Billy was a good-natured man who had a high level of tolerance for Gwen if she made a fuss about their position on the bill or the quality of accommodation. She sometimes cancelled bookings to make way for holidays in the south of France.[2] In general, though, Gwen seems to have maintained a good level of professionalism, and despite a series of escapades in the company of Audry and Tallulah, she and Billy kept up a touring schedule throughout the UK in 1928.

They had recorded a song for Vocalion in 1926, though, that would lead to a rare public disagreement between the pair. 'Masculine Women, Feminine Men' was a topical comedy number about the reversal of gender stereotypes.

Masculine Women, Feminine Men,
Which is the rooster, which is the hen?
It's hard to tell 'em apart today. And say...
Auntie is smoking, rolling her own,
Uncle is always buying cologne.
You go in to give your girl a kiss in the hall,
But instead you find you're kissing her brother Paul.
Go to a party, most any place,
Dad sings soprano
Mother sings bass.

Gwen sang the last line in full throaty basso profundo. By 1929 it had become an established part of their repertoire, but when Billy and Gwen began singing it at a run-through onstage at the London Coliseum in January, manager Sir Oswald Stoll objected, saying it was far too risqué. He told them to cut it.

Gwen said no – she wouldn't perform at all if they didn't include it.

When it came to that point in the show, Billy started playing the intro to a different song and, true to her word, Gwen picked up her cello, slung it on her back, walked off the stage and out of the theatre.

It was announced that Gwen had been taken ill, but reporters found her dining with friends at the Kit-Kat Club in the Haymarket, so the affair was hard to disguise and, according to Jill Mayerl, Billy was very annoyed about it.

That Gwen should so publicly take a stand over this particular song shows how strongly she felt about her right to perform lyrics that reflected her queer world view. Stoll's objection to the song may have been entirely in character, but it is tempting to assume that, in banning it, he might also have been influenced by the prevailing mood of censoriousness in the British Establishment which would soon come to a head.

Billy at least must have forgiven Gwen and regained his sense of humour about this kind of subject matter, for a few months later they recorded another number with a similar theme.

'We Can't Blame the Bobbies for That' again questioned

gender roles in a list of topical issues for which the police (the song declares) could not be expected to take responsibility.

The old channel tunnel has bobbed up again
But we can't blame the Bobbies for that
So under-paid typists can swim there by train
But we can't blame the Bobbies for that
No more on the deck of a steamer we'll slide
'Cos up to date Pullmans to France they'll provide.
With a footpath for Scotsmen laid down at the side
But we can't blame the Bobbies for that.

Our ladies today all resemble the men
It's hard to distinguish twixt rooster and hen
If sexes keep changing new trouble begins
And ladies won't suffer for gentlemen's sins
Mama will play billiards while papa has twins
But she can't blame the Bobbies for that.[3]

A few months earlier, an advertisement for their performance in Cheltenham read:

Gwen Farrar and Billy Mayerl are artistes who have struck out with an original line of entertainment and they stand without a rival, so unique and perfect are their performances that they will go down in posterity as creators of a new art in entertaining.[4]

The turnout was poor, though, when they appeared in Bedford, home turf for Gwen, in November 1928. Here we see she is reprising her dog impressions:

Whether she was giving us the 'plopping' of rain... or imitations of a puppy in 'The Puppy Dog Blues', her work was altogether delightful and she is also probably a very good world's second to Mr Mayerl in syncopation. Her cello playing is good and altogether, the small audience found it a disappointment when she and Mr Mayerl finished at 10.45 p.m.[5]

Gwen and Billy may well have been guests of Gwen's sister Marjorie and her companion Peggy at Chicheley Hall after this concert. The two women were still together, discreetly enjoying life away from the spotlight, though Marjorie (unusually for a woman) held the position of Master of Fox Hounds, along with younger sister Kathleen, in the Oakley Hunt. Gwen's life was a world away from her country-dwelling younger sisters, but they remained close.

At the same time Gwen continued to maintain a loyal friendship with Tallulah. On Sunday 22 January 1928 they had been together at the Stage Golfers' Ball at the Savoy Hotel. The caricature artist ES Hynes depicted Tallulah dancing disdainfully with Gerald du Maurier, and Gwen looking doubtful in the clutches of London Hippodrome manager Frank Boor. The jowly older man surveys Gwen through his monocle while his right hand seems to take forceful possession of her bottom.

Gwen's face registers alarm. She looks the viewer straight in the eye, in a clever depiction of her ironic stage 'take'. Calling out men for sexual harassment was something Gwen could only do through the medium of her comedy, via meaningful looks and the lyrics of the songs she sang.

When she did so, unsurprisingly, it was her behaviour (not the men's) that was criticised.

> Gwen Farrar seemed to have some rather low songs on
> this occasion – or am I wrong in attributing meaning to
> descriptive phrases like that of the man who tells you he'll
> be a father to you 'till father tries how much farther he can
> go' or the soldier who 'tries manoeuvres on your flank'?[6]

Holier-than-thou puritanism was on the rise and it expressed itself in a multitude of ways. This coincided with the registration period of the new electorate. The law having changed, women between the ages of twenty-one and thirty were, for the first time, being added to electoral rolls. Men in positions of power were nervous and scornful of what they perceived to be a volatile new voting demographic.

Another caricature, towards the end of the year, by the same artist, shows just the kind of thing the Establishment deplored: Tallulah and Audry Carten focusing on Gwen as she sits smoking, arms folded, in a nightclub. They occupy a table with an anonymous man who, like the couple on the adjacent table, are looking attentively at Gwen, Tallulah and Audry. The large man at the piano is Rex Evans, who would feature more prominently later in Gwen's career. The title of the drawing, 'London Nights: At the Café Anglais', adds to the impression that this is a typical scene. It was a milieu that was under intense scrutiny. The suspicious minds of the men of the Establishment had recently reached fever pitch and the police had opened an undercover investigation that centred on Tallulah and her set.

Undercover officers from Scotland Yard spent the day observing Tallulah on Sunday 22 July 1928 'in the company of various people connected with the theatrical profession'[7] on a day out on the Thames near Maidenhead, Berkshire. Audry had a younger brother, Kenneth, who was at Eton College. Tallulah, Audry and Gwen were in the habit of driving over to the school to smuggle him and his friends out at weekends. Somehow things got out of hand and it was reported in the press that a number of boys had spent the night with Tallulah at a nearby country club. This caused great alarm in the corridors of power, especially when several senior boys were expelled on account of it.

The country club in question was the Café de Paris at Bray, whose brochure was scrutinised by the CID officers charged with investigating the case. A copy is included in the Home Office file on the matter. Inspector George Yandell reported that it was 'a rendezvous of the fast and smart set', adding that Tallulah (also referred to as 'the Alien') was 'exceedingly well known (there)'.[8]

Another inspector on the case reported, 'Although it is rumoured in theatrical circles that Miss Bankhead is regarded as a sexual pervert, it has not been possible to gather any information to confirm this.'[9]

The matter was referred to Sir William Haldane Porter, head of the 'aliens' branch of the Home Office, who carried out his own investigation and reported what he was told by an anonymous informant:

She is both a Lesbian and immoral with men... Her
'circle' is a centre of vice patronised by at least one of
the most pronounced Sodomites in London (the name
was given) and that it was the considered opinion of the
more respectable American actresses in this country that
she was doing them a great deal of harm as people might
be inclined to think that they were tarred with the same
brush.[10]

The case was passed to the chief legal advisor to the Cabinet, Sir
Earnley Blackwell, and the permanent under-secretary of state
at the Home Office, Sir John Anderson. In the end they agreed
with the headmaster of Eton who thought it best if the whole
thing was hushed up to avoid a scandal.

This curious file on Tallulah, now stored at the National
Archives in Kew, also contains a joke. Tallulah received a
telegram from an admirer: I WANT YOU FOR MY WIFE. So she
wired straight back: IS SHE BEAUTIFUL?

Also contained in the file is a mysterious empty envelope
marked ON HER MAJESTY'S SERVICE on which seem to be inked
the words 'Correspondence other acts T Bankhead + Gwen
Farrar (Drug Addiction)'. This scrawled note appears be dated
15/07/32. The recipient of the envelope writes in pencil
underneath that it came to him empty, so the intriguing
contents are destined to remain unknown.

The prurient men of the Establishment involved in the
investigation, with their moral panic and double standards
would, within months, seize on something in black and white
to prosecute. Radclyffe Hall's sincere and worthy attempt to
portray the life of an introspective lesbian writer was published
on 27 July 1928 and by September was the subject of intense
controversy. The prosecution and subsequent banning of *The
Well of Loneliness,* on the ludicrous grounds of obscenity, would
serve to stir up yet more moral outrage.

In the face of this, Gwen, Audry, Tallulah and their set were
undaunted. They continued, in their own incorrigible way, to
unnerve the authorities. Having shocked the country's elite by
allegedly corrupting their sons at the country's most exclusive

boarding school, they now gleefully set about the task of morally compromising a minister of religion.

Early in October Tallulah and Bea Lillie accepted Charles Cochran's unlikely invitation to an evangelical rally held by the American celebrity preacher, Aimée Semple McPherson, at the Royal Albert Hall. McPherson believed even 'pleasure-made sons of Satan were hungering for something solid'. The remedy, she claimed, 'was the old undenominational revivalist faith based upon the whole Bible and nothing but the Bible'.[11] She appeared with the support of an organisation called the Elim Foursquare Gospel Alliance.

Tallulah hooked up with the glamorous and publicity-hungry evangelist, and the press enjoyed reporting sightings of Sister Aimée in such incongruous company. 'Miss Aimée McPherson seems to have had a social, if not an evangelical success,' said the *Graphic*. 'The question is who is converting who to what?'[12]

Tallulah Bankhead was appearing in her twelfth West End show, *Her Cardboard Lover*, opposite Leslie Howard. They were having sex, despite Howard being married. His excuse, that he 'didn't chase women but… couldn't always be bothered to run away' probably rang very true in this case.

In her autobiography, Tallulah says of Aimée Semple McPherson:

> Bea [Lillie] and I were curious about her piety, her sincerity. Were they genuine or sham? … Aimée came to my house after my performance of *Her Cardboard Lover*… Gwenn [*sic*] Farrar, Leslie Howard, Audry and Kenneth Carten, and I tried in vain to trick her into admitting some peccadillo. We admitted to depravities and excesses – mostly invented – to test her tolerance. She shrugged them off. 'I don't mind those things so long as you don't hurt anyone else by doing them,' she said.
>
> Aimée was fascinated by Bea and her witty sallies and comments… [and] expressed concern because she had not seen [her] before her departure for Southampton.[13]

So Tallulah, Gwen, Audry, Leslie and Aimée all jumped in a car at midnight to head to the south coast. It was terribly foggy and they had to drive at a snail's pace. They reached Southampton at dawn and went aboard the ship on which Bea was about to set sail. Aimée gave her a signed copy of the Bible and they all wished her farewell on her voyage to the States. Coming back, the fog was even thicker and they didn't reach London until two in the afternoon. Fearing they had much to hide, they all agreed to keep quiet about the trip. Journalists, however, had got wind of the excursion and hounded each of them.

> Gwenn [sic] Farrar denied that she'd been on any party. This put her on the spot because Audry Carten told the same reporter: 'You'd better ask Miss Farrar about the party.'... These contradictions spurred on the reporters.[14]

One journalist wrote sarcastically:

> Aimée and Tallulah and Gwen Farrar and Audry Carten. I'll say she was in the safest company. I'm afraid Aimée's Foursquarers may misconstrue her midnight slumming. They don't understand such boyish tricks. I don't suppose they've heard of emancipation.[15]

A statement from Mr EJ Phillips, secretary of the Foursquarers declared:

> I can only say that it seems very strange. I do not understand Sister McPherson's actions. I can only suppose she went after Miss Bankhead and Miss Lillie because she thought they would be good catches.[16]

Tallulah's inclusion of this story across several pages of her autobiography suggests that, in her very eventful life, this mischievous escapade was a highlight – but perhaps, to get the full fun of it, you had to be there.

The iconoclastic friends were still close a year later when they starred in a charity matinee, organised by Gwen, in what may have been an ironic gesture of contrition, or at least a public relations exercise. It took place at the Lyric Theatre, Shaftesbury Avenue, on 26 November 1929, in the presence of the Duchess of York. Audry and her sister Waveney wrote a sketch for the occasion which Tallulah performed with Elsa Lanchester (actress wife of the gay film star Charles Laughton). Audry also acted – a rare occurrence by this time – playing a nun in an extract from a play, based on a book by Daphne du Maurier's grandfather. Gwen played Schubert's *Serenade* on the cello. The event was reviewed in the *Stage* under the heading 'Gwen Farrar's Matinee'.[17]

If Audry, Tallulah and Gwen had contrived to look aloof in the photograph that appeared in the *Tatler*, no one told Elsa Lanchester, who sat beside them, alert and engaging in her maid's costume.

Tallulah went on to perform Audry and Waveney's sketch around the country, using these appearances to raise cash to cover her outstanding Inland Revenue bill, before she left for America at the end of 1930.

Reviewing her performance at the Palladium, a critic wrote, '"Always Apologise" is written in an easy and natural manner. It is a subtle jest, freshly observed and delicately pointed.'[18] The sketch sent up the seriousness of Scandinavian playwright Henrik Ibsen as, Hedda Gabler-like, Tallulah's character emoted and raged histrionically in an argument with her husband about something very trivial.

'Miss Bankhead is at her very best in the mock emotionalism of their modernism.'[19] Audry and Waveney's sketch derived its humour from exploiting the gap between European dramatics and polite British behaviour. True, it relied on its sophisticated audience having seen an Ibsen play to get the joke (an example of 'highbrow' art being mined for its entertainment value in a so-called 'middlebrow' context) but it also provided a great vehicle for the wide-ranging dramatic talents of their friend Tallulah. In generating, performing and producing material themselves, these women were successfully blazing a trail that bypassed theatre's traditional male gatekeepers. It was a route that Gwen would continue to follow with varying levels of success.

However, she was beginning to be featured in the press as much for her social life as for her performing. A photograph

Gwen at a fancy-dress party next to hostess Olivia Wyndham (with guitar) – both in breeches

from June 1929 serves to confirm her as an official member of the Bright Young People. She is standing next to their high priestess, the photographer Olivia Wyndham.

Olivia was a good friend of Cecil Beaton and of Stephen Tennant, one of the most flamboyant Bright Young People. His brother David was married to Hermione Baddeley, the young dancer who had appeared with Gwen and Norah in *The Punch Bowl*.

Kind-hearted and entirely lacking in snobbery, Olivia was a creative and generous socialite who brought together all the different cliques that constituted the BYP. Like Gwen, she came from an aristocratic background. She was a photographer, part of London lesbian subculture, a heavy drinker, and a drug-taker – the archetypal Chelsea Bohemian.[20] She knew Gwen well and, given the freedoms of the age, they may well have been occasional lovers.

The financial crisis that followed the Wall Street Crash in 1929 hastened the backlash against the Bright Young Things. Conspicuous wealth, independent youth, theatricality, effeminacy

Offstage at the Annual Theatrical Garden Party (L to R):
Charles Laughton, Betty Pollock, Elsa Lanchester, Cedric Hardwicke,
Cathleen Nesbitt, Noel Coward, Gerald du Maurier, Edmund Gwenn

in men, masculinity in women, began to be highlighted as signs of decadence and degeneracy. The *Well of Loneliness* trial was not the only court case that alerted the public to queer behaviour. On 25 April 1929, Colonel Barker, born Valerie Arkell, was sentenced to nine months in prison for perjury. Barker had married a woman and creatively invented a heroic military career to match his male identity.

Two lesbian friends of Gwen, Susan Dudley Ryder and Marjorie Bagot, were smeared with innuendo by the papers when they stood charged with smuggling spirits on their yacht at Dover, 'dressed in the garb of sailors'.[21] A customs officer who searched the women's floating quarters was quoted as saying: 'The atmosphere was very unsavoury.'[22]

This censorious atmosphere seeped insidiously through all strata of society. On the subject of gay people, one Bohemian author wrote, 'God knows they abounded in our set, but to normal people it was a failing not to be discussed and certainly not boasted of by "queers".'[23]

The actor/producer Sir Gerald du Maurier inveighed against

homosexuals. Given his views, it is amusing to see his evident discomfort when photographed with a group of actors all in drag for a show at one of the annual garden parties in aid of the Actors' Orphanage, of which he was the president.

There was a growing awareness of the new tendency of psychologists to account for homosexuality as a disorder rather than a crime. This pathologising had the effect of making the public increasingly suspicious of masculine-presenting women.

Prurient and bigoted reporting in certain newspapers fuelled an increase in homophobia. The public knew something, but not enough to allay the fear, suspicion and mounting hysteria that the newspapers were only too happy to feed. It was in this climate of highly derogatory reporting that Joe Carstairs decided she had had enough of public life and moved to a private island in the Bahamas.[24]

At the same time Olivia Wyndham astounded her friends by moving to Harlem to live in a *ménage à trois* with Edna Lewis Thomas and her husband. Edna was an acclaimed African-American singer of spirituals, 'a pioneer exponent of the serious music of the plantations'.[25]

She had broadcast on BBC radio, in the same concert as Norah on 28 December 1926, and early in 1928 she brought a solo show to St Martin's Theatre.

> No sooner did Edna Thomas appear... and her melodious, coaxing voice had chanted 'Swing Low, Sweet Chariot', than she had us in the hollow of her hand... We came away enchanted. Edna Thomas, single-handed, had unveiled a corner of a hidden world to us.[26]

Olivia was completely smitten. She sought out the singer in New York City and lived with her and her husband until he died and they were able to spend the rest of their lives as a devoted lesbian couple. Decades ahead of their time, the two women took part in a survey of homosexuals in 1937. Under a pseudonym, Edna described how Olivia (here called 'Pamela') tracked her down:

> She was persistent, to the point of annoyance. She finally

came to my house and I had the most exciting sex experience of my life. It has gone on for five years because it's so very satisfactory. Pamela is one of the finest women I have ever known. She has come to be very, very dear to me, not just for sex alone. It's just a very great love. She is tender and gentle as I have never known any one else to be.[27]

If there were any doubt about Gwen's credentials as a Bright Young Person then her inclusion in a photo shoot at Olivia's home in October 1929 should allay all uncertainty. In a contest between beer and cocktails, she is pictured on the side of beer. The cheerleaders for cocktails are socialites Edward Gathorne-Hardy and Elizabeth Ponsonby, a woman who so embodied the hedonistic, entitled, wild-eyed qualities of the age that she became the model for Agatha Runcible in Evelyn Waugh's iconic novel on the era, *Vile Bodies*.

As they worked their way through a barrel of beer and a tank of cocktails, everybody at this photo shoot seems intoxicated. Gwen is in the company of some serious alcoholics.

While Gwen was making a name for herself as a debauchée, Norah, was busy recording sweet, conventional ballads with titles like, 'When My Dreams Come True' and 'Just Like Darby and Joan'. She had considerable success with these hits, though privately she thought such sentimental repertoire 'awful, dreadful, heartbreaking'. When she had the opportunity, she did not shy away from saucier repertoire, such as the deliciously queer 'Yes Sir, I Prefer Brunettes', or the song that Gwen had taken a stand for, 'Masculine Women, Feminine Men'. Norah went so far as to contract with De Forest PhonoFilm to record on celluloid her performance of this song at the piano.[28]

She had also taken over the title role from Gertrude Lawrence in George Gershwin's musical *Oh Kay!* for a UK tour. This was the first show since the Charlot revues where Norah was required to dance, and she was very grateful to her co-star, the actor Paul England, who had to lift her. 'I didn't fancy myself as a very great dancer, but I got away with it thanks to Paul. He was marvellous. Ooh, I felt like Pavlova.'[29]

Norah received all-round positive reviews. The critics recognised her great versatility and the tour was a success.

While appearing in Sheffield she became the guest editor of a page in the local newspaper, supplying one long article each day for a week, under the headings: 'Why I Collect Antiques', 'Music and Millionaires', 'My Faithful Pal – Why Forbid Dogs on Tram Cars?', 'A Few Celebrities' and 'Books That I Avoid'. We learn that Norah adores dogs and, as a child, her ambition was to marry a vet, so that she could be his assistant. She is so attached to her West Highland terrier, Sammy, that she has turned down further work in America rather than put him in quarantine. She even holds dog parties where Sammy's canine friends are brought round to play at her flat.

When discussing her reading habits, Norah recommended Aldous Huxley, Beverley Nichols and Dornford Yates, adding:

> Fairy stories are still my delight; they always have been. I adore Hans Christian Andersen and even now cannot read the story of the mermaid who loved the Prince without wanting to cry... The children's verses by AA Milne are very delightful, *Alice in Wonderland* too.[30]

But, at the very start of her book choice, under the heading 'The Sex Novel' Norah says:

> I detest any form of censorship and in the recent controversy on *The Well of Loneliness*, my sympathies are with the gifted authoress. Having read the book I do say it is beautifully written and the style is delicate and restrained in the extreme.[31]

It was bold for Norah to stick her neck out on this matter, especially when we remember how much she valued the approval of her entire fan base, not to mention her own parents.

The editor of the *Sunday Express* was waging a war on the novel, calling it 'a seductive and insidious piece of special pleading designed to display perverted decadence as a martyrdom inflicted upon these outcasts by a cruel society'.[32] He famously said he 'would rather give a healthy boy or a healthy girl a phial of prussic acid than this novel'.[33]

Earlier that month a feature writer in the *Tatler* had said:

> The Home Secretary is to be congratulated on having
> secured the suppression of *The Well of Loneliness*... The book
> is mischievous and unwholesome and... injurious to public
> morals. The female 'invert', hitherto regarded as a hysterical
> half-wit, is by Miss Radclyffe Hall described as the victim of
> a pre-disposition or pre-natal taint.[34]

Norah had nothing to gain and much to lose from defending
the book. What is more, she made this statement, not in passing
during an interview, but deliberately in a feature article. In
calling the book 'beautifully written, delicate and restrained',
Norah does not reveal whether or not she found parallels
between the novel's central character and Gwen, but she can
hardly fail to have been moved by the depiction of lesbian
love blossoming behind the lines, the young couple setting up
home with their pet dog, and Stephen's eventual self-sabotage
of the relationship.

If this made her feel sentimental about her partnership
with Gwen, she did not let it show. When a journalist had the
temerity to suggest that, despite her success as a solo artist, he
still missed her double act with Gwen, Norah retorted:

> There is not the least likelihood of Gwen and I ever getting
> together again... it simply would not pay us to go back into
> partnership. We can both earn more apart than we did as
> a double act, and that was the only reason for the split.
> Pounds, shillings and pence must come before sentiment in
> business.[35]

The summer of 1929 found Norah performing as a solo artist
on a variety tour with the talented Irish multi-instrumentalist
and band leader, Debroy Somers.

In cinemas, sound had arrived. Theatres were experiencing
unprecedented competition and Norah made a plea to audiences
not to defect:

> It is my greatest wish that [people] should not let the
> 'Talkies' harm the theatre by taking all the audiences away.

It is a very serious thing for theatrical people that houses
that have been theatres for years, and in which I myself
have appeared with many happy memories, are turning
over to talking pictures. What's going to happen to all of
us?[36]

What was going to happen to Norah was panto. She played
principal boy Colin in *Mother Goose* at the Theatre Royal, Leeds,
alongside a young man who would go on to become an iconic
pantomime dame, George Lacy. He and Norah were now 'King
of Pantomime' Francis Laidler's biggest stars.

Playing Huguette in tunic and tights had been the perfect
audition for principal boy, but now, instead of being a lovelorn
victim, she was the driver of the narrative. Colin (as with Dick
Whittington, Aladdin or Jack and the Beanstalk) was a likeable
boy on a quest for riches and romance. The audience willingly
suspended its disbelief with regards to her gender for the added
frisson of the love scene between Colin and principal girl Jill.
Norah was in her element. Rather than hark back to the style
of yesteryear she brought a touch of Peter Pan–inspired boyish
realism to the role. As one newspaper noted:

Norah Blaney swaggers, she strikes heroic attitudes, she is
the very model of noble beauty and within a few minutes
we are on her side against all the powers of evil.[37]

Another paper called her a 'regular lad';[38] and there was scope
for her to do what she was most famous for:

Miss Blaney at the piano scored an instant success with her
clever topical verses on local people and affairs.[39]

Producer Laidler had at first thought this might interrupt the
flow of the show, but Norah settled for an upright instead of a
grand piano and when it was wheeled on and she sat down –
as Colin – to tinkle the ivories, it became a natural part of the
action.

With local jokes, Norah was forging a relationship with the
people of Yorkshire which she cemented with appearances at
charity and community events and interviews in local papers.

She observed, in one such article, that pantomime in the north still felt like an important component of Christmas, whereas in London the public were more blasé about such traditions.[40]

She was asked by the *Leeds Mercury* to help answer the question, 'What Sort of Men Do Women Like Best?' Apparently, 'Miss Norah Blaney... found some difficulty in giving definite shape to her ideas on this question.'[41] She eventually replied, 'Men who are much-travelled, well read and broad-minded. I like to make friends with men who are willing to be my pals – not my lovers.'[42]

Mother Goose was an enormous success. Norah was earning the princely sum of £300 per week (about £18,000 in today's money) and the performances were packed. People came, not just from Leeds, but from all over Yorkshire.

On 4 January 1930 the show made history by being the first pantomime broadcast by BBC radio and the longest theatrical broadcast yet (except for opera). It was relayed all over the country, giving it the widest audience of any pantomime ever.

Picking out one of Norah's songs, 'I'll Keep off the Grass No More', the critic from the *Yorkshire Observer* said, '[It] is as finely done as this type of thing can be. A distinctive work of art in its own genre.'[43] The song was sung defiantly by Colin when told by Mother Goose to stop courting her daughter. It was full of references to topical things – plus fours, cocktails, wireless licences – and it gave Norah the chance to smuggle in a saucy line that was more personal to her than the panto's family audiences might have imagined: 'You can tell all your vicars, I've seen Tallulah in her cami knickers.'[44]

Colin's heart, though, was set on Jill and he won her affection in the end:

> Joan Brett is a soft-toned girl of wistful beauty with just the right kind of voice. Inevitably she has a lover. On the stage he is Colin, and in private life he is Norah Blaney. Miss Blaney is the more modern type of principal boy... when she is there the audience know it.[45]

Knowing he had scored a hit, Laidler immediately contracted

the same cast to perform in the same roles the following Christmas, at his flagship venue, the Bradford Alhambra.

When the run ended in February, Norah wanted to work, but was unable to take on a role that might conflict with her commitment to go back into panto the following Christmas. She stayed in Yorkshire for a couple more weeks, continuing her partnership with George Lacy by adapting some of their panto banter into a double act which played at the Leeds Hippodrome. Then she had a week as a solo turn in Sheffield. She renewed her acquaintance with the readers of the *Sheffield Mail*, when, in upbeat mood, she expounded on her new philosophy: 'I have come to the conclusion that stage teamwork is more important than personal success,'[46] she said. This showed a marked change of heart since the interview she gave about pounds, shillings and pence.

> I know that some of you in Sheffield would be only too glad of the chance to get some hard work. But to those of you – the big majority – who are in work, I would say, do as much as ever you can. It is the great cure for unhappiness, worry and disappointment. I turn to work instinctively as the remedy for all ills... It is better than medicine.[47]

The start of a new decade was a good time for resolutions and a fresh approach to life. Norah had always believed in self-motivation but now she was acknowledging the satisfaction of working in a team. As the wild and heady 1920s gave way to the more sober 1930s and she approached the age of forty, Norah recognised that her days of stardom would eventually come to an end. Ever pragmatic, she knew that to continue to enjoy the stimulus of the theatre work she loved, she would have to promote herself as an eager team player rather than rest on her laurels.

The same Christmas when Norah was playing Colin in Leeds, Gwen, Billy and Tallulah were sharing a bill at the Brighton Hippodrome, causing the *Daily Sketch* to remark, 'Brighton seems to have had about the gayest Christmas week of any place in England.'[48]

Tallulah, like Norah, sensed the start of the new decade was a time for change. She planned to head back to the United States. Gwen, with her almost canine faithfulness to friends, felt life would never be the same without Tallulah at the centre of her world. Gwen loathed the States and had no wish whatever to follow her, but she sensed with sadness that an era was coming to an end. Joe Carstairs had already left England to live on her island in the Bahamas, although she still maintained a London flat; and Olivia Wyndham had gone to live in Harlem with Edna Lewis Thomas.

Audry, who was now working successfully in a playwriting team with her sister Waveney, agreed with Tallulah that Gwen must not be abandoned or she would sink into despair and alcoholism. Quite possibly Audry carried a sense of guilt for the part she had played in splitting up Blaney and Farrar; perhaps she hoped to make amends by helping to draw them back together. Gwen's partnership with pianist Billy Mayerl was no longer the novelty it had been for audiences, or for Gwen. Besides, Billy had a new project – a highly successful piano teaching academy, selling sheet music and instructions by mail order – as well as invitations to record with other artists as the dance band era began to take off.

Tallulah worked her way through lovers with scarcely a backward glance, but she felt towards Gwen a guilty sense of duty and fondness, much as one might to a very faithful, characterful and affectionate dog. She thought of capable, hard-working Norah, and the way she had got out of bed to come to entertain party guests in her sensible tweeds. She was not the sort of person to shirk responsibility. Would it perhaps be possible to find a way to gently return Gwen to her former owner?

*Gwen (with Norah's dog Sam) and Norah
on the roof of the London Hippodrome, 1930*

PART V
REUNITED
1930–32

Gwen and Norah reunited, 1930

~ 12 ~

WE'LL CLING TOGETHER

One night in mid March 1930, Gwen was at the Hotel Splendide on Piccadilly for the jazz cabaret when she spotted Norah in the vestibule. 'They began a friendly conversation and Miss Blaney invited Miss Farrar to her suite of rooms.[1] There was a piano in Miss Blaney's suite. It was irresistible.'[2] Within days they had agreed to perform together again.

Perhaps it was not just the piano that was irresistible, but also the reassuring familiarity of each other. It was gorgeous to reaffirm their queer kinship and become lovers again. There is something delightful about their pose in a room with a hastily made bed and a piano in unusually close proximity. Both of them eye the camera with the intense satisfaction of a couple enjoying a special private affinity.

It seems likely that Tallulah, perhaps with Audry's help, encouraged and facilitated Gwen and Norah's reunion. The time for it was ripe. Once they began spending time together again, they found that miraculously, in this first spring of the new decade, they started to enjoy something very like their old relationship.

They were pictured arm in arm on the roof of the London Hippodrome, and side by side at a party at Ivor Novello's. They went to a dog show at Olympia, meeting up with Gwen's sister Marjorie and her companion Peggy (who were showing their prize schnauzers, Chicheley Colin and Chloe).

Norah and Gwen with Marjorie and Peggy's schnauzers

They posed looking lovingly at each other, as they had ten years earlier, while the newspapers happily announced: BLANEY AND FARRAR: PARTNERS AGAIN, LONELY NO LONGER.

One particular article, preserved ever since in Gwen's scrapbook, deserves close attention – as a remarkable record of their reunion and a surprising example of what they were prepared to divulge about their friendship. First the interviewer set the scene, in Norah's hotel suite, where the pair had received her 'to talk about their life together and apart'.[3] She noted their contrasting styles: Norah was dressed in a beautifully embroidered Chinese skirt and jacket, reclining on a couch, smoking, while:

> Miss Farrar, whose severe coat and skirt suggested the masculine garb she adopts on the stage, sat upright at a table, making sketches of frocks which will in time be worn by Miss Blaney on the stage.

Norah said:

'Gwen and I are modern people and we want to forget that
we ever parted, now that we have joined forces again... Our
life together was like most people's lives together or apart.
We generally breakfasted, lunched, dined and supped like
them and occasionally drank a cocktail. We have no dietetic
fads to talk about, like so many entertainers and actresses
have today, and we spent an appreciable amount of time
preparing and rehearsing our songs, for the public demands
novelty and we have to be up-to-date.'

After talking about the topical element in their act Gwen added:

'I will tell you one thing about our life together which
few people suspect and I did not realise until we had
gone our respective ways apart. I had a strange sensation
of loneliness which I couldn't understand. I didn't know
which way to turn – like one feels when one is first learning
to ride a bike.'

'And I had the same sort of feeling,' confessed Miss
Blaney. 'I felt as if I was writing with my left hand and
that's a thing I can't do.'

'There was another thing separation taught me.' Miss
Farrar's voice took on a tone of deeper seriousness. 'Well, as
I knew what Norah could do, I realised more vividly than
ever her versatility. She can go into all sorts of shows and
make good in them all. You remember she followed Gertie
Lawrence in *Oh, Kay!* ...'

'I often wonder if versatility is any good to anyone on the
stage,' smiled Miss Blaney, puffing out a cloud of smoke. 'If
I have versatility, Gwen has a strong personality.'

'That's a friendly way of saying I can't get away from
myself,' laughed Miss Farrar.

The interview continued in a similar vein. Past rivalries had
turned to mutual appreciation. It ended with Gwen in ebullient
mood – 'There's no knowing what we may do now we are
together again!' – and Norah, practical as usual, declaring that
they were being offered a larger salary than ever before.

203

Onstage with Billy Mayerl, Gwen always wore dresses, but she was about to return to a very masculine look. Norah promised: 'Gwen is going back to her trousers while I shall keep to my skirts.'[4]

But fashions had changed. When their act began, the trouser suits and cropped hair had been absolutely on trend, but the androgynous look for women, which had been so widely adopted, was now out of fashion. Wearing trousers was more likely to be associated in the public imagination with the kind of snide insinuations that surrounded Radclyffe Hall, Joe Carstairs and Colonel Barker.

Once they started appearing onstage together again, Gwen's style began to be called out by critics. 'Norah Blaney exquisitely frilly in a white silk evening dress... and Gwen, mannish and rather glowering in black pyjamas.'[5] She was no longer a fashion maker, but an oddity.

Their old friends Jack Hulbert and Ciceley Courtneidge were putting on a new edition of their revue *The House that Jack Built*. It was to take over the Winter Garden Theatre, scene of Norah's long run in *The Vagabond King*. They asked Gwen and Norah to appear to launch the revitalised show. Rehearsals got under way.

Gwen suggested a special number to mark their reconciliation. With Billy's permission she altered the lyrics of his love song, 'Sunshine and Rain', and rehearsed it with Norah. Gwen did away with the saccharine conventional clichés of the original lyrics ('Our two hearts beat as one... Our love nest we'll feather'), replacing them with words more concrete and relevant to their situation, offering a recap of their relationship history, including a direct reference to themselves as a pair: 'When a couple quarrel they will both declare, "We will never speak again!"'... Then they'll say the disagreement's ended, All the broken threads of friendship mended.' She kept in the powerfully physical word 'cling' from the original chorus, leaving audiences in no doubt as to the closeness of the relationship.

On opening night, Gwen gave Norah a gift: a beautiful necklace – 'one side a shining curve of jet, and the other a brilliance of paste'.[6] Of course, with its gleaming cut glass next to the lustrous dark gemstone, it matched the white and black 'magpie' colours which had always been the hallmark of their act. This love offering signified the attraction of opposites, the irresistible magnetic pull they had felt for each other since that fateful train journey to France thirteen years ago. The necklace acted as a physical symbol, solemnising the new vow Gwen had written for them to sing to each other each night, with the audience bearing witness: 'We will endeavour to cling close forever, we never will sever again.'

The audience seemed as delighted as the couple:

> The reception they received must have convinced them of their good fortune in rejoining one another in their unique entertainment. Recalled again and again, they closed with an amusing skit on the drawing film *Mickey the Mouse* [sic].[7]

Norah's article on teamwork had been a manifesto for the year ahead. She was practising what she preached: the power of togetherness and hard work. She and Gwen were busier than they had ever been: back in a West End show together, taking on cabaret bookings and charity performances, judging fashion shows, picking winning raffle tickets at boxing matches and making new records.

When the legendary, warm-hearted, larger-than-life artist Sophie Tucker came over from New York to star in Jack Hulbert's next revue, *Follow a Star*, Gwen and Norah became her friends:

> Darling old Sophie, she was really rather a character... a very kind, sweet person. She used to entertain during her breakfast, which was always taken in bed. Gwen and I (I don't know why we were favoured, but we were) were always invited to have breakfast with her. There she lay, in bed, with telephones all round her and eggs and bacon all over the place.[8]

Norah very likely moved back in to 217 King's Road and imposed some order, marking a decade since they had excitedly taken up residence there in the first place. Norah's parents, Molly and Walter, still living in Barnes, undoubtedly had concerns about what people might think.

Gwen and Norah made their rapport increasingly evident in their act, almost as a deliberate challenge to critics, one of whom sounded a sour note: 'Everyone was glad to see the two actresses together again, but they make a mistake if they think that the audience is in the least interested in their private affairs.'[9]

'Love, love, love, love, everybody falls in love,'[10] sang Gwen and Norah in ecstatic harmony at a recording session in April. Then they gave a bluesy lilt to a soulful night-time lament about sexual frustration:

> If you ever wake from your sleep
> And you hear someone softly weep
> Honey it's only me moaning for you.[11]

When Gwen took up the melody on her cello, she coaxed the strings with the coolest jazz bowing action and knew exactly where to lay on the vibrato. Norah dropped into her lower register for a final chorus, as Gwen lent her deep contralto and surprisingly sweet mid-range notes to the sumptuous, romantic final harmony.

> And as long as we're far apart
> Hear this song of an aching heart
> Honey it's only me,
> Moaning for you.
> Ooooooooh oooooh![12]

Next came 'My Love Affair' in which they harmonised the opening bars and chorus, then took a verse each. The tone is deeply romantic, until, halfway through, in trademark style, they jazz the piece up, doubling the speed and syncopating wildly, before coming together in harmony again for the final rubato.

When they came to record 'The Moon is Low' in July, they sang with utter sincerity:

> Gwen: Alone we two, our camp fire gleams
> Tonight we will find the trail of our dreams

Norah: The purple hills, this call of the west
Your face close to mine, our lips are pressed.[13]

At the end of this piece they perfectly impersonate the twanging of ukulele strings. It's light-hearted but done with immaculate artistry. Raising the banal to the level of high art, these were coded performances, a celebration of camp. The very fact that they were such accomplished musicians, performing cheap popular tunes with total commitment, gave them popular appeal, yet also sent a subversive signal to those with a similar sensibility. Their enjoyment of the theatricality of 'passing' as a 'regular' couple is evident in Norah's statement about Gwen going back to her trousers, while she kept her skirts. Norah's embodiment of traditional femininity and Gwen's complete lack of self-consciousness as her own unique, authentic self, helped the audience accept them as a romantic pair they could relate to.

The new act was full of songs that linked to their own relationship. 'Don't Tell Her What Happened to Me' spoke directly to the awareness they each had of the other's activities during the period they were apart, with its exhortation to 'Tell me where she is, tell me where she goes, tell me what she does, tell me who she knows, but don't tell her what happened to me.' And its appeal to 'Let her remember me as I used to be, when her love for me made me strong and free.'[14]

Strong and free they were again now, reunited – the guardians of each other's individuality.

'A Cottage for Sale', about a couple and their dream home, proved to be a huge hit when they introduced it at the Glasgow Alhambra.

They alternated reflective romantic ballads with upbeat songs as they publicly celebrated their reunion with lyrics about clinging to each other, moaning with longing in the night and pressing their lips together in passionate embrace.

Elsewhere in popular culture, though, a new novel, *Loveliest of Friends*, came with the following dire warning about the perils of sapphic coupledom, practised, as the writer saw it, by:

... twisted freaks of Nature... so choked with the weeds of viciousness and selfish lust that... they regard their victims as mere stepping stones to their further pleasure. With flower-sweet finger-tips they crush the grape of evil till it is exquisite, smooth and luscious to the taste... leaving their prey gibbering, writhing, sex-sodden shadows of their former selves, conscious of only one ambition, one desire in mind and body, which, ever festering, ever destroying, slowly saps them of health and sanity.[15]

In a climate where that book was a bestseller,[16] what self-belief and courage it took to carry on, putting themselves onstage, trusting that their professionalism and innate sense of self-worth would carry them through. The enthusiastic response they received from audiences was proof that the public could see past what it had been taught to believe, that it could forget bigotry and prejudice and respond instinctively to love.

In London they played at the Palladium and the Victoria Palace. They received hyperbolic billing in Folkestone as 'The World's Greatest Lady Entertainers'. When they performed at the Buxton Opera House, 'Tallulah... (who had much to do with the reconciliation of this long-estranged pair)... dashed on to the stage in a tennis dress and beret and finished singing the song for them. To the huge delight of the audience.'[17]

Sometime during 1930, the tobacco company R&J Hill produced a series of thirty cigarette cards celebrating 'Music Hall Celebrities Past and Present'. With an enormous number to choose from, living and dead, they featured Gwen, looking imperious over her horn-rimmed spectacles.

The wording on the back of her card is of interest, whether it was coined by Gwen herself or by a marketing person. Reference is made to her old act with Norah (but not Billy) and to her work in revue.

She delights in making weird noises with her voice, much to the discomfort of her partner. She has deserted the Music Halls several times for Revues but always to return to her 'first love.'

It is not hard to interpret this as a veiled reference to Norah, especially when the timing of the release of the cards coincided so perfectly with their reunion.

Norah was not included in this set of cards, but by the time she recorded 'Say "Oui" Cherie' later in the year, with its teasingly provocative lyrics, she was firmly associated with Gwen once more in the mind of the public:

> Imagine just a little love nest for two
> Keeping our affair strictly entre nous.

Though she recorded this and 'Love is Like a Song' with a full orchestra, one could just as well imagine her making a loving appeal to Gwen to add one of her plaintive cello obligati after these lines:

> Love is like a song played on many heartstrings
> But the words will always be
> 'I love you.'

In the middle of 1930, this busy reunion year, full of travelling, recording, broadcasting and the bliss of being back together, Norah woke to find her name in the papers for an incident quite beyond her control.

Under the heading 'Night Adventure on the Brighton Road' readers learned that Norah's husband, Philip Durham, had been held in police custody following a high-speed car chase. According to Durham, his car broke down on the way to Brighton, so he decided to spend the night in it. Unable to sleep, he got chatting to a policeman who flagged down a passing car and instructed the two men inside to give Durham a lift. The men drove at terrifying speed – eighty miles an hour – were pursued by police and skidded to a halt just feet in front of a road block set up to stop them. Durham told the *Evening News*, 'I rang up my wife a moment ago and she laughed about it. She wouldn't have laughed if she had been in the car. I shall never accept a lift from strangers again.'[18]

The *Daily Mirror* included a photograph of an anxious Durham, thin-faced, with chiselled cheekbones, a long nose and dimpled chin, captioned 'theatrical manager… unknowingly asks for a lift'. It was designed to raise readers' curiosity and suspicions and it was not the sort of publicity that Norah wanted.

Wonder Bar opened at the Savoy Theatre in early December. Gwen and Norah took centre stage with their usual cabaret turn, performing both during the show and in the interval. Gwen also had a role within the action of the rather thin plot. She played a timid, eccentric cabaret singer, Josephine, who carried around her knitting and, at one point, was coaxed out from her hiding place under the piano to sing a comic song about her failed love life, called 'I'm Alone in a Crowd'.

> He was my man
> When we began
> We had a plan to wed
> But now he shakes his head
> He declares that I must lump it
> He's too busy with his trumpet.

It was typical of the self-deprecating songs that were Gwen's speciality. The couple's sexual incompatibility was expressed in a further suggestive musical metaphor: 'Though I dearly loved that fellow, He's all sax and I'm all cello.'[19]

Gwen had ample chance to camp up the pathos of mismatched Josephine, conducting the band with a knitting needle as she sang. By contrast, when joined by Norah for their cabaret numbers, she showed her true self, musically partnered to perfection.

She and Norah were very well reviewed, but critics were not happy with the format of the show. One wrote: 'The resemblance to a cabaret was so strong that after a while one began to wonder if it wouldn't be jollier at an actual restaurant, instead of watching a mimic one.'[20]

Surprisingly, given its lukewarm reception, *Wonder Bar* ran for well over 150 performances, went on a UK tour and was later made into a movie.[21]

Of course, Norah was still committed to her pantomime

contract. André Charlot, producer of *Wonder Bar*, offered to pay Francis Laidler £3,000 to release her, but he refused. Bradford people had already booked to see her; the King of Panto would not disappoint them. Norah did just ten nights in *Wonder Bar* before reluctantly leaving Gwen and the show, with a promise to return.

An accomplished musician called Peggy Cochrane took her place at the piano, but, said Norah, 'She couldn't sing for nuts [and] she and Gwen loathed each other.'[22]

Soon after she arrived up north, Norah spoke to the *Yorkshire Observer* who published the 'Confessions of Miss Norah Blaney'. She answered a series of questions including, 'What is your life's greatest sorrow feared?' Norah replied, 'I agree with Miss Edith Craig. My life's greatest sorrow – I have not had it yet – would be the loss of my greatest friend. I won't say who it is. It is a lady.'[23] Edith Craig, Ellen Terry's lesbian daughter, had been interviewed by the paper the week before and had indeed said the loss of a female friend was her greatest fear, but Norah was more emphatic.

She and Gwen spoke to each other on the telephone every day. They shared ideas. Norah included a new comedy song in the panto, 'Never Swat a Fly'. Days later, Gwen tried out the same song in *Wonder Bar.*

In January Gwen recorded 'If I Had a Girl Like You'. Other female singers had substituted 'Boy' into the lyrics. Gwen stuck with 'Girl'.

> I've been looking for someone to love, someone just like you.
> I've been asking the stars up above to find someone like you.
> Now that I have found you dear I always want to keep you
> near me.
> I've waited a lifetime, I've hated the night-time
> Those longs nights have made me blue
> I wouldn't be waiting, I wouldn't be hating if I had a girl
> like you.[24]

The contradiction in the lyrics, between the definite, 'Now that I have found you' and the uncertain, '*If* I had a girl like you' matched Gwen's unease at Norah's absence. This was the first time they had been apart since their passionate reunion nine months earlier. They were happy, hectic months, but Gwen was all too aware that there was no marriage contract binding Norah to her and that the pressures of the outside world could intervene as they had done in the past.

Norah had been working non-stop. Quite apart from all the performing, travelling and broadcasting, she had been dealing with a wayward husband, anxious parents and an emotionally intense Gwen. She was now geographically at a distance from them all, which may have been a relief.

After the enormous success of *Mother Goose* in Leeds, the cast were under pressure to promote and deliver their spectacular entertainment again, this time in Bradford. Norah arrived at rehearsals word perfect. Expectations were high, and the cast did not disappoint. Critics were again struck by Norah's brilliance, calling her 'dashing' and 'breezy',[25] 'very convincing' and 'an ideal boy'.[26]

Onstage she exuded optimism: 'To hear her sing "There's a Good Time Coming" is to believe every word of it!'[27] But behind the scenes Norah was run down, irritable and suffering a great deal of pain from a blister on one toe. Privately she wondered how long she could go on in this exhausting profession where everything depended on her appearance of vitality.

The theatre used the services of an elderly local doctor, who was treating her toe with poultices. Norah lost her temper backstage at a matinee when an over-zealous call boy, who only came in as cover on Wednesday afternoons, rang an alarm bell in her dressing room because he thought she was about to miss her entrance. In fact she was in the middle of a particularly frantic quick change. Norah let the boy (who was eleven) know 'exactly how great a sin he had committed'. Subsequently, 'The stage manager and other important backstage people were embroiled and in the confusion the boy was sacked.' At the end of the show, when Norah heard the child had been seen in floods of tears, she made the stage manager promise to reinstate him. 'You must send him a postcard tonight. I can't bear to think of the poor boy spending a week thinking he has been sacked.'[28]

Norah was less forgiving of the elderly doctor when it became clear that her foot was getting worse. He didn't know what to do.

As it happened, a few weeks earlier at a first night, Gwen, who had an easy way with titled people, had introduced Norah to Yorkshire-based Lord Moynihan, President of the Royal College of Surgeons. Norah mentioned she was heading to Bradford and presciently quipped, 'If I get appendicitis, p'raps you'll operate on me!' Moynihan had replied that the best surgeon in Bradford was Basil Hughes. The name had stuck in Norah's head and now she asked the doctor to get hold of him.

Hughes examined Norah in her room at the Midland Hotel and said she must leave the show. 'You can't dance with a foot like that.'

She was booked into the Duke of York's Nursing Home, known locally as Hughes' Home, as Basil was in charge. He went to London overnight to operate on a diplomat. All this was a worry for Norah, who had brought a maid with her to Bradford. Fortunately the maid would look after her beloved dog, Sam, but Norah would have to keep on paying her hotel bill. Private nursing homes did not come cheap. She would have the expense of that and the doctors' bills, on top of the hotel, and she did not know whether Laidler would continue to pay her fee. Worse was to follow.

Hughes returned the next day and told staff to prepare the operating theatre. The bumbling poultice doctor was roped in to administer the anaesthetic.

Decades later, Norah told Roger Wilmut the dramatic story of what happened next.

> On the table I had a cardiac arrest. Six and a half minutes. All sorts of funny things happened. I died and he [Basil] brought me back to life again... operated on my heart – stuck something into it and I recovered. I didn't go back to the theatre for nearly a fortnight.[29]

The papers were not given the whole story. They just reported, light-heartedly, on her recovery from a septic toe. A photograph appeared in the *Yorkshire Evening News* of Norah sitting cheerily in her nursing-home bed surrounded by flowers.

Norah's understudy, Madeleine Mars, came to visit, bringing Sam the dog. Norah's first question was whether the call boy had got his job back.

The reporter wanted to know details of her operation, but Norah made light of it:

'When I was recovering consciousness, I gazed dreamily at the surgeon, whose face was hidden by a mask and sang, "I remember you from somewhere."' She hid the fact that she had nearly lost her life. 'The Matron says she will have to set a limit to the number of visitors... my room is like a cocktail party!' She said she had received letters from all over the country and added, 'Gwen Farrar, my partner... sends me a telegram every day to cheer me up.'[30]

Gwen, alone at 217 King's Road, could not include in a telegram all she wanted to say to Norah. One senses that she wanted to tell her that she loved her, missed her, worried about her and never wanted to be apart from her again. Last time, the split was Gwen's fault – she had been unkind and foolish to leave Norah without warning in America. Reuniting had saved her and the past nine months had brought her more joy than she could remember. At first Norah hadn't seemed to mind that people knew they were in love. She was older now and could stand up to her parents. She was her own person and Gwen loved her for it. But if Gwen had overstepped the mark and been too demonstrative (and who could blame her for wanting the world to see how happy they were together?) then she was sorry.

The young lyricist Rowland Leigh[31] knew at first hand the secrecy and pain of homosexual love. He had written the lyrics of a song Gwen heard Carl Brisson sing every night in *Wonder Bar*. It perfectly expressed what she wanted to say to Norah. Gwen chose to record it herself and she arranged and rehearsed a tender cello obligato passage to go with it. Going in to the

Columbia studio on 16 January 1931, Gwen was aware Norah was lying in a hospital bed, but could not have known the drama that awaited her on the operating table that very night.

> I long to tell you all that I feel
> Every ideal of mine dear
> If I but dared to I would reveal
> Love by some subtle sign.
>
> If I were brave and said what I meant
> Would you resent my true love?
> Would you be angry, shy or content
> If I should say to you...
>
> Tell me I'm forgiven for daring to sing
> Our love is a thing apart.
> Tell me I'm forgiven for spreading the news
> I'm happy to lose my heart.
> Tell me I'm forgiven for daring to show
> The rest of the world I love you so.

The following Monday, Basil Hughes inspected his patient's foot. He sent everyone out of the room. This is how Norah remembered the conversation that followed:

'Do you know why I sent them out?'

'I don't know.'

'Because I had a dream about you last night. I dreamed I married you.'

'Oh well, you're all right because dreams always go the opposite and I've got a husband anyway.'

'Where is he?'

'Oh, I haven't lived with him for years.'

'Haven't you had a divorce?'

'I can't be bothered.'

'Oh well, we'll see about that.'[32]

Norah's vivacity had charmed him in a very short time. With her talent for lively conversation, even in adversity, she had found they had things in common. He was a talented all-rounder and high achiever; tenacious and hard working. He was musical, had a degree in maths from Cambridge University and had worked as a teacher before switching to medicine. He had been awarded the Distinguished Service Order in the war for his heroic work in military hospitals, becoming famous for his delicate and speedy work as a surgeon, saving countless lives. His book, *War Surgery from Firing Line to Base*, was a medical classic.

Despite witnessing horrors in the conflict he was good-tempered and cheerful. He looked after himself, taking care with his diet. He was medium height, average build, with an exceptionally kind face and an unassuming, relaxed manner. At fifty-two, he was fifteen years older than Norah. He was divorced, with no children. His first wife, like Norah, had been much younger than him.

When Norah was well enough, he took her out in his soft-top motor car to Baildon Moor. It was too cold to put the roof down but the weather was sunny and bright. Norah had spent very little time in the countryside and at first she found it bleak and uninteresting. But she loved seeing her sociable little dog, Sam, race about on the moor with Basil's dogs, while he told her the romantic pre-history of the place with its bell pits and mysterious cup-and-ring marked stones. He pointed out kestrel and golden plover, reed buntings, meadow pipit, lapwing and skylarks. He drove her to nearby Shipley Glen. Norah was amazed how easy it was to reach Bradford city centre again from the wilder open spaces. It took less than fifteen minutes – not because Basil drove recklessly – on the contrary, she felt very safe with him at the wheel. It was flattering that a doctor (not to mention one who had saved her life) should take a genuine and companionable interest in her. How impressed her parents would be when she told them that a member of the profession she had admired all her life was paying her such close attention.

By the end of January she was ready to share more of what had happened with the press. They reported: 'The surgeon told Miss Blaney that she was not only lucky in still possessing her foot, but was really fortunate to be alive.'[33]

Norah's injury and enforced recuperation had given her a

much-needed rest and she was seeing the world in a new light. She had been made shockingly aware of her own vulnerability and how easily her career and even her life could have been cut short. She owed everything to Basil Hughes and now this gentle, likeable, cultured, highly respected man, far from playing the aloof professional (as perhaps he ought), was courting her, relieving the boredom of her convalescence and reassuring her that from now on everything would be all right. He waived his fee and the cost of the nursing home. There was no more direct route to Norah's heart. It wasn't that she easily took monetary favours – she had never taken advantage of Gwen's wealth. But this was different. Being courted by Basil matched an image she knew would play well with the public: famous actress with handsome, wealthy, life-saving admirer.

Norah went back to *Mother Goose* on 26 January 1931 and would finish the run before returning to London and *Wonder Bar* in March. She began rehearsing new numbers each morning over the telephone with Gwen. A local journalist was intrigued to know how this worked. Was it difficult?

> No, not really. You see, Miss Farrar and I have been together so long that we just sort of sense each other musically speaking, even if we are 200 miles apart. Usually we rehearse while we are in our bedrooms – Miss Farrar in her bedroom in London and myself in my Bradford hotel. There is a piano near my telephone... I play a few lines... Then Gwen may sing a few lines. So we get along famously. We play the songs through, fix up the harmony and decide which line each other of us shall sing.[34]

One of them was 'Just a Little Longer'.[35] (Did Gwen but know the irony of the lyric.)

Everyone who loved Norah – her parents Walter and Molly, and, of course, Gwen – felt huge gratitude to Basil Hughes for saving her life. They greeted him like a hero and liked him immediately when he came to London to see Norah in *Wonder Bar* in March.

Norah told Wilmut, 'He'd never seen me act before. There

wasn't a seat in the house so they put a chair in the wings for him. Saturday night. When he heard all the cheering he said, "You'd never give this up, would you?"'

'What for? Why should I?' she asks.

'Because I thought you might marry me.' Norah recounts his words without emotion. 'Would you miss it?'

'Yes, I should miss it.'

'In that case I'll give my work up.'

'You couldn't do that!' Norah's reaction is full of awe and emphasis, in contrast to her matter-of-fact delivery of the rest of the story.

She continues in the same dramatic vein, recalling how she had said to Basil, 'My thing is only make-believe! Yours is real! You're curing people!'

'Oh, I'd do cancer research,' was Basil's casual reply.

'What about money?' enquired Norah, true to form.

'There's no problem there.'

'Well, I'll have to talk to Gwen about it.'[36] The pain in her voice as she says this is unmistakable.

Basil's readiness to sacrifice the career in which he was so respected made Norah feel more appreciated than she had ever been before. Even the tumultuous applause of an audience and Gwen's adoring gaze could not induce in her a greater feeling of self-worth.

This unlooked-for marriage proposal had the potential to solve a number of problems. Philip Durham was a liability. She had paid him an allowance of eight pounds a week for several years and was glad to have an excuse to divorce him. The bad publicity around his Brighton escapade had been embarrassing.

Molly and Walter would disapprove of a divorce but then how could they object to her marrying Basil? True, she might have to move north, but she would be mistress of her own house and free for the first time from the proximity of her parents. Finally, as she weighed up the pros and cons, Norah was forced to admit Gwen's drawbacks: her infuriating refusal to broadcast on the radio, her insistence on being top of the bill, her untidiness, her lack of care for her appearance, her reckless

Norah with Basil Hughes

driving, her dependency on alcohol and her undisguised devotion. Love Gwen as she did, Norah was scared of being all and everything to her forever. Getting back with her had felt so good, so comfortable, so much like old times, but she knew Gwen was growing increasingly dependent on her. What future was there in that for Norah, except as an emotional prop, seen by the world as one half of a faded, ageing couple of old maids? Or, as the prevailing rhetoric on lesbians would have it, 'inverts', 'sex perverts', 'crooked, twisted freaks of Nature... slowly sapped... of health and sanity'.[37] Only the most courageous and thick-skinned could remain immune to (what we now call) internalised homophobia, when church, state and popular culture preached such loathing. Added to this was the discourse around ageing. Norah, approaching her thirty-eighth birthday, had to decide whether to grasp a fresh opportunity or look forward to residing in an underworld of past glories where subterfuge was poor defence against deep social and sexual shame.

Norah faced the difficult task of explaining her decision to Gwen. Speaking in 1981 she recalled with great sadness and love:

219

Gwen was wonderful about it. She said, 'I've always got Sir George' – she always called her private money 'Sir George' – 'and you've saved nothing, you've spent all your money. I think you ought to marry him. We've got to the top. We've done what we wanted to do. So why not?'[38]

Money is Norah's default term of reference. It is surprising, given how much it's on her mind, that she has spent it all; but less so that she speaks about this marriage as a financial arrangement. It neatly skirts the unspeakable reality of her betrayal. Gwen's plea, 'Tell me I'm forgiven for spreading the news our love is a thing apart,' has fallen on deaf ears. Norah has emphatically chosen not to continue publicly as Gwen's lover, not to forgive her for being so obvious about their partnership, but to make the clearest public statement possible that her own kind of love is not 'a thing apart', but the conventional, heterosexual sort.

Despite this personal betrayal, Norah was determined to honour all the professional contracts they had signed. It is greatly to her and Gwen's credit that they never fell out in public during the awkward year that followed.

Quite probably they were still lovers. Norah was not physically attracted to Basil.[39] He did not regard Gwen as a serious rival and Gwen had little pride when it came to her overwhelming love and affection for Norah.

Gwen's sadness and hangdog resignation to Norah's impending desertion is almost palpable in the *Wonder Bar* publicity photographs of April 1931. (Contrast these with the playful excitement of their Mickey Mouse fooling a year earlier.) For these photographs they visited the studio at 22 Old Bond Street of their friend Dorothy Wilding. She was a contemporary whom they had known since 1923 when she had produced a series of publicity shots for the *Midnight Follies*. The following year she had taken the photograph of Gwen and Norah gazing at each other on the cover of the 'Come Back' sheet music.

By 1931 Wilding was one of London's best-established and most respected portrait artists, a favourite of Tallulah and the Prince of Wales.[40] She believed that women were natural psychologists and thus superior in the art of portraiture, 'better able to portray their own sex than men… because they are not deceived by artifice in women, and so get to the soul of the sitter'.[41] She had an innate sense of drama and shrewd judgement of character. Cecil Beaton, who admired her greatly, said she was motherly, funny and smart.[42]

She wasted no time in catching up with her friends' news, chatting between shots. Gwen's hurt and Norah's preoccupation are visible in every picture. In marked contrast to earlier photographs, the pair can no longer look each other in the eye.

Their onstage dynamic mirrored offstage emotions so closely that they acted out their personal trauma, performing a version of the drama of their breakup in their improvised poses for Wilding's camera. Gwen was accustomed to playing the unrequited lover role for laughs and she slipped into it with ease, but throughout the shoot was constantly reminded that this role was now her reality. Gwen looks over Norah's shoulder as she reads a private letter. Gwen poses, hunched on a separate plinth from Norah, or looks down wistfully from her moral high ground at Norah, dreamy and detached below.

They stand back to back, arms folded. Norah checks back with anxious eyes to see Gwen dejected, hands in her pockets, eyes cast diagonally downwards, a picture of childlike self-pity. They sit side by side, Gwen's chin planted firmly on her palms, her wrists touching. A ring is visible on the little finger of her right hand – lesbian code. Norah frames her own face in two clenched fists, defensive, her eyes smiling with the smug, mischievous confidence of a person with two lovers on the go. In the most poignant shot of all, Gwen rests her chin on Norah's bare shoulder and nestles her forehead into her cheek in a silent plea to turn the clock back. She looks resignedly past the reunion gift – the necklace, set off to perfection by Norah's V-necked blouse. Her eyebrows are raised, her face smudgy with emotion. Dorothy Wilding captured it all.

One is tempted to imagine that, for Gwen, what hurt so much was not only Norah's betrayal, but the fact that this proved the bigots right. Lesbian love was doomed to failure. Happiness was fleeting. The bliss of their reunion was replaced by the dull knowledge that Norah was slipping through her fingers. Gwen had been relegated from first place in Norah's affections to second best. She faced a bleak year ahead, working with Norah, but with the prospect of her marriage to Basil and her retirement from the stage looming inexorably.

The critics of lesbian relationships set up a self-fulfilling prophesy. By condemning them as self-indulgent, destructive and doomed, they deliberately stifled them, denying women self-respect, social status or a framework in which their love could thrive. Only total discretion, to the point of denial, could protect a lesbian partnership – and that was made much harder by being in the public eye. It helped enormously to be less known but to have private means. In this respect Gwen's sister Marjorie and her companion Peggy, securely away from the limelight at Chicheley Hall, were in the best situation of all.

On 16 June, Gwen and Norah were both present at the Annual Theatrical Garden Party in aid of the Actors' Orphanage, held in the gardens of the Royal Hospital, Chelsea. Actors and public alike could 'refresh themselves at Mr André Charlot's Wonder Bar, or lose money at Mr Carl Brisson's Gambling Den in the consoling presence of Misses Norah Blaney and Gwen Farrar'.[43]

As well as continuing to perform in *Wonder Bar*, Gwen and Norah did spots in Sunday shows at the Folkestone Pleasure Gardens and Brighton's Palace Pier. They headlined a Midnight Cabaret at the Dorchester Hotel and celebrated *Wonder Bar*'s success at a gala in a Piccadilly restaurant.

In June Norah recorded two of the most heterosexual songs she ever put on vinyl. In 'Oh Mr Porter' and 'Our Lodger's such a Nice Young Man' she adopted a Cockney accent and exaggerated performance style. Years later she resented it when people thought these music hall songs (dating from the 1890s) were her usual kind of repertoire.

The second half of the year was taken up with a tour of *Wonder Bar*. They took in the London suburbs, Wimbledon, Golders Green, Hammersmith, before travelling further afield to Glasgow, Edinburgh, Manchester, Liverpool, Nottingham and Birmingham.

In Leeds, the venue was the Theatre Royal, scene of Norah's original hit in *Mother Goose*. This was a chance to see her fiancé and make plans. However, Norah's abiding memory of *Wonder Bar* in Leeds did not involve Basil, but instead, a shared joke with Gwen – about Danish actor Carl Brisson – that made her laugh every time she recalled it.

> Carl was all right but he wasn't exactly what you might call noted for his modesty – he loved himself to death. When we were on tour with *Wonder Bar* and we were all lined up for the final curtain, we bowed down together all holding hands. He would say, with his head down, 'Speech!' Then he'd look up with a beautiful smile as much as to say, 'Well if you must insist, I'll make a speech.' He'd walk down to the footlights and make his speech. Tilly [his sister] was up in the gallery to lead the applause. After his speech one night she called out, with a Danish accent that certainly didn't sound like an authentic Leeds voice, 'Ve are very glad to see you back Carrl.' A saucy member of the company – a boy who didn't care what he did – said, 'Good old Tilly!'[44]

Norah had a strong claim to be a favourite with the Leeds audience following her recent pantomime hit. This perhaps explains why she so enjoyed making fun of Brisson's arrogance.

By the end of the tour Gwen was carrying round yards of yellow knitting – all sorts of different stitches and slightly mismatched shades of wool. She kept on knitting when the tour had ended and she and Norah were back doing variety dates. It became something like a security blanket.

Norah's engagement to Basil was made public just before Christmas 1931. Newspapers in Bradford and Leeds reacted with particular excitement to the news. The wedding date was set for 20 February.

In the run-up to Christmas, Gwen and Norah performed at one of their old London haunts, the Victoria Palace, still introducing new songs and keeping their act up to date. Ciro's Night Club was their home for a couple of weeks in the New Year. There were excellent reviews. Gwen and Norah were going strong.

The parting of the ways, 1932: Leslie Henson between Norah and Gwen, Connie Ediss to their right (Leeds Mercury)

Then came a week at the Palladium, where fifteen years earlier Norah had begged the manager to let her include her friend. Now, on their final night in the huge and iconic West End theatre, there was not a spare seat to be had. A newspaper reported:

> The couple, who presented one of their distinctive double musical turns, were given a tremendous ovation, and Miss Blaney had to make a speech. The house was thronged, and every item by the pair, who were making the last of thousands of joint appearances, was cheered to the echo. They received many curtain calls and finally came through the tabs to receive handsome bouquets. When silence fell Miss Blaney's speech was short but to the point.
>
> 'I want to thank you for the wonderful way we have been treated all these years. I now want to say "Goodbye" and give my love to you all. Bless you, and be as sweet to Gwen as you have been to us both.' Miss Farrar, it should be explained, is remaining on the variety stage as a single turn.[45]

224

London Nights: At the Café Anglais

Audry, Tallulah and Gwen at the table on the left are dwarfed by Rex Evans at the piano, ES Hynes, Bystander, 28 November 1928

FROM LEFT TO RIGHT (AT BACK): MR. R. H. GILLESPIE, SIR FRANCIS TOWLE AND MISS EDNA BEST, MR. FRANK BOOR AND MISS GWEN FARRAR. (IN CENTRE): MR. FRANKLYN DYALL AND MISS MARY MERRILL, SIR GERALD DU MAURIER AND MISS TALLULAH BANKHEAD, MR. JACK SMITH AND MISS PEGGY O'NEIL. (BELOW): MR. ERNEST TRUEX AND MISS VERA LENNOX, MR. A. W. BASKCOMB AND MISS SYLVIA LESLIE.

In another Hynes caricature, Gwen is in the clutches of Hippodrome manager Frank Boor (top right) and Tallulah dances with Gerald du Maurier (at the centre of the circle), Illustrated Sporting and Dramatic News, 28 January 1928

*Gwen drawing a caricature of herself, Sketch, 1927, and reunited with Norah
as Mickey and Minnie Mouse in* The House that Jack Built, Bystander, *1930*

Norah wears a necklace from Gwen as they play together in Wonder Bar, *1930*

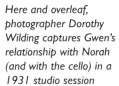

Here and overleaf,
photographer Dorothy
Wilding captures Gwen's
relationship with Norah
(and with the cello) in a
1931 studio session

Gwen and Norah during the time they spent preparing for their Abbey Road
recordings, February 1935, and (below) a publicity shot of Gwen the next
year in which a spaniel wears her glasses

But it was not quite the end, for later that night, Norah had another send-off:

> Miss Norah Blaney and Miss Gwen Farrar played together
> in a speciality act on Saturday night for the last time
> before Miss Blaney becomes a bride. The occasion was the
> 'Green Room Rags' at the Shaftesbury Theatre, which is
> an entertainment reserved for stage artistes and friends.
> Showers of good wishes greeted Miss Blaney before the
> close, on her marriage this week at Prince's Row Register
> Office to Dr Basil Hughes, of Bradford.[46]

A ceremonial farewell handshake between the duo was staged and photographed, with their mutual friend Leslie Henson looking skywards as though in silent prayer, while confirmed spinster Connie Ediss rested a consoling hand on Gwen's shoulder.

Then, finally, a week later:

> The marriage took place quietly... at the Prince's Row
> Register Office, London, of Mr Basil Hughes, a Bradford
> surgeon, son of the Rev John Edward Hughes, Vicar
> of Cheswardine, Shropshire, and Mrs Philip Durham,
> professionally known as Miss Norah Blaney. The bride was
> accompanied by her parents and Miss Gwen Farrar, who
> was for so many years her stage partner... There was a
> luncheon party for the guests at the Berkeley Hotel after the
> ceremony. A wedding reception had been held the previous
> evening at the home of the bride's parents... The famous
> partnership of Blaney and Farrar, now finally at an end,
> is world known. Miss Farrar is desolate at losing her stage
> companion, and has not yet decided on her future plans.[47]

Gwen looks very sad in the photographs taken outside the register office, in striking contrast to her carefree manner at Norah's wedding to Philip Durham ten years earlier. This was a cruel blow. If Norah had plotted to take revenge on Gwen for her desertion in America, she might have done exactly this: reunite with her, only to drop her less than a year later, when Gwen had done nothing but reciprocate Norah's love. But of course that had not been Norah's intention; she would never have deliberately planned to hurt her lover and friend.

Norah's mother, Molly, beams her approval upon this respectable marriage. Norah knew her parents would rest easy now that their only child was secure and comfortably off in the care of a suitable man. She had even managed to convince herself that this was what she wanted. Looking across at Gwen, though, she could see her behaviour was punishing her. How long before it would be Norah's turn to ask, 'Tell me I'm forgiven'?

*Wedding day: Gwen, Basil Hughes, Norah,
and Norah's mother Molly*

PART VI

IF LOVE WERE ALL

1932–44

In a publicity stunt for After Dinner, *Gwen poses with children beside a giant model of Wallace Beery in* The Champ

Gwen as the woman judge of the future in a sketch set in 1980

~ 13 ~

AFTER DINNER

G wen knew she had to do something spectacular and prove, all over again, that she could thrive on her own. She began writing sketches for a revue which she would produce and appear in. She was also working with Audry Carten on a production of her latest play, *Gay Love*. Tallulah Bankhead, meanwhile, was in America enjoying an affair with the beautiful, boyish, accomplished stage artist, Hope Williams.

Gwen's cello, as always, was a consolation. Daily practice gave her some mental relief from the misery of losing Norah. In a photograph from the April studio session with Dorothy Wilding, Gwen seemed to come alive and look far younger, almost childlike, when she played.

Two weeks after the wedding, Gwen headed north in her car. She was billed to appear in Ilkley, a Yorkshire town about fifteen miles from Bradford Moor where Norah was settling in to Basil's house.

'I've got to take a partner,' Gwen wailed down the phone to Norah, evidently resorting to desperate emotional blackmail, for Norah eventually relented, 'Oh I can't bear that. I'll go with you and I'll sing too.' The local paper continued, 'She stayed with the Hughes and when the night came she went to Ilkley where she was billed "with partner". When the anonymous partner stood up it proved to be Norah Blaney herself.'[1] The bandleader that night was the great Jack Hylton. It was a night to remember for Ilkley Dance Club.

What Gwen found when she visited was Norah happily homemaking for Basil in his large house, Moorlands.[2] Basil was very often at the hospital. There had been no honeymoon, as he was too busy.

Seeing Norah settled there made the fact of her departure a reality. Though Gwen had managed to prevail on her to sing at Ilkley, she knew that such tactics would not persuade Norah to change her mind again. Married life in the countryside clearly appealed to her. Gwen had grown up in the great outdoors, but for her friend it was a wonderful novelty to take moorland walks with the dogs and enjoy the big skies and great vistas.

Norah was still affectionate with Gwen, intimate even, when the occasion allowed. But she was committed to staying married. Gwen knew that she would have to accept the friendship on Norah's new terms or give it up. She drove back to London resigned and unhappy.

For local journalist Joyce Mather, Norah's presence in Bradford proved a godsend. She filled her column in the *Leeds Mercury* with news of her homemaking activities. We learn from Joyce that Norah now went to bed much earlier than she used to and got up at seven to have breakfast with Basil before he went to work. In the daytime she typed letters for him, played the piano and exercised the dogs.

Mather promised to tell her readers more about the Hughes' home another day, before concluding her article by mentioning the locket Norah wore containing two pictures of Basil. 'He wears one too! We're both frightfully in love with one another and we're not ashamed of it. I must be in love, you know, to get up at seven o'clock in the morning.'[3]

Gwen, meanwhile, was getting into trouble. In mid June in Arundel, her car glanced the wing mirror of a motorcyclist she was overtaking. He was knocked off his bike and spent three weeks in hospital. 'She was fined £10 for driving a car without due care, and £2 for driving without a licence... It was stated that there were eight previous convictions against Miss Farrar for motoring offences.'[4]

Gwen had always been a reckless motorist, since starting

to drive without any formal lessons in the days before safety training was a priority. With the roads relatively free of cars and the vast majority of drivers being men, Gwen seemed to regard being behind the wheel as an enjoyable statement of her individuality, and an expression of her anti-authoritarian approach to life, forgetting a duty of care to other road users. Driving was an entertaining sport for her – and for any brave passengers who dared to travel with her.

At the end of June, Gwen was at the Annual Theatrical Garden Party with a sideshow she had devised called 'Hit the Hat'. The Pathé footage[5] makes this look like a terrifying game in which she stood, pulling comedy anxious faces, behind a painted stage flat, while laughing people threw sponges at her in an effort to dislodge her top hat. The intertitle announces there are no prizes for guessing who this lady is!

Another mark of continued fame came with Gwen's inclusion in a set of caricatures by the artist known as 'Tom Titt' covering the walls of the Caviare Bar in Green Street (now Irving St), Leicester Square. This was unveiled in June 1932 and showed Gwen in trademark style alongside Bea Lillie, Gertrude Lawrence, Noel Coward and Gladys Cooper.

Gwen's revue idea was taking shape. It was to begin at 9 p.m., allowing audiences to dine properly beforehand. It would be called, appropriately enough, *After Dinner*. Her backers were two aristocratic young men, Sir Hugh Smiley[6] and Edward, Marquess of Donegall[7] who suggested that society girls be included in the cast, as they might attract their well-off friends to see the show. This sparked a furious row, with theatre critics wading in, before the show had even opened, to correctly point out that there were plenty of out-of-work professionals who deserved the work ahead of amateurs.

Another young man, Lance Lister,[8] became involved as a producer. He denied that amateurs were to be cast and set about pulling the show into shape with Gwen and Rowland Leigh, who had written the lovely lyrics to 'Tell Me I'm Forgiven'.

Auditions were held for professional dancers and singers. In Yorkshire Joyce Mather's paper published a story that, on a trip to London, Norah got herself anonymously admitted via the stage door to the theatre where auditions were taking place. She was too late but, disguised under her hat, she told a sad story about how far she had come. The message was relayed to Gwen who said, 'Let the poor kid have a go, she's come a long way.'[9] Hilarity ensued when Norah identified herself.

Gwen went to lengths to advertise the show, even posing with school children in front of a giant model of American film star Wallace Beery. This was for a sketch in the revue spoofing his hit film *The Champ,* with Gwen impersonating the cute nine-year-old boy actor, Jackie Cooper.

This was not the only intriguing idea in a show whose modernity was marked by the prominence it gave to women. Besides the team of twelve well-drilled, highly professional, tap-dancing, platinum blonde chorus girls, there were four strong comedy character actors: Gwen, Hermione Baddeley, Betty Frankiss, and Elsa Newell. They appeared as 'The Four Marx Sisters' in a spoof that took the critics by surprise. Another sketch – ahead of its time – was the 'Assizes 1980' in which Gwen played a High Court judge presiding over an entirely female-run court. In this futuristic vision, a man is tried under the Male Persons Act for daring to attend a women's football match.

Besides these sketches, Gwen, with her knitting from *Wonder Bar* (now twenty yards long), wandered the stage between scenes knocking things over. She played the cello and sang a self-deprecating song. Most striking of all, reclining on a chaise longue in a blonde wig, she did a stunning impression of Greta Garbo in her latest hit movie, *Grand Hotel.*

The first try-out of the new revue happened in September at the King's Theatre, Southsea, seventy-five miles from London on the south coast. Half the cast were flown down by Lord Donegall in one of his light aircraft, while Gwen, Hermione and her husband raced them in a car.

All did not go well with the show and the local paper was not kind:

> The production last night was badly fumbled. Not only
> were there scenic and lighting troubles... but there were

missed lines, slipshod acting and a lack of slickness vital to a show of this sort.[10]

Gwen and Lance Lister had a week to tighten things up before the show's next port of call – Leeds. There Joyce Mather wrote:

> Hearing that a rehearsal of *After Dinner* was in progress, I went round to the Grand Theatre this afternoon to look for Mrs Basil Hughes, knowing full well that if Gwen Farrar was in the cast, her former partner, Norah Blaney, would be there to watch.[11]

Norah was recuperating from an operation, but would be attending the show twice – on the Wednesday matinee and then the final performance on Saturday 'to wish the show luck before it opens in London on the 12th of next month'.[12] Mather naturally discussed Norah's operation for her readers, saying Basil had performed the appendectomy. 'It is unusual for a surgeon to operate on his wife. Mrs Hughes however insisted.'[13]

Norah had good reason to keep it in the family. This operation was most likely a hysterectomy following complications from her earlier abortion.[14]

Gwen was naturally nervous about Norah's reaction to her show. In a photograph of the pair taken at the theatre, they look at each other, but awkwardly, not touching. Norah, despite her recent surgery, looks rather more robust than Gwen.

The *Yorkshire Post* thought the revue was good in parts but still needed some cutting. The next stop was the Theatre Royal, Birmingham, where a critic remarked that it was a mystery 'to see Miss Gwen Farrar in what is, for her, a restrained mood. There is ample opportunity and need for the producer to exploit her comic genius to the ultimate improvement of this show'.[15] It was in Gwen's power, as the self-styled 'deviser' of the show, to take a more commanding role in *After Dinner,* but, as a decision-maker and manager of actors, she struggled to muster the supreme confidence that used to characterise her stage appearances. The impression PL Travers had given that Gwen 'would go her own serene way if the world were falling to bits around her' was turned around. Gwen seemed to be falling to bits while the world went its own way.

After Dinner arrived at the Gaiety Theatre, London, on 12 October 1932. The theatre itself was run down, a shadow of the place it had been in the 1890s when it hosted the immensely popular 'girl' themed musicals that Norah had seen as a child, and considerably more dilapidated than when Gwen and Norah had made their revue debut there eleven years earlier.

Norah made the trip down to London to support Gwen on opening night. Fashion writer Florence Roberts noted that she was wearing 'the quaint necklace… which Gwen Farrar had given to her on the night when they resumed the stage partnership which is now, finally, broken'.[16]

The reviews in London were not too bad. This was not the disaster that *White Birds* had been. 'On the whole the revue is better than many that have made smash hits.'[17] Critics praised Gwen's impersonation of Garbo and appreciated the work of the chorus. They remained frustrated by the show's patchiness and some felt it could use a male compere.

After Dinner suffered by comparison with Noel Coward's revue, *Words and Music*, which was running concurrently and contained the great writer's most popular songs, 'Mad About the Boy' and 'Mad Dogs and Englishmen'. Unable to compete with sheer genius, *After Dinner* folded within three weeks.

Gwen was given little credit for her ambition and ingenuity in devising and staging a revue that put women at the heart of the comedy. It was far ahead of its time. The press preferred to mock the audience of supportive friends who turned out on the first night than to take the piece seriously. Gwen and her friends were lampooned for 'making whoopee'[18] and being 'more modern than the moderns'.[19]

Back in Yorkshire Norah kept herself busy, making celebrity appearances for charities and the like all over the West Riding. On 13 August Joyce Mather informed her readers that Norah and Basil had finally been able to get away for a belated honeymoon in Scotland. Then, when Norah returned to her good works, Mather depicted her as a dim-witted wife:

She was as vivid as ever, a pleasing decoration for the platform... Primed, one suspects by her husband... Miss Blaney gave a learned little speech on serums and tumours and other medical matters illustrating her point of our debt and duty to the animals.[20]

This was in the autumn of 1932, when Norah wowed the locals by bringing Ivor Novello with her to open the RSPCA bazaar. Novello stayed with Norah and Basil at Moorlands; photographs suggest he visited them on more than one occasion.

In the week before Christmas, Mather updated her readers on the holiday plans of her favourite local celebrities. Mr Basil Hughes 'will be taking his turn at voluntary hospital duty... Mrs Hughes, therefore, is going up to town on Thursday... returning on Boxing Day... Her stay in town will be divided between her parents and her old friend and stage partner, Miss Gwen Farrar.'[21]

Whether this was a mark of Gwen's need or Basil's altruism, it was fortunate that the two women were able to spend Christmas together. If Norah was as content with her new domestic arrangement as she always maintained, one imagines it ought to have been a sacrifice to spend her very first Christmas of married life away from the home she had lovingly decorated. Instead she was at 217 King's Road, the subtext of her trip, a plea from the heart: 'Tell me I'm forgiven.'

She and Gwen had been unable to catch up properly in the week of *After Dinner* at the Grand. Here was a chance for them to be in their original home, without any commitments, just together again. And of course Gwen welcomed her delightedly.

Most certainly they would have gone to see their friend Cathleen Nesbitt in *Children in Uniform* which was running at the Duchess Theatre. The play contained stirring scenes as schoolgirl Manuela publicly declared her passionate love for a woman teacher; followed by affirmative words as the teacher tried to defend the girl from the headmistress's punishment: 'What you call sin, I call the great spirit of love which takes a thousand forms.'[22]

It must have been invigorating for them to sit in the

audience and see, at last, a public endorsement of their kind of love. But on Boxing Day it was time for Norah to return to Bradford to see in the New Year with Basil. As a distraction from the pain of separation, Gwen was off to the races. She liked to visit Sandown Park in Esher and Hurst Park, near Hampton Court Palace.

Gwen was co-producing Audry and Waveney Carten's *Gay Love* which was soon to open at the Q Theatre near Kew Bridge. Margaret Bannerman played Gloria. She had been a friend for a long time. (Norah had acquired Sam from her as a puppy when he needed re-homing after disgracing himself by killing a neighbour's chickens.) *Gay Love* was a particular success for Bannerman and transferred for several weeks to the Lyric Theatre, Shaftesbury Avenue.

Just as they had with *After Dinner*, the critics were disparaging about the 'hysterical' audience of friends on the first night. They called the writers 'lighthearted ladies', demeaning both Audry and her sister, whom they nicknamed 'Permanent Waveney'.[23] This kind of sexist sneering was endemic, but the Cartens had the last laugh, for the production succeeded and they sold the film rights and saw the play adapted into a movie the following year starring Florence Desmond and Sophie Tucker.

On 12 June in Regent's Park, Gwen again set up her stall for the Annual Theatrical Garden Party. 'Gwen Farrar's "Hit the Hats", a funny variant of the coconut shy, was a popular offering'[24] said the *Stage* reporter, estimating that twelve thousand people attended the event.

Norah, meanwhile, had slipped back happily into her round of good works. Her down-to-earth approach matched the no-nonsense Yorkshire temperament and, although she enjoyed her dual status as a former stage star and wife of eminent surgeon, she did not take herself too seriously. Mather reported on her presence in Shipley to open a branch of the YMCA:

> The Lady Mayoress turned to her and said apologetically, 'I don't know what to call you – Miss Blaney or Mrs. Hughes?'
> 'Call me Florrie Forde,[25] if you like,' replied Miss Blaney.[26]

Gwen with Audry Carten at the races

Norah celebrated her fortieth birthday on 16 July 1933 quietly
– secretly perhaps, as she had lied about her age on both her
previous marriage certificates. She may have been with Gwen,
who had turned thirty-six two days earlier. It seems likely that
they would meet to mark the occasion of their joint birthdays,
if only to rue the passage of time. Both knew that hard work
was the key to future happiness, but they were equally aware
that their glory days were behind them. Gwen was sinking into
alcoholism and occasional despair.

On 19 August the *Stage* reported on Gwen's non-appearance
in Weston-super-Mare:

> Miss Gwen Farrar, who was billed to appear last Sunday, was
> unable, owing to illness, to do so. She is ordered a complete
> rest for six weeks or two months by her doctor.[27]

Fearful of Gwen's dependence on her and knowing Audry
would step in, Norah threw herself into more Bradford ventures.
Months earlier she had joined the Bradford Amateur Operatic
and Dramatic Company and rehearsals were well under way

for their production of *The Vagabond King* in which she was to play her old role, Huguette. In a kind of travesty of her former triumph, she slightly injured her hand again in an accident with the dagger. If that was all too familiar, she did something else that was strikingly new. She allowed herself to be selected as the Conservative candidate for Bradford Moor in the local elections – one suspects more in a spirit of feminism than through any particular commitment to party politics. In this role she experienced a baptism of fire.

> A heckler caused no little trouble and some amusement. After asking Mrs Hughes several questions, one relating to public assistance which she admitted she could not answer, he persistently interrupted the proceedings until Alderman TJ Robinson answered his questions. Mrs Hughes said... 'Bradford was the means of bringing true happiness to me and my real home and I want to do something for Bradford in return.' At the end of the meeting Mrs Hughes said she was glad her first meeting was over. 'I have had lots of ordeals, terrifying first nights, but tonight I really felt more frightened than I have ever done before.'[28]

Norah lost to the incumbent Labour councillor but was able to reflect positively on the experience:

> My friends told me I should never stick coming up here, but what with having rotten eggs thrown at me at election meetings, being snapped to death at rehearsals, and opening bazaars, life is just full of colour and adventure, and I have never been bored for a minute.[29]

By this time Gwen had rallied. Throughout December and over Christmas she had a cabaret spot at the Café de Paris with a new accompanist, Anne Denys.[30] Just the other side of Leicester Square at the Café Anglais a remarkable French cabaret artiste, Suzy Solidor, was also performing. Gwen most certainly witnessed openly lesbian Solidor deliver her sensational set which included the songs 'Ouvre' and 'Obsession':

Every woman that I know
I desire from head to toe
In my fantasies I hope
They'll all be mine.
Soon my thoughts begin to drift
Underneath the skirts I'll lift
And the places that I'll kiss
That are forbidden. [31]

By singing in French, Solidor got away with it. She was the toast of the sophisticated smart set, 'a French cabaret artist with a husky voice and so much charm that her personality is described as devastating'.[32]

Gwen appeared, as a last-minute addition, in André Charlot's revue *How D'You Do?* at the Streatham Hill Theatre. With the stage appearance and a radio broadcast Gwen's year had started well, but on 7 March she fell over, hit her face on a door and broke her nose. It was the kind of injury that suggested she was under the influence; and it meant an operation and a short stay in a nursing home to recover. Remarkably, by Good Friday she was sufficiently recovered to head a variety bill at Brighton Palace Pier, and then at Eastbourne Pier on Easter Day.

In her scrapbook, a cutting from this period states Gwen's ambition to be 'a kind of female Harold Lloyd'[33] and says, to that end, she was having a story written around her personality. The cartoon shows her bounding along, grinning, her cello on her back, in the direction of Hollywood. It was an exciting aspiration.

When a set of cigarette cards was produced by Gallaher in 1934, Gwen and Gracie Fields were the only two artists to appear in both the Music Hall series from 1930 and this latest collection, 'Champions of Screen and Stage'. Greta Garbo, Katharine Hepburn, Tallulah Bankhead, Clark Gable and Marlene Dietrich were just some of the other stars featured in the pack.

In June 1934 Gwen supported the Annual Theatrical Garden Party again. She did not revive 'Hit the Hat', but this time worked in a team with colleagues from her recent Charlot appearance and the Waters Sisters, running 'Cabaret Sports'. In the past year Elsie and Doris Waters had begun what would turn out to be a meteoric rise to 'national treasure' status, thanks to their broadcasts on the BBC as Cockney friends Gert and Daisy. They were first inspired to develop their act, which originally consisted of Doris on the piano and Elsie on violin, by watching Norah and Gwen blend musical numbers with witty repartee. Now they were radio stars.

Perhaps the success of her imitators inspired Gwen to drop her antipathy to broadcasting. When the opportunity arose to be involved in a radio adaptation of *Wonder Bar*, she and the BBC producer lost no time in persuading Norah to take part. She came to London to rehearse with Gwen and the recording took place in early October. Thanks to a photograph in the *Leeds Mercury* we know that Norah wore her special gift from Gwen: the black and white necklace.

Wonder Bar had top billing in the *Radio Times* when it was broadcast in October, with an audience of millions and numerous repeats. One review read:

> A notable feature of the evening was the reunion of Gwen
> Farrar and Norah Blaney, who had a substantial share of
> the last part of the show to themselves and who revived
> 'It Ain't Gonna Rain No More' with red-hot topical verses,
> and, so, with a merry swing, sent *Wonder Bar* to its climax.[34]

Back on the variety circuit Gwen briefly formed a double act with her friend Rex Evans, the larger-than-life pianist, raconteur and singer from the Café Anglais. With great panache and irony they included the jaunty number, 'Keep Young and Beautiful (if you want to be loved)'.[35] The song's reference to a Marcel wave was right on trend – as was Norah, who sported this fashionable hairstyle in a photograph of the *Wonder Bar* recording.

Up in Bradford, Norah, still a leading light of the Amateur Operatic Society, had a role in Noel Coward's *Bitter Sweet*. As Manon, the French cabaret singer who has seen better days, she sang Coward's most poignant and autobiographical song. Gwen travelled north to watch the performance from a box in the Alhambra.

> I believe in doing what I can
> In crying when I must
> In laughing when I choose
> Hey ho, if love were all.[36]

How hard it must have been for Gwen to sit alongside Basil watching Norah perform a song about the devastating compromises that life demands of queer lovers. Coward wrote with insight. He had been a lover of Prince George since 1923. Just as Gwen had (twice) watched Norah get married, Coward was about to be a guest at the Royal Wedding of George and his bride Marina on 29 November 1934. His gift to them was a copy of his complete works.

Another gay male writer and friend, Beverley Nichols, had written Gwen and Norah a song inspired by a heartbreak of his own. 'Another One Gone' poignantly expressed the agony of a doomed part-time love affair.

> A little story, a little passion
> A little glory, then out of fashion
> Why is it never true love forever?
> Why must we always sing the same song?[37]

Gwen and Norah were going to record this song in February 1935 and they spent the early weeks of the year working together on this and several other pieces.

Gwen had a new address. While her London base remained the King's Road, she began renting a country house in Effingham, Surrey, not far from her old friend Teddie Gerard. Grove Paddock was a cosy three-bedroomed brick cottage with a low tiled roof and leaded-light windows overlooking a large garden with a swimming pool. Norah seems to have spent so much time there with Gwen in the winter of 1934–35 that local shopkeeper Lena Bridger was under the impression they were co-habiting. Speaking in 1971 she recalled:

> Two actresses, Gwen Farrar and Norah Blaney, lived at the
> Paddock. They were characters. They used to dress up and
> walk up the village, and all sorts of peculiar things, for
> those days anyway.[38]

Mrs Bridger's comment reveals a mixture of excitement and mild rebuke that was typically English – lesbianism was a taboo subject which she could only bring herself to allude to obliquely. But with Basil deeply involved in his medical work in Bradford, evidently there was no barrier to Norah and Gwen spending many days and nights together as companions, colleagues and lovers, perfecting the material they would take into the recording studio. It seems Norah was making all the compromises she could to her marriage in order to be with Gwen, to work with her and to win her lasting forgiveness.

They celebrated Valentine's Day in their old Chelsea home, having motored up from Effingham. The next morning they drove to the converted Georgian town house, five miles away, that housed HMV's Abbey Road studios. (Opened by Sir Edward Elgar four years earlier, this was where Norah's hero Pablo Casals would record his Bach cello suites.) The work Gwen and Norah had put in over the preceding weeks paid off and the result was the finest recording they ever made.[39]

Norah took the vocal part in 'Another One Gone' with Gwen supplying a tender, yearning cello obligato before Norah's exquisite final top note. There followed two tightly rehearsed medleys of 'Old Favourites', displaying their full range from satirical ('It Ain't Gonna Rain No More' and 'In Our Little Garden Subbub'), through character comedy ('Toreador'), vocal tricks ('Ukulele Lady') and animal impressions ('Who Tied the Can on the Old Dog's Tail?') to romantic ballad ('What'll I Do?'). After a display of ludicrous guttural and nasal clowning, Gwen switched mood to hum along, with great simplicity, behind just two phrases from Norah's greatest hit: 'What'll I do when you are far away and I am blue?' and 'When I'm alone with only dreams of you that won't come true, what'll I do?'[40] The effect is stunning.

For their final number they carefully crafted their own take on a song which Bing Crosby and Leslie 'Hutch' Hutchinson had just recorded (with words by African-American lyricist Jo Trent), 'Maybe I'm Wrong Again'. Gwen and Norah were the only artists to record it as a duet, adding their own beautifully balanced harmonies to the deceptively simple lyrics about forbidden love rekindled. It matched their personal circumstances to perfection. With its almost casual acknowledgement of transgression, 'Maybe I'm wrong again' and its exultant conclusion, 'Let me be wrong again', in Gwen and Norah's hands this lilting ballad becomes a paean for queer love, the most significant and tender statement of their feelings for each other that they were able to put on record.

> Maybe I'm wrong again
> Playing with love again
> Maybe I'm wrong again
> Believin' in you
> Let me be wrong again
> For I love the thrill
> That comes when you love again
> When two hearts are still yearning.[41]

The critic in the *Surrey Mirror* wrote:

> The names alone are enough to tell you that this is a record not to be missed, and when you hear it, you will be even more delighted. 'Maybe I'm Wrong Again' and 'Another One Gone'... make this record a sheer delight.[42]

Another paper reviewed the record, along with new releases by Gracie Fields and Cicely Courtneidge, under the title 'Four of our Great Comediennes'.[43]

Norah was working to promote the new disc back home in Bradford, but she was unable, of course, to be explicit about the pain of her double life and the encoded message of queer love contained within its grooves. Instead she quipped, in an interview with the *Leeds Mercury,* that she had just taken up golf, so 'Another One Gone' perfectly expressed her feeling about lost balls.

It seems likely that the extended period of togetherness over the winter had raised Gwen's expectations. She had begun to

The six Farrar sisters at the wedding: Marjorie, Helen, Kathleen, Ella, Gwen and Muriel

forgive Norah for deserting her, but hopes of a future together were dashed again when Norah returned north.

In a complete reversal of the professional rivalry of a decade earlier, Norah now actively promoted Gwen, in an attempt to help find her work and distract her from her misery. Norah's co-star from *Oh Kay!*, Paul England, had written a screenplay for a movie featuring Jack Hylton and his dance band. Contacts and networking paid off as the film's director, Leslie S Hiscott, who had previously directed *Gay Love*, cast Gwen in the role of Miss Peachum.

She Shall Have Music was made at Twickenham Film Studios, conveniently situated, for Gwen, between Chelsea and her house in Effingham. The film was declared 'an obvious winner'.[44] Hylton played himself, first encountering Gwen doing sprightly pull-ups as Miss Peachum, the gym mistress in an academy for beautiful young girls. Next she is at the centre of the action as Hylton and his band accompany the young blonde leading lady (June Clyde as Dorothy) in a catchy tune, 'The Run Around'. Dressed in a mortar board and gown, Gwen delightfully and wordlessly acts the strict schoolma'am,

Penrith concert: the Bradford amateurs are scribbled over; to their right are Muriel, her father-in law, Gwen looking askance, and Norah

gradually seduced by the syncopated music. She taps her feet, puts her mortar board at a jaunty angle and jiggles in her seat, all the while flirting deliciously with Dorothy. At the end of the piece we are supposed to believe she has fallen in love with Hylton. Gwen did her absolute best to bring out Miss Peachum's love of the ladies but her character is ultimately sent doggedly, dejectedly and unrequitedly in pursuit of the man.

With this film in the can, Gwen headed for Chicheley Hall on 29 April. The year 1935 had started well and she was off to a joyous family occasion, the wedding of her youngest sister, Ella. Four hundred people packed Chicheley's small Church of St Lawrence. Fittingly Marjorie acted the role usually taken by the father of the bride, giving Ella away. The six Farrar siblings were reunited in a photograph.

Muriel invited Gwen and Norah to come and stay with her in Cumbria, and in November they did just that, with Gwen stopping off at Moorlands en route. Muriel had asked them to appear at a British Legion event in Penrith's Alhambra Cinema, so Norah brought three of her Bradford Amateur colleagues along to perform too. In an awkward photograph of the occasion, kept in Gwen's scrapbook, the faces of the amateur friends have been scribbled over. One of them, Bessie Pratt (third from left), later made Norah godmother to her only child. If the scribble was Gwen's, was she motivated by jealousy, class snobbery or professional elitism? She looks away from the camera, pointedly in the direction of Bessie and her friends.

By the end of February 1936 it was reported in the *Daily Herald* that Gwen was seriously ill in a London nursing home. Then everything went very quiet. She recovered sufficiently to come home, but kept an unusually low profile.

Audry Carten had met and fallen in love with an outstandingly attractive, enigmatic and aristocratic young drama student, Caroline Paget. If Gwen felt jealous, she knew that it was counter-productive to her relationship with Audry to let it show. Here was another relationship in which she was now forced to play gooseberry.

When it came time for the Annual Theatrical Garden Party neither Gwen nor Norah took part. It is conceivable that Gwen had made a jealous scene about Bessie Pratt and the Bradford amateurs and that she and Norah had not seen each other since the previous November. As she had often done in the past when she felt rejected, Gwen threw herself into a new project. This time it was another film.

In *Take a Chance*[45] she played Lady Emily Meriton, in hounds-tooth tweed, enjoying an obvious (and not unsympathetically written) lesbian relationship with Binnie Hale's character, Wilhelmina (Bill) Ryde. These characters run a garage together and may have been inspired by Joe Carstairs and her X Garage colleagues. As an on-screen couple, Emily and 'Bill' have a warm familiarity, even enjoying a hug, and their partnership is taken for granted by the other characters, who regard them merely as slightly eccentric. Sadly and predictably, though, in the end, the implication is that they each find romantic fulfilment with a man.

After shooting had finished in September, Gwen took a brief holiday in Paris. There she spent time with Dolly Wilde, by now a forty-year-old socialite whose chief accomplishment was contributing to Natalie Clifford Barney's regular Friday salons the 'iridescent bubbles of her humour... lightning-swift retorts [and] devasting arrows of wit'.[46] People were enchanted by Dolly, and the striking resemblance she bore to her famous uncle Oscar.

*Gwen, Norah, Audry and an unknown woman
driven by Basil at the Spinsters' Rally*

American author Djuna Barnes, in her rude, affectionate celebration of the Paris lesbian community, the *Ladies Almanack,* re-christened her 'Doll Furious', while 'Lady Buck-and-Balk' and 'Tilly Tweed-in-Blood' were hilariously cheeky satirical versions of Una Troubridge and Radclyffe Hall. In reality 'big, beautiful bedridden Doll'[47] was a drunk and a heroin addict who sponged off other people. Gwen fell deeply under her spell.

Back in Bradford, amongst a far less privileged group of single women, Norah was involved with the newly formed National Spinsters' Pensions Association, a grassroots organisation founded by local working-class activist Florence White. Basil gave speeches in support of their campaign for fairer pensions for spinsters.

The association also had a social side. On 13 January 1937, Norah hosted a party for four hundred women to mark the opening of the Spinsters' Association Club. Florence White 'sensed a feeling' amongst the women that a social club was desirable. Many lived alone and 'friendships struck up at these gatherings... may result in members rooming together, an economic as well as a social move'.[48]

When the day of the Spinsters' Rally arrived on Saturday 5 June, Gwen and Norah were at the head of a procession leading three thousand women (most of whom had fond memories of the duo's heyday) across central London to Hyde Park. Audry came too and, in a newspaper cutting, she and her old rival Norah seem quite comfortable perching, with Gwen, on the back of Basil's car as he acts as chauffeur.

The crowd sang 'ditties outlining their demands'[49] and Norah performed a song Gwen had composed for the occasion (ending with a neat pun on the name of the health minister):

> We spinsters are a happy lot
> And do the things we should.
> We should be far happier
> If only Kingsley-Wood.[50]

Six months later, on 8 January 1936, in surroundings that look not at all like the dark-panelled interior of Gwen's Chelsea home, a very patient springer spaniel is photographed wearing Gwen's glasses. The lampshade is awry and Gwen is drunk. Could this be the elegant white home of Gwen's neighbour, Syrie Maugham, or perhaps the house Joe Carstairs owned in Mulberry Walk? It is a publicity shot ahead of Gwen's first public television appearance. Having helped Logie Baird ten years previously, perhaps she was the natural choice as one of the earliest artists broadcast by the BBC from Alexandra Palace. Her twenty-minute act is listed in the first ever television supplement to the *Radio Times*.

In February Gwen appeared in *Die Fledermaus* with the Carl Rosa Opera Company as a guest artist, in a role that the *Era* said 'might have been written for her'.[51] This was possibly a veiled sneer since Prince Orlofsky's aria is all about throwing parties and drinking to excess, but in as much as it was a trouser role (a male role in opera traditionally sung by a woman), it did suit her well. After her performance at the People's Palace in the Mile End Road, she was invited back to join the company again at the Brighton Hippodrome.

The celebrity casting continued when Norah was offered

a trouser role of her own by the company. She played Siebel, the romantic young man bringing flowers to his beloved in the opera *Faust* at the King's Theatre, Glasgow, in April, and again when they came to the Bradford Alhambra.

Gwen meanwhile had sailed away on 9 March 1937 aboard the *Queen Mary*, arriving two weeks later in New York. From there she flew to Miami and met Ruth Baldwin who accompanied her in a light aircraft to Joe Carstairs' private island, Whale Cay, ninety miles to the east.

From an overgrown, deserted wasteland Joe had master-minded the construction of a working community with a shop, a school, a port and roads leading to white sandy beaches. It was now a livelihood and home for the two hundred or so black Bahamians who had come from neighbouring islands to work on the project. In 1936 work was completed on Joe's large Spanish villa–style home, on the southern tip of the island.

Gwen arrived just as Joe was in the middle of receiving 'a steady stream of friends from England and America, sometimes twenty at a time... her parties were riotous'.[52] Tallulah, Greta Garbo, Mercedes de Acosta and Marlene Dietrich all visited Joe in this period.

Ruth Baldwin, still Joe's favourite girlfriend, came often, but did not stay long. She preferred the house Joe had bought her in Miami, from where she could visit bars and lead a wild life of drinking and drug taking. Her London home, also paid for by Joe, was 5 Mulberry Walk, just a stone's throw from Gwen's in the King's Road. It was here that Gwen and Ruth returned together on 21 April 1937. They had travelled, in neighbouring cabins, on board the *Berengaria*.

Ruth was a lively, handsome, round-faced woman, seven years younger than Gwen. According to Carstairs' biographer, Ruth was 'promiscuous and possessive. She freely spent Joe's money... She was a heady, stormy woman, and it seems that her public wildness was matched by a private wilderness'.[53] It's difficult to know who was chaperoning whom on this long journey back from the Bahamas. It seems likely Gwen and Ruth were sleeping together. What none of them knew, as they bade farewell and thanks to Joe at the start of their journey, was that Ruth and Joe would never see each other again.

The house in Mulberry Walk had a forbidding exterior, brick, modernist and stark, but inside it was spacious and inviting, with exposed staircases extending up the sides of large rooms and huge windows at the rear overlooking the small walled garden where Joe had once kept penguins. It was a good house for parties and Gwen knew it very well.

Ruth and Dolly Wilde were friends and, with their voracious appetites for alcohol and drugs, were an increasing distraction to Gwen as she endeavoured to get back to work. It was as if these women were making manifest in their lives society's dire warnings about the mortal dangers of lesbianism. Here was the self-fulfilling prophesy: external homophobia becoming internalised in a vicious circle of self-loathing, fed by the hateful moralising rhetoric of the Establishment, leading to numbing debauchery, a vortex of self-pity, fear and incapacity, which provided more evidence to bolster the vile bigotry of society's 'moral' commentators.

The stage was set for tragic scenes in which Gwen was to be a hapless key player.

~ 14 ~

SUBMERGED

On 14 July 1937, Gwen turned forty. There were tensions. Dolly Wilde, increasingly present at 217 King's Road, perceived Gwen's old friends – among them Norah, Audry and Caroline – as a threat. She did her best to create a rift between these 'theatrical people' (as she disparagingly described them) and the coterie of herself, Gwen and Ruth Baldwin.

On 31 August, Ruth, Dolly and unspecified others were gathered at Gwen's to listen to a radio broadcast from the Yankee Stadium, New York. The British heavyweight boxing champion, Tommy Farr, was challenging the American Joe Louis for the world title. The BBC broadcast the tense fight with live commentary into the small hours.

Ruth Baldwin was suddenly taken ill. A taxi took her the very short distance home to Mulberry Walk, but by dawn she was dead of a suspected involuntary overdose. Very likely Gwen or Dolly were with her, for they wasted no time in telephoning Joe, saying, 'You'd better sit down...'[1]

There was almost nothing in the papers, except one piece which reported that no inquest would be held.[2]

Joe was able to board the fastest of ocean liners, the *Normandie*, bringing with her the precious doll, Tod Wadley, which had been a gift from Ruth years earlier. She asked for Ruth's body to be embalmed and laid out in a room full of flowers at Mulberry Walk. The doll was set beside her body as if in vigil. The funeral took place at Golders Green cemetery.

Gwen must have been involved in these arrangements and have felt a sense of guilt that Ruth's death had occurred, so to speak, on her watch. But far from acting as a corrective to her self-destructive behaviour, Ruth's sudden demise led Gwen to drink more. The tragedy played on.

Gwen found herself drawn closer to Dolly in mutual consolation. By early November they were in Paris together, visiting Natalie Clifford Barney and drinking heavily. A journalist from the *Tatler* spotted them amongst a crowd of revellers at the Bagatelle Club, and was sneering about Gwen's outfit: 'Josephine Baker was looking tropical in a jade green suit... Gwen Farrar in a suit of the material men choose for wedding trousers.' She added that with Gwen was 'Dorothy Wilde, in whom fin de siècle veterans find Uncle Oscar's features'. [3]

Still a lover of Natalie Barney, Dolly constantly played her and Gwen off against each other. Natalie had gained her first impression of Gwen thirteen years earlier from Romaine Brooks' unkind letter about her throat problems and drinking habits. It was an impression that stuck with Natalie. Though Gwen made several trips to Paris with Dolly, even staying in Natalie's house, she failed to endear herself to the great lady. Gwen could not compete in the self-confidence stakes with this woman who reigned supreme in her home on the Left Bank, where, in *The Well of Loneliness*, Radclyffe Hall had immortalised her as Valérie Seymour:

> Valérie, placid and self-assured, created an atmosphere of courage, everyone felt very normal and brave when they gathered together at Valérie Seymour's. There she was, this charming and cultured woman, a kind of lighthouse in a storm-swept ocean.[4]

Gwen fell into the role of obsequious underling. In a place where she should have felt 'normal and brave', clever, well-read and thoroughly musical Gwen was instead the victim of dismissive snobbery. Natalie's appreciation for artists and intellectuals did not extend to stars of popular culture and

Gwen with Dolly Wilde, Tatler

she had very little time for Gwen, who found herself having to fawningly apologise for some *faux pas* committed (certainly under the influence of alcohol) while staying at her house in the Rue Jacob. Gwen's innate instinct for comedy had perhaps resulted in some misunderstood grimace or other buffoonery that backfired, or perhaps there had been a drunken outburst about the sleeping arrangements. She wrote:

> I am afraid I can never apologise enough for my extremely bad manners to you. I can only hope that you will one day realise it was driving nearly to distraction and if I may coin a word 'over love' that caused them. May I thank you for your sweetness and divine hospitality.[5]

Dolly's manipulation of both her lovers was further enabled by her poor state of health, caused by her drug addiction. Gwen's letter to Natalie continued:

May I ask you one favour and that is to let me know how
Dolly is... If there is anything I can do you know you have
only to let me know and I will provide any facilities and get
in touch with any of her friends... Please try and forgive me
and realise my only aim and ambition in life is for her to be
cured, really cured, because I really love her as much as you
and shall worry always until she is well.

Yours always,
Gwen Farrar[6]

Gwen was sincere in her desire to help. She consulted the
celebrated surgeon Ivor Back whose wife, Barbara, was an old
friend. Even Norah's husband Basil Hughes was called on to
examine Dolly and, at one time, it seemed she would travel to
Bradford for surgery. No stone was unturned in offering Dolly
medical diagnosis and support. There is no record of what
Norah thought of Dolly.

Meanwhile Gwen was briefly involved in producing two
short plays by women[7] under the title *Destination Unknown*.
Reviews were good for the second of the two, which starred
Hermione Baddeley and had a short run at Richmond Theatre.
'The two plays are very well produced by Gwen Farrar. She
makes the most of the first one and keeps the fun of the second
moving at a brisk pace.'[8]

Just after Easter 1938, Norah and Gwen were contacted
urgently by a BBC producer to see if they would step in at short
notice for a live radio broadcast to replace, not for the first time,
the Duncan Sisters,[9] who had dropped out. They agreed to fill
the gap but, according to one critic, Gwen's performance let
the side down.

They sounded to me like a couple of mediocre artists giving
an 'impression' of Blaney and Farrar. Not bad for Blaney, I
would have said, but not a bit like Farrar. In fact poor Gwen
seemed entirely submerged throughout the act. When the
pair of them were singing together she could hardly be
heard at all. Listeners who did not know this clever couple
in the past must have thought the turn a big leg-pull.[10]

'Submerged' was an insightful term, for Gwen was sinking into a quagmire of domestic chaos and emotional turmoil. Dolly told Natalie:

> She is unused to grappling with everyday details of servants, house etc. She had two maids for years who did everything for her and a secretary. The former robbed her outrageously and went and she can't afford the latter now.[11]

In May Gwen surrendered the lease on her cottage, Grove Paddock, in Effingham, salvaging reams of headed notepaper which Dolly then used to write disloyal letters to Natalie. 'Gwen's love is suffocating me... I feel a prisoner.'[12]

Fortunately, Dolly was sometimes abroad. Gwen had a few weeks of sanity with Norah, first running a 'Tinkers' Stall' at the Annual Theatrical Garden Party, now under the management of Noel Coward, then opening a garden party in the grounds of Norah's new house, Woodlands, in aid of Bradford Civic Theatre.

In October 1937 Norah and Basil had moved a few miles down the road to this beautiful mansion in Baildon. Woodlands was the perfect place for Norah to entertain old friends if they were travelling north and Basil soon celebrated his sixtieth birthday there. The house had extensive grounds which Norah loved. The gated estate had a lodge for the gardener, a mews for a coachman or chauffeur, vegetable gardens, tennis courts, and even a piggery. Norah enjoyed the services of a lady's maid and there were kitchen staff.

Norah had plenty of famous friends she could have called on to perform the task of opening the fête, but she knew Gwen needed the stimulus of the work. The sun shone and twelve hundred people came to enjoy sideshows, brass bands, refreshments and performances by Norah's 'unsalaried artist' friends. Gwen wisely thought better than to object to the amateurs' entirely justified presence at this local jamboree.

Arthur Prince, the ventriloquist, was there, so Gwen and Norah had a reunion with their music hall mentor. Coincidentally there was another connection: 'Mr Hughes was the surgeon who decided in Salonika, that it would not

255

be necessary for Arthur to lose his legs, as was feared after he received serious wounds.'[13] He pledged support for the Civic Theatre, whose president, the playwright JB Priestley, declared such democratically run, non-commercial ventures represented 'a dramatic movement of immense social importance'.[14]

Linked with such serious ventures as the Civic Theatre and the Spinsters' Association and mindful of her responsibilities as the wife of a highly respected surgeon, Norah would hardly have risked her social status by inviting Gwen to open the event if her friend had become the undisciplined and obvious alcoholic that starts to emerge from Dolly's accounts. It seems likely that their mutual love and loyalty helped Gwen to stay sober for the day. If so, it is a great testament to their bond.

There was no permanent place for Gwen, though, in respectable Bradford. Norah had made her choice, on the side of convention, when she married Basil six years earlier. So, in late July, Gwen went on holiday with Dolly, to Étretat, Normandy, whence Dolly wrote to Natalie from the Hôtel de la Plage:

> Why are we here? Because Gwen's aunt[15] has a charming
> villa and her sisters and friends come every year so that
> there is 'homelife' going on at the various villas and we
> are not confined to the bare seaside aridity of two hotel
> bedrooms... No clothes are needed and we saunter down
> to bathe and laze: play tennis in the afternoon late, return
> to English teas with softly hissing big silver teapots and hot
> scones in covered dishes etc – then meet for dinner, stroll to
> the casino and sit in the warm outside 'in the wings' of that
> stage setting with its cardboard cliffs. I feel much happier
> here than I have for a long time as Gwen, who loves open
> air life, golf etc. gets rid of her burden of love more easily,
> than turning round and round in the squirrel cage of her
> suffering in London.[16]

Dolly has set the scene but she is anxious to assure Natalie that this is no romance:

> Alas! I am out of love and [Gwen] is more than ever in its
> throes – (I state this as her personal obsession and madness

rather than my personal triumph and have no vanity ever
as you know!) She is so sweet and so unselfish to me, that I
feel her sorrow all the more, being able to do nothing about
it and sometimes my sense of her constrictive suffering
weighs me down and I feel I must live on my own. To 'love'
someone is, it seems to me, as painful as to be in love and
to witness pain in that person is to have a perpetual ache in
one's heart. She does everything to look after me.[17]

Still solicitous, Gwen brought Dolly, who had no permanent
home of her own, back to the King's Road. From there Dolly
wrote to Natalie, complaining, 'If only there were two bedrooms
here so that some privacy of life could be sustained! ... I long
for the Rue Jacob days and your rhythm of ordered life.'[18]

Dolly's friends were quick to offer solutions. Natalie asked
her back to Paris. Joe Carstairs offered her the use of her house
in Mulberry Walk. Gwen fixed up a maid's room at the top
of her house for Dolly to use as a bedroom. Always playing
Natalie and Gwen off against each other, Dolly wrote declining
Natalie's offer:

> If I went to Paris I feel all the rowdy lot would get in
> again and through loneliness [Gwen] might fall back
> into unhappy habits – late nights, drinking etc. I know
> that sounds great weakness on her part – but only
> companionship or work keeps her straight... While working
> she is always as good as gold and it is unfortunate that the
> last two years she has not worked.[19]

One of the few outside observers to comment on this increasingly
toxic situation was Dolly's old friend Honey Harris,[20] who felt
that it was Dolly who relied on Gwen:

> Everyone tells me that GF is a hopelessly bad friend for her
> from the point of view of environment and habits of life,
> but at the same time she does provide a sort of homelike
> companionship and security against loneliness which I
> personally think is very important for Dolly – and I don't
> think one could alter or ought to try to alter anything just
> for the time being.[21]

Dolly wanted everything both ways. She craved privacy but needed to be the centre of attention. She blamed 'theatrical people' for Gwen's problems, yet knew that work was good for her. She complained about Gwen's bad habits but was herself abusing drugs and leading a life of chronic indolence.

By January 1938, suffering from 'a complete paralysis of all will power with worries becoming unduly exaggerated',[22] Dolly alternated between complaining about Gwen and praising her to the skies. She wrote to Natalie: 'I must say this time Gwen has been wonderful in looking after me... She is doing a hundred things about getting order and discipline into the house and couldn't be sweeter.'[23]

Natalie sometimes sent Dolly chocolates, but on one occasion these were misappropriated by Djuna Barnes. Dolly complained to Natalie that Barnes had given them to 'a candy-eating friend' who had eaten the lot.

In the same letter Dolly wrote:

> I cannot stay with Gwen as her inability to cope with
> the slightest domestic detail and intermittent lapses into
> drinking make me too nervous... Please don't ever mention
> anything I tell you about all this to her. She is lonely and
> very unhappy without me and in many ways self-sacrificing
> but it's that enormous mixture of complete unselfishness
> and complete selfishness. [24]

A week later Dolly was able to move into Mulberry Walk and from there she told Natalie:

> Gwen and I have parted for good... The burden of her love
> and need for me, plus her many lapses into drunken idiocy –
> the strain of trying to run her house, her affairs etc. not only
> sapped my vitality but made me sometimes drink too much
> out of sheer hopelessness. A slovenly, impossible atmosphere,
> with the constant worry of someone incapacitated through
> drink driving the car, arriving home hours late etc. under-
> mined what little discipline a 'Wilde' possesses... Now that
> we have parted, I am rung up all day by her friends telling me
> that she has 'wasted' a year of her life with me.[25]

While Dolly's account is undoubtedly one-sided, it provides a valuable insight into some of the issues Gwen might have faced, on a less exaggerated scale, in her relationship with Norah. Certainly her reckless driving and late nights, her alcoholism, her failure to manage the household and her emotional dependency seem to be traits that pre-date the relationship with Dolly.

One wonders who the loyal friends were who took Gwen's side in the fallout with Dolly; certainly Audry and Caroline, possibly Norah too, although she never mentioned Dolly in later life. How disheartening for them that within just a few weeks the hopelessly dysfunctional pair were back together again. In August Gwen informed Natalie:

> I am writing to tell you that I have been looking after
> Dolly all the time and that last week a miracle happened.
> Suddenly she settled down at the home, cut off all alcohol
> (+ drugs are practically nil) came out of her depression and
> became her real old self – brilliant, happy, gay, amusing and
> divine, such as I have never known her.[26]

She signed off, 'My love always, Gwen.'

Natalie's replies to Gwen came on postcards crammed in a spidery hand, tetchy and anxious.

Gwen's optimism about Dolly's recovery was short lived. Dolly was now going from doctor to doctor and clinic to clinic seeking a cure for symptoms that included cysts in her armpits and chronic addiction. It was an expensive business and her friends, including Gwen and Natalie, were shouldering the costs.

With Dolly no longer living with her, Gwen was able to regain some emotional balance and in June 1939 was sufficiently organised to put in an appearance at the Annual Theatrical Garden Party. There Noel Coward sang songs from *Bitter Sweet* and judged the dog show; Dame Sybil Thorndike ran 'Fishers for Fizz'; Elsie and Doris Waters conducted a bargain sale; while Douglas Byng, Hermione Baddeley and Joyce Grenfell[27] entertained. It was a baking hot, sunny day and she cannot have been idle for, the *Stage* reported, 'Gwen Farrar was looking after her ice-cream tricycles.'[28]

But history was about to intervene. Three months later Hitler's armies invaded Poland, and Britain entered the Second World War. Almost immediately Gwen rediscovered a sense of purpose. She set up the 'Farrar Entertainment of Troops Fund' and helped organise a concert at Chelsea Town Hall where she topped the bill with none other than Beatrice Lillie. She made plans to perform again with Norah.

By December Joyce Mather was able to report: 'Mrs Basil Hughes... has joined up with her old stage partner, Gwen Farrar, I hear, and now spends much of her time helping to entertain the troops in the south.'[29]

With Norah's absence, Mather has lost access. The choice of the words 'I hear' suggests a disappointed journalist whose information has come from a third party. Perhaps there is even a hint of innuendo in her report. But she is relieved to be able to reassure her readers that 'Mrs Hughes will be at home for Christmas'.[30]

It seems clear from Mather's report that Norah has travelled south to spend time with Gwen, just as she had in the winter of 1934–35. There are reminders, too, of the summer of 1917, for plans were made for Gwen and Norah to entertain troops across the Channel. On 10 May 1940, the German invasion of France put paid to that. It seems Gwen and Norah spent a good deal of time together in Chelsea, and at Chicheley Hall, where Gwen now had an apartment. There were occasional performances at army bases in the UK, though evidence of this is hard to find as times and locations were kept secret for security reasons.

On 24 May, the agent Harold Holt wrote to a BBC producer about Gwen and Norah in a bid to promote them: 'I was at a concert with them last night with a programme full of stars and they had an amazing success holding up the bill for quite a while.'[31]

He added:

> I have just had a talk with Norah Blaney and Gwen Farrar and they are quite agreeable to broadcast in any programme you care to present them at the same fee as they had when they were last with the BBC.[32]

Norah must have been confident that Gwen was competent to perform, despite seeing the toll that alcohol had taken on her mental and physical health. Neither she nor the agent would have risked their reputations on an act that was no longer first rate.

The sobering fact was that, even though they were rehearsing new and topical material and Gwen was now willing to broadcast, the BBC were no longer interested. The offer to perform at their old fee was declined.

With rationing now in force and Basil needing support for his war work in Bradford, Norah returned home. The separation was a big blow for her, but a desperate, perhaps fatal one for Gwen, who returned to London to live amidst the shattering noise and danger of nightly air raids. When they parted at the end of May 1940, it is hard to believe that Norah was abandoning Gwen forever. But she could not help her; or not without wrecking her own life for an outside chance of rehabilitating her friend, whose worst challenges were, in any case, self-inflicted. It had been Gwen's choice to join the hedonists in 1923 with their jagged sophistication and Gwen's choice to leave America in 1926. If she chose to drink herself to death now, there was nothing Norah could do about it.

In reality Norah did not articulate these brutal thoughts. She loved Gwen more than anybody else in the world. She cared for her and wanted to help. But the winter together had not been easy, with both of them succumbing to jaundice and then flu. With the war on, Norah admitted to herself, as she approached her fiftieth birthday, that she felt safe and relatively happy with her dependable husband.

Basil was running a military hospital with two thousand beds and Norah set about organising entertainments. She enlisted Elsie and Doris Waters and was tremendously impressed that after performing they visited each soldier in the ward, promising to call on their families when they were on tour. This was when they told Norah that her double-act with Gwen had been their inspiration.

Norah rolled up her sleeves in other practical ways. Within

a few weeks, her war work was being reported in the national press. The headline in the *Daily Mirror* read: 'Actress is dustman now.' While Basil was busy seeing patients, Norah was driving a dustcart, giving regular workers a break by helping to collect 'useful scrap' from housewives. They were reportedly 'surprised to see the trim figure of the actress' who had cast off her expensive gowns for 'old overalls and a sou'wester'. Norah said: 'It may seem strange for a woman, but we have to do all kinds of things these days.'[33]

She was indignant about what happened next:

> I was told that the subject came up for discussion at Baildon Council meeting and it was decided that I must not be allowed to drive the dustcart again. Some of the councillors thought it was not 'quate nace' [*sic*]. Apparently it doesn't matter about the war and getting on with an urgent job. It is a stupid and petty attitude to take. I liked the dustmen. We got on well together. All right. Now I shall find myself some other useful war work.[34]

She hosted a party for some old theatre friends in June 1941 which was written up in the *Stage* as 'a remarkably fine lunch... an example of what one can do with a little attention'.[35] Afterwards she sang one of her old compositions:

> When Norah does 'Mabel's Pigtail' you see the Margate bandstand and the happy pre-war holiday crowd on a hot afternoon; you see Stanley Kirkby who ran the show... the whole of the picture passes before your eyes as Norah does 'Mabel's Pigtail' with her own descriptive interpolations. A delicious experience especially in these days.[36]

Leslie Baily, a BBC producer and journalist who specialised in nostalgia programmes, wrote to ask if she remembered performing at St George's Hall in Liverpool. There is no record that she ever did so, but she sent him a delightful, self-deprecating reply:

> I don't remember. If the truth were known... I probably was such a triumphant Royal FLOP that like the determined

Norah on the dustcart

little woman I was, I said to myself, 'Now, Norah, my dear, let us bury this inglorious event in your career once and for all' and promptly forgot it there and then. If you hear what happened, you might let me know. I am always interested in me!

P.S. If I did sing there, then I should think I must have sung my epoch-making, soul-stirring number 'Mister Bear' because it was the only one I knew![37]

In August 1940 the French star Alice Delysia was performing in Leeds and visited Woodlands for lunch. She had 'the most lovely pair of legs in the world', Norah recalled decades later, before recounting how, on the occasion of Delysia's visit, her own left arm was broken and in plaster. To help out, Delysia cooked lunch, starting with an omelette. But she was not *au fait* with war rationing. Eggs were no problem because Norah and Basil kept chickens. But, Norah recalled, 'She used all our butter for the next two weeks.'

Another French-speaking visitor during the war was the comedy writer and performer Jeanne de Casalis.

263

'Oh dear Jeanne, what fun she was! I did know her very well,' Norah told Derek Hunt emphatically and with great delight, recalling how she had asked Jeanne about her recent wedding.

'What on earth do you want to get married for? Why bother?'

'Well, you see, it's so much easier with the ration books.'[38]

On another occasion Norah improvised a hat out of a hot-water bottle cover. She wore it to a smart Sunday lunch in Harrogate, but with her irrepressible instinct for comedy, at the end of the meal she couldn't resist revealing her secret to the assembled guests.

Norah was insulated from danger in the Yorkshire countryside, but the war came very close to home for Gwen when, at the height of the Blitz in November 1940, a bomb fell on Sloane Square Underground station, killing thirty-seven people. Caroline, Audry and their friend Grizel Niven,[39] who had all enlisted for the Auxiliary Fire Service, saw some horrifying sights as they joined the effort to recover the injured and dying.

It seems Gwen's 'Fund to Entertain the Troops' absolved her from the kind of hands-on active service her friends were engaged in.

Life in London was seriously disrupted. Bombing raids were frequent and there was enormous damage to property and loss of life. Many streets were permanently lined with piles of broken glass, like snow swept into the gutters.

Through it all, Gwen seems to have maintained her reputation as a theatre producer. In April 1940 she had directed one of Audry's pieces[40] at the Embassy Theatre, Swiss Cottage. Cecil Beaton showed Gwen the script for a psychological thriller by his friend Enid Bagnold (later of *National Velvet* fame), who was pleased to hear that Gwen liked it.[41] However, nothing came of this and the drama was later staged by a different producer.

Gwen organised at least two concerts in Bedfordshire, before and after Christmas: the first was at her father's old school, Bedford Modern. Betty Pollock, the impressionist, joined her on the bill. The second took place on 7 January 1941:

A very successful concert for troops and the Home
Guard was held in the Bury Hall, Pavenham, on Tuesday.
Lady Luke... introduced Miss Gwen Farrar, the famous
comedienne and organiser of the party of artists who are
travelling round giving concerts to troops...They gave an
excellent show, which was very warmly appreciated by a
crowded audience.[42]

The location of these concerts suggests Gwen was spending
more and more time at Chicheley Hall, and she was certainly
there for Christmas, with Marjorie and Peggy. Her youngest
sister Ella may have been there too. Tragically Ella's husband,
Sir Thomas, was killed in Cairo less than two weeks into the
New Year. Their little boy, Andrew, had just turned three.
Gwen's family, who had suffered such losses in the First World
War, were now grieving again.

Gwen was back in London, drinking heavily, when in
February she tripped over a sandbox outside the entrance to
the Royal Court Hotel during the blackout, injuring her right
thigh to the extent that she was on crutches for weeks.[43] Dolly
Wilde was staying at the hotel, running up a large bill in
Gwen's name. Though Gwen was no longer infatuated, she was
too kind-hearted to abandon her completely, especially as, by
this time, Dolly was seriously ill with cancer and was addicted
to sedatives as well as heroin. There was a row with the hotel
management who chased Gwen for payment through the
courts. She counter-claimed for damages, insisting they ought
to have marked the sandbox with luminous paint. The hotel
said the collision was due to her own negligence, implying she
was drunk. The judge thought so too, adding insult to injury.
He decided in the hotel's favour and Gwen had to pay up.

Arrangements were made for Dolly to rent a room at 20
Chesham Place in Chelsea – a more affordable option. There on
9 April she died alone in the night. The inquest recorded an open
verdict. Dolly's biographer, Joan Schenkar, has examined the
coroner's report in depth, even exploring the possibility that a
woman friend administered a fatal heroin injection. She does not
rule out that Gwen may have done this inadvertently, although

she believes that, still on crutches from the sandbox accident, her arrival or departure from Dolly's room would have been noticed.

Natalie Clifford Barney wrote a poem in memory of Dolly, expressing her view that her death was not suicide and that she died 'with friends less fond than I'.[44]

Gwen did not deserve Natalie's scorn. She was one of very few people at Dolly's funeral on 15 April 1941 in the Catholic section of Kensal Green cemetery. Mourners were deterred from attending by a particularly destructive air raid the night before. Gwen struggled across the graveyard on crutches. Even in her grief she would have managed an ironic smile when the priest pompously turned and announced, to the two or three mourners, 'We will now form a procession.'[45]

The Blitz finally ended a month later but the war dragged on and air raids continued. Freed from her toxic relationship with Dolly, Gwen began to function better. Before long, Betty Pollock became her lover. She was very thin and tall and bohemian-looking – 'wore veils with spangles, long trailing clothes in autumnal colours and more scarves than a conjurer'.[46]

Betty had a son, Adrian, but was now divorced and more or less retired from the stage, where she had been the most gifted and daring mimic. She was a friend of Cathleen Nesbitt and had appeared with her in drag alongside Gerald du Maurier in the *Nick of Time* revue at the 1932 Garden Party. Radclyffe Hall described her in a letter in 1937, relating how infatuated she seemed to be with Naomi (Mickie) Jacob, the butch lesbian novelist, who had acted in Audry's play *Fame*.

> [She is] a mass of make up and breathtaking scent. But in a queer rather frightening way... beautiful – marvellous eyes, but looks like a vampire, very long and thin then hungry and passionate! ... It is evident that [she] is dementedly in love with Mikkie [*sic*]... Can you beat it![47]

That particular passion now a thing of the past, Betty was spotted out with Gwen in June 1941 by a journalist from the *Tatler* who stated the obvious: 'Elizabeth Pollock in very red hair. Gwen Farrar in trousers...'[48]

In October and November Gwen managed a couple of solo radio broadcasts for the same producer who had engaged her and Norah at short notice in 1938. Perhaps she had not let the side down on that occasion so badly as the *Daily Mirror* critic had made out.

Betty Pollock was a much better influence on Gwen than Dolly had been. She was funny and talented and, like Gwen, well connected in both high society and the theatre. They shared similar friends and interests. Betty was kind, generous, loving and loyal. Her son Adrian McConnel later wrote, 'I do not think she ever made an enemy in her entire life.'[49] At the time of their relationship, Adrian was making the transition from prep school to senior school. With his military father fulminating against the evils of the London theatre scene, Adrian's life in the school holidays was uneasily split between two warring parents in different homes. It is a mark of Gwen's closeness to Betty that Adrian was aware of her presence in his mother's life. His loathing for her was still evident sixty-five years later. A mild-mannered man who spoke fondly of his mother's other women friends, Adrian became visibly angry at the thought of Gwen and would not expand on his deep-seated revulsion for her, beyond a few angry words about her drunkenness and (alleged) cruelty to children.

Gwen's nephew James, five years older than Adrian, told a different story. He thoroughly enjoyed Gwen's company when he finally got to know her and was old enough to share her appetites.

> He was at Sandhurst and used to take off for London on Friday evenings with friends on motorbikes. They used to gather at the Moore Arms pub in Cadogan Street… Amongst the din he heard a distinctive voice, unmistakably belonging to a Farrar – all six sisters had carrying voices and this one sounded much like Marjorie. On being quizzed, she acknowledged to being Gwen. They met often after that, carrying on the evening drinking in the back room until about 3 a.m.[50]

James further recalled that any women Gwen described as 'not of my persuasion' would be passed on to him. Girls were a shared interest for Gwen and James, as for Noel Streatfeild who indulged her teenage nephew with trips to the Windmill Theatre to watch the famous showgirls: 'She was the only woman in the theatre... but she enjoyed herself.'[51]

The BBC had moved its recording studios to Bedford Corn Exchange and there Gwen and Norah broadcast together live (for a modest fee) for the very last time in a radio programme about the history of the London Coliseum that went out on 3 June 1943. There was no final visit to nearby Chicheley Hall. It had been requisitioned at ten days' notice to become a top-secret centre for spy training. Marjorie and Peggy had gone north to live in Cumbria, not far from Muriel.

In London, Gwen had some sittings with the distinguished portrait artist Gerald Kelly. Perhaps she wished to leave behind a likeness of herself by a great artist to match the portrait Giovanni Boldoni had painted of her mother in the 1880s.

On 11 January 1944 she made her will. It is not known what prompted her to draw up this document, but she must have been aware that her ever-increasing alcohol consumption was taking its toll. She had witnessed the sudden deaths of Ruth and Dolly and wanted to face the end at least prepared.

She bequeathed £2,000 to her nephew James, who had been posted abroad, leaving his 500cc motor bike with her for safe keeping. She arranged to leave £6,000 to her youngest sister, the recently widowed Ella, and half that to each of her other sisters. She was most generous to her lesbian friends. Her old flame Audry would receive £13,000; and her current lover Betty Pollock (named as Mrs Elizabeth McConnel) a huge £18,000, plus all her clothes and jewellery, except her pearls. Those would go to Norah, along with £2,000. She believed of course that Norah would be well provided for by Basil. Another bequest of £3,000 would go to Joan Griffiths,[52] who had written some sketches for *After Dinner* and been a passenger in Gwen's car on the occasion of at least one motoring mishap. Gwen bequeathed her cello to the Royal Academy.

In 1944 there were eight hundred deaths and forty thousand injuries from bombing raids in Kensington and Chelsea alone, so Gwen put herself at risk by staying in London. To economise she shuttered up her beloved house in the King's Rd and moved into a flat. Number 16 Arundel Court, Jubilee Place, was just a few yards from Betty's house at Elystan Place. Grizel Niven also lived in Jubilee Place and they used to play cards and the board game Halma together. From June London was attacked intensively by V1s or Doodlebugs in a relentless terror bombing campaign. If one of these bombs (small forerunners of the cruise missile) passed overhead making its characteristic buzzing sound, the observer was safe, but when the buzzing stopped, anyone in the vicinity knew that the bomb would fall and explode at any moment. They were terrifying, but not as deadly as the V2 rockets which followed, so swift that their victims would not hear them coming at all.

Despite the air raids some London theatres remained open and on 4 October it is likely Gwen attended the opening night of a play by Esther McCracken, *No Medals*. Possibly Norah came down for this too. The contemporary play, set in wartime England, contained a poignantly understated scene where a couple said goodbye to each other for the last time. Norah later chose this play, with its interesting range of parts for women, to direct with the St Austell Players. One likes to think that Gwen and Norah spent their last evening out together at the Vaudeville Theatre, scene of their early triumphs in *Pot Luck*, *Rats!* and *Yes!*, and that they savoured the occasion and parted on the best of terms.

Beverley Nichols recalled:

> The last time I heard from [Gwen] was at midnight, when the telephone suddenly rang. I answered it and was greeted by the sound of a cello, playing 'Softly Awakes My Heart'. I said, 'Stop it, Gwen darling' – for it could be nobody else – 'and go to bed.' To which she replied, 'I've got a temperature of a hundred and four.' So I said I was very sorry but she must go to bed and stop playing 'Softly Awakes My Heart' which was not one of Saint-Saëns' best, anyway. But she

269

went on and on. And she *had* got a temperature of a hundred and four, and very soon afterwards she died.[53]

Gwen's nephew, Andrew Watson, unaware of Nichols' account, remembered that Gwen played the cello down the phone to him and his mother just before Christmas 1944. And Charles Duff says Gwen made an imploring gesture, arms outstretched towards Audry, as they parted on Christmas Eve, a kind of unspoken 'Don't leave me' that haunted Audry afterwards.

Gwen was not alone, but playing cards with Grizel (according to Betty's son Adrian) when she suffered a stroke in the small hours of Christmas morning. She was taken straight to St Mary's Hospital, Paddington, where she died the same day.

We do not know how Norah, up in Bradford, found out the dreadful news. It may have been Grizel, Betty or Audry who called her, or else Gwen's sister Marjorie. If she had been made aware earlier in the day that Gwen had been rushed to hospital, then Christmas Day would have been a sombre affair, spent fearing the worst. Or perhaps she had no prior warning, and the news came and shattered the festivities, making Norah run for the privacy of a darkened room to sob out her shock and grief.

James, Andrew and the other nephews and nieces were told Gwen had died in an air raid. It was easier to bear than the truth of her alcoholism. As the writer of her obituary put it:

> In a period of theatrical and social triumphs, of fête and flattery, of hectic parties... she laid up heavy debts to her constitution, never robust, with which she would never come to terms. Her last few years were troubled with ill-health.[54]

A cremation service took place at Golders Green Crematorium on 28 December. It is not known who attended. We have the crematorium record which gives Gwen's age, accurately, as forty-seven, and tells us her ashes were removed.

The air raids which had been such a relentless backdrop to her final years had a last devastating impact on her legacy when Gwen's beloved cello, along with James' motorbike and perhaps the urn containing her ashes were lost in the wreckage of an explosion some months later.

An anonymous friend wrote, by way of tribute, 'She had so much talent, lovely perception, sense of humour, and pathos, appalling pathos... deep kindness and understanding,' [55] going on to make an affectionate canine reference. Cecil Beaton was to say years later, in anticipation of his own epitaph: 'Save me from the well-meaning friend whose grief is drowned in clichés, or the amateur who wrote of Gwen Farrer [sic]: "She loved dogs, was very like a dog."'[56] But whoever wrote it did so lovingly, in a sincere and truthful attempt to describe the nature of a unique friend who repeatedly put love and loyalty before personal pride.

Augustus John, whose initial response to Gwen's 'coal-heaver' voice had been so negative, had grown to love it. Eight years after her death he wrote, 'She was the up-rooted one, the changeling... the play-girl of the moon, the proud pilgarlic,[57] perverse and adorable being... Come back and talk to me Gwen!'[58]

On 24 December in 1947, 1949 and again in 1953, this entry from Betty Pollock, Gwen's last love, appeared in the In Memoriam section of *The Times*: 'Gwen Farrar, in loving memory, in very loving memory – Betty.'

Norah in her London flat c.1976 with Sir Gerald Kelly's portrait of Gwen

PART VII

ONCE AN ARTIST…

1945–83

Norah and Basil's home at Vounder Farm in Cornwall

~ 15 ~

I WAS KNOWN AS NORAH BLANEY

There is nothing to tell us how Norah mourned for Gwen or even if she was able to get to her funeral. There is nothing in print in any archive, in any newspaper or on any recording from Norah for six and a half years. We know she moved with Basil to Cornwall at the end of the war and that from her home near St Austell she wrote, by hand in 1951, this letter to a man at the BBC.

Dear Mr Holland,

I see by my *Radio Times* that Gwen's and my voices are to be heard in your programme on the Light Programme *These Radio Times* on Saturday, October 6th. Perhaps the programme has already been recorded, in which case I am wasting my ink, to say nothing of your time. But just in case – may I? On the rare occasions when someone plays one of my records in *Family Favourites* or some such thing, I note with dismay that the most depressing and unflattering record is always put on, such as a cracked and squeaking period piece like 'It Ain't Going to Rain No More' or myself bellowing 'What'll I Do?' or, worse still 'Oh, Mr Porter'. I wondered whether it would be possible to put a nicer record on. I have several in good condition, a very nice one, 'Maybe I'm Wrong Again' (it was Gwen's favourite) – I could send them to you immediately if you have not got them in the BBC library. Please. Sometimes I listen to some agonising record of us, and I have to rush away and shut myself in a dark woodshed to blush it off – and I'm sure my beloved Gwen turns in her grave. We were not really good broadcasters. Gwen was so essentially a stage artist and so much was lost of her funny antics and our bits of by-play.

Sad – all these ghosts appearing.

Best wishes to all who may remember me (if they are still able to get about!).

Yours sincerely,
Norah Blaney
P.S. Excuse me, I have to go and milk a cow.[1]

Norah and Basil were living at Vounder Farm, a fifty-six acre property near Par with a modest farmhouse and outbuildings, which years later would become part of the Eden Project. Derek Hunt says the move was partly motivated by Norah's continued closeness to Daphne and Angela du Maurier. A local, Freddie Rowe,[2] remembers seeing Norah and Angela at Menabilly, Daphne's enchanting Cornish home, when he took a pony there to be ridden by Daphne's younger daughter; and a Christmas card addressed to Norah and Basil from Daphne is signed 'a crumb from Scroop'.[3] It dates from 1950, just weeks after Daphne had, with difficulty, torn herself away from a holiday in Florida with Gertrude Lawrence. (There Daphne had given in to what she called her 'Venetian tendencies'. In her vocabulary, 'Venice' stood for lesbian love and 'Cairo' for heterosexual sex. As she wrote to a friend the following year, 'I glory in my Venice, when I am in a Venice mood, and forget about it when I am not.'[4] Like Norah, Daphne had a husband she was fond of.)

Basil had taken a course in agriculture. He and Norah had sold up in Baildon in July 1945, bought a splendid seaside home in Carlyon Bay, and were now running Vounder Farm themselves. There really were cows to milk and a tractor to drive. Norah's parents, Molly and Walter, both in their eighties, had come to live in a terraced house nearby at 52 Par Green.

Just as she had in Bradford, Norah quickly involved herself in community events. The St Austell Players still celebrate her for the impact she had on their newly formed organisation in 1946:

> Our first full-length play was *Fresh Fields* by Ivor Novello...
> it was so popular... it brought in the handsome profit
> of £58. Norah Blaney, who directed, was a distinguished
> pianist and musical comedy star and was once described
> by the *Daily Mail* as 'London's most versatile actress'.
> She directed two more full-length plays for us: *Dangerous
> Corner* in 1947 and *No Medals* in 1948.[5]

Norah remembered:

> They got me to produce the amateur dramatics – they were
> all sort of schoolmasters and postmen and bank clerks. Fun.
> Lovely. We thought it would be a good idea to do *Dangerous
> Corner* because there are a lot of nice parts in it.[6]

Norah knew JB Priestley from the days when they were both involved in the Bradford Civic Theatre.

> I wrote to Mr Priestley, told him we were doing this play...
> and he wrote a charming letter... I hung it up so they could
> all read it and, ooh, they were thrilled to bits.[7]

Norah was a judge at the National Town Criers' Championship held at St Columb Major on 6 August 1949. About two thousand spectators were present. She was an adjudicator at local music festivals and ran courses for the Cornwall Drama Association.

In 1952 Norah's father Walter died, aged eighty-eight. Then Basil became ill with cancer. They had to give up the farm and move to London for his treatment. Norah's mother Molly came back to London to live nearby. Basil died, aged seventy-five, on 21 November 1953, fondly remembered by colleagues and patients and mourned by Norah. She had really loved this gentle, interesting, capable man.

Much of his money was left in a capital investment to his niece and nephew and Norah was by no means well off. Her share was £500 in cash, a quarter of the sum Gwen had left her. It is unclear how much access she had to any of the other funds Basil left in trust.

Whether or not her financial situation was perilous, she certainly felt she needed to look for work. In July 1954 she sent this letter to Norman Carrell at the BBC:

> Dear Mr Carrell,
>
> I have been advised to write to you regarding the possibility of you being able to offer me any radio work; classical accompanying, and so forth. I have had a great deal of experience. I am not an amateur. Before I left the stage to marry I was known as Norah Blaney. I can of course play swing if required. I should think I might be useful. Can read anything at sight.
>
> I have recently lost my husband and I'm living in London. I would be glad of something to do!
>
> Yours sincerely,
> Norah Hughes[8]

Six weeks later, the reply to this humble letter was not encouraging:

> Dear Madam,
>
> We regret very much that we are unable to offer you any classical accompanying work. We have five staff accompanists on full contract and a large panel on which we may call for ad hoc arrangements, which regretfully are very few and far between.
>
> Norman Carrell[9]

Undaunted, Norah submitted a tape recording of herself singing. An internal BBC memo reports:

> Undoubtedly Norah Blayney [sic] still has a great deal of charm and a typical, not over-strong musical comedy voice of the late 20s period. She is nevertheless still obviously an artist, and of course just as obviously not the sort of artist which we are very likely to be able to use in our normal output.[10]

While many people in Norah's position might have given up, in typical style she persevered. After a career gap of twenty-eight years, it would take several years of writing similar letters before she found professional performance work.

Meanwhile an old school friend, Winifred (Biddy) Johnson, noticed Basil's obituary in *The Times* and contacted her, saying, 'You must do something. You must write.'

Johnson had set up *Woman and Home* Magazine in 1926 and was now a major figure in Fleet Street. Her success was due to two secrets: 'She knew and loved her readers and she switched her deaf aid on to a flat battery whenever male executives ventured to tell her how to run her paper.'[11]

Biddy chivvied Norah. 'I want a story about two identical twin girls. They must be contrasting.' Norah's first attempt came back with blue pen all over it, but Biddy gave her a few hints and told her to try again. Norah stuck at it.

In the end 'Nora and Tilly' became one of the magazine's most popular features and she continued writing the stories for twenty years. An extract shows the twins were well-behaved, money-conscious little girls with a friend called Paul. They had a pony each and a dog. When they wanted to enter a charity pet show, they asked their daddy for the entrance fee. 'The trouble is it is a shilling for each animal so it does rather mount up.'[12] Norah's preoccupation with money is evident again.

In London Norah met up with another old friend, Barbara Back, a close confidante of the gay writer Somerset Maugham, who found herself similarly adrift financially when her surgeon husband, Ivor Back, died. She took to writing gossip and beauty columns in the *Daily Mirror*, a job for which her style and social connections made her perfectly well suited.

Norah recalled twenty years later: 'She came to me one night[13] and said, "Do you know there's a picture of Gwen at Sir Gerald Kelly's?"' Sir Gerald was president of the Royal Academy of Art and he welcomed Norah to his Marylebone house to see the portrait. 'I was stunned. I thought it was so lovely. Gwen as I remember her so well.' Sir Gerald let Norah buy the portrait for very much less than the going rate and it was hanging on the wall in her flat when Derek Hunt interviewed her. 'I'm very proud of owning that,' she told him.[14]

In 1956, Norah's resilience paid off when she was cast in a comedy feature film, *Who Done It?* The movie was written as a vehicle for a young comedian who would go on to be world famous for his character's puerile sexual stereotyping, but who, in the early 1950s, made a meteoric rise from Southampton-based pub comic to Television Personality of the Year – Benny Hill. Tibby Clarke, who had won an Oscar for *The Lavender Hill Mob*, wrote the screenplay for *Who Done It?*, which would turn out to be one of the last Ealing Comedies.

Norah was not alone among respected stage actors of her era who appeared in this movie. Ernest Thesiger was also in the cast. Norah's role, known simply as 'The Actress', suited her to a tee. Benny Hill played Hugo Dill, a would-be private detective whom the actress approaches because she mistakenly thinks he is a theatrical agent. She is seeking new representation following a row with her agent.

'He's very good at handling women. But then I'm sure you are too?' Dill gets the wrong idea and thinks she is chatting him up. Norah makes the most of her one scene in the film and adapts to the more subtle acting technique required by the camera. This was no small task after years of playing to vast audiences.

In real life Norah's agent was Kenneth Carten – the younger brother of her erstwhile love rival Audry Carten, with whom she was now friends. Kenneth had started his career acting in walk-on roles in *Wonder Bar* and *After Dinner.*

In 1957 he found Norah work on a daytime TV programme that had run for two years with a variety of hosts. Norah was involved in monthly episodes of *Mainly for Women Twice Twenty: A Magazine for Older Women* between September and December. For most of these the host was Jon Pertwee, an actor who would go on to achieve cult status as the third Doctor Who.

Norah's role was to play songs on the piano at the request of members of the studio audience. She did this with evident delight. No video footage survives but there is an audio recording in which Norah can be heard urging the audience to sing along.

After some familiar songs, she introduced a new one, 'I wrote the tune myself... I hope you like it.'[15] She sang:

> I wore my heart upon my sleeve
> For all the world to know
> That you were mine....
> I wore my heart upon my sleeve
> But you were not the kind
> To understand my mind.

The beautiful melody belongs to an earlier age. There is no indication of when she wrote it. The lyrics may also be hers, containing an allusion to the all too familiar lesbian experience of falling for a heterosexual woman ('not the kind to understand my mind').

Reprising 'All Alone', Norah earnestly encouraged the studio audience to join her at the point where Gwen's cello had previously supplied its sublime harmony. Her excitement is palpable, but so is her sadness:

> All alone every evening
> All alone feeling blue
> Wondering where you are
> And how you are
> And if you are
> All alone too.[16]

In 'Cottage for Sale' she narrowly avoids bathos:

> Our little dream castle
> With every dream gone
> Is empty and silent
> The blinds are all drawn.[17]

It was sad, in real life, for Norah to look back on the grandeur of 217 King's Rd and Woodlands, knowing that she could never aspire to live in such a large property again. Finding a permanent base for her new solo life was problematic. When she first moved back to London she rented a flat at The White House, Regent's Park, a very grand spot that proved too expensive. In early 1954 she wrote to a BBC producer acquaintance: 'I'll go and be a lodger with a girl friend of mine who has a nice little mews cottage near Marble Arch'[18] (possibly Barbara Back who lived at 8 Connaught Place). That never happened, but instead she found 'a nice roomy flat with a studio where I can get my beloved piano installed'[19] at 3 Kara Lodge, Newton Road. It was less than two miles from her childhood home in Hammersmith and her widowed mother Molly came to live close by.

In 1957 Norah was cast in a small part in a television play. *The Critical Point* was 'a cryogenic murder mystery',[20] which centred on a scientist volunteering himself as a guinea pig for 'hibernation anaesthesia'.[21] Described as 'spine-chilling in more ways than one',[22] the production left JC Trewin (writing in the *Listener*) 'afraid to approach the refrigerator'.[23]

Norah caught up with her old friend Beverley Nichols, who was writing a nostalgic book about the 1920s. In it he recalled Gwen with great humour and affection and lamented her passing, adding, 'But Norah Blaney is still with us, as pretty as a picture and as clever as a bundle of monkeys.'[24]

Norah's customary vivacity and resilience had sustained her through the difficulties of widowhood and the sense of invisibility she experienced when trying to restart her career. In 1959 she approached the new decade with a conviction that life held plenty more excitements and challenges.

~ 16 ~

WAITING IN THE WINGS

It was old friend Noel Coward who made possible Norah's return to the West End after nearly three decades away. He told her:

> You're going to come back into my play. Once an artist, always an artist. I've got to have you in the show because you can play the piano, you can sing, you can act without knocking into anybody.[1]

The play was *Waiting in the Wings,* set in a home for retired actors (called The Wings), based on Denville Hall in Middlesex. The director was an American lesbian, Margaret Webster, known as Peggy, who was in London with her partner, novelist Pamela Frankau. Peggy liked Norah immediately when she met her at the audition ('She is a little duck!')[2] and could see she was trying hard, early in rehearsals, along with the other elderly performers:

> Very occasionally they fasten triumphantly on a move...
> that belongs to a quite different scene... otherwise they
> float about with expressions of agonised apprehension...
> because it *is* a very confusing play.[3]

It opened on 7 September 1960 at the Duke of York's Theatre – the same stage on which, thirty-six years earlier, Norah and Gwen had starred in *The Punch Bowl.*

Photographed with his arm round Norah, and beaming delightedly, Coward said in the accompanying interview in the *Stage*:

> Edith Day, Norah Blaney and Mary Clare were stars, are
> stars and always will be stars. They are also extremely
> good actresses. That is the point. There may be a special
> interest for some people in the audience in seeing these
> wonderful players, just because they are stars, but so far as I
> am concerned, the chief thing is that I am sure they will be
> wonderful in their parts.[4]

The role of Maudie Melrose was written as if for Norah,
including a pastiche song, 'Miss Mouse', that recalled, at least
in its title, Norah's own composition, 'Are You There, Mr Bear?'
Waiting in the Wings was very much a tribute to the generation
of stars Coward remembered from his youth. He had been a boy
actor in the days when Norah performed 'Mabel's Pigtail' and
in the play Maudie is remembered singing 'a most enchanting
song, dressed as a school girl'. There are even allusions to a
performing partner 'poor Dolly Drexel' who had 'no middle
register'.

The brightest and most encouraging resident of The Wings,
Maudie provided piano accompaniment to some of the play's
most poignant moments and, like Norah, could improvise and
play by ear.

Of the opening performance of this, his fiftieth play, Coward
wrote:

> It was one of the most moving first nights I ever attended...
> each member of that remarkable company gave to my play
> their shining best and for me, together with the majority of
> the audience it was a great night in the theatre.[5]

But to the critics the play was dated; and Coward was hurt by
their failure to acknowledge the strength of the performances
and how well audiences responded to the piece. It ran for 188
performances.

The piece was unusual in offering fourteen roles for women,
compared to only three for men. Later, Coward's biographer,
Sheridan Morley, wrote, '*Waiting in the Wings* has moments
of near-Chekhovian dignity'[6] and went on to quote Coward
saying: 'The play... contains... the basic truth that old age

needn't be nearly so dreary and sad as it is supposed to be, provided you greet it with humour and live it with courage.'[7]

Norah embodied this message, as did her mother, Molly, who was now well into her nineties.

Dame Sybil Thorndike played the lead role in the play with 'unswerving truth, restraint, lack of sentimentality and sheer beauty'.[8] She and Norah became friends. They shared a love of piano playing and found a music shop whose manager encouraged them to go in and play. Peggy Webster wrote, 'If allowed to reach the piano together, [they] would settle down to a four-handed Bach jam session which took a lot of stopping.'[9]

One day, during the run of the show, a BBC producer approached Norah to ask if she and Dame Sybil would play their duets on the wireless. When Norah got to the theatre that night she put the idea to Thorndike who said, 'Oh my dear, I'd love to do it, and I don't want a fee.'

In typical fashion where money was concerned, Norah affectionately told her, 'Shut your trap! We're going to get a fee, mate, and we'll share it.'[10]

They played a jig from one of the Bach Suites and Khachaturian's *Waltz* in a programme broadcast on 25 January 1961, each receiving a fee of twenty-six guineas.

In a light-hearted interview Dame Sybil credited Norah with being her 'instructor', adding, 'You've been a pianist all your life.'

'Don't rub it in,' retorted Norah.

Dame Sybil, Norah and the cast of *Waiting in the Wings* were not the only ones playing actors looking back at past glories. In 1962, Norah's old friend Cicely Courtneidge played a cameo role in the movie *The L-Shaped Room* – a performance that would have struck a chord with Norah, for the character of Mavis was a lady living alone in a flat, recalling the love of her life who happened to have been a woman. Attitudes to homosexuality were very slowly beginning to change.

For Norah, a big break was just around the corner. It would see her working with a much younger company of actors and would take her away from her London flat for almost a year.

Norah had an audition at the Royal Shakespeare Company and was cast in their 1962 season at Stratford-upon-Avon. The company included Eric Porter, Ian Richardson, the young Vanessa Redgrave, Judi Dench, Diana Rigg and Maroussia Frank, who played one of the witches in *Macbeth* alongside Norah. She remembers Norah being a good raconteur, telling the story about the *Wonder Bar* company visiting Leeds with Carl Brisson and his sister's heavily accented interjection from the gallery.

Audry Carten and her partner Caroline were still together, almost thirty years on, and they took Caroline's eleven-year-old son Charles with them to see Norah at Stratford. Although he had been rather put off Norah on an earlier visit to her flat when she had snapped at him for fingering her piano, he was prepared to forgive her when he saw her marvellous, funny performance as what she called the 'bitchy witch'.[11] Audry's brother Kenneth was now so well established as an agent that he had Laurence Olivier and Vanessa Redgrave on his books. This didn't stop him paying Norah a marvellous compliment, after her performance as the Hostess in *The Taming of the Shrew*, when he told her, 'You are my favourite Shakespearean actress!'[12]

Her best part was in *Measure for Measure* in which she played the mouthy brothel keeper Mistress Overdone. Maroussia Frank says this was 'right up her street and she did it splendidly'.[13] The critic Caryl Brahms captured the joy of this performance in her review:

> Miss Nora [*sic*] Blaney's brazen wreck of pleasure, Mistress Overdone, tittupping across the stage in offended, gin-sodden grandeur, a magnificent and unrepentant barque at sea, the high seas having played havoc with her finery.[14]

In his introduction to a 1964 edition of the play for the Folio Society, theatre critic Harold Hobson made particular mention of Norah's 'very juicy performance'.

As a company member, Norah was unafraid to speak her mind. At a large and serious meeting called by the RSC's director, Peter Hall (later to be knighted and called 'the most important

*Norah as Mistress Overdone with Ian Richardson in the RSC's
1962 production of* Measure for Measure

figure in British theatre'), Norah somewhat inappropriately
complained about her dressing room's proximity to the toilets:
'You can hear everything from first fart to final trickle.'[15]

Diana Rigg recalled:

> I shared a dressing room with Norah and adored her. We
> were a most unlikely duo to share – youth and age... Norah
> flashed a large diamond ring one day and said, 'Be sure to
> get one of these for yourself.' It was the only advice she
> gave me and I have failed to follow it.[16]

Norah's season with the RSC led to a healthy run of theatre,
television and radio work in the 1960s, during which time she
was still writing the 'Nora and Tilly' stories for *Woman and Home*.

She recorded, on one occasion, with the great star Elisabeth Welch, and recalled:

> [I] loved her and admired her, ooh what a lovely artist! On this occasion [Welch] had brought her dog with her. He was a wire-haired fox terrier called the Colonel. How she'd been allowed to get him inside the studio, don't ask me, but anyway he was there. He was a sweet dog. When the time came to record, he started to try and run across the studio floor. It was polished and very slippery, but he couldn't get a grip. Elisabeth and I saw this dog and I can't tell you how funny it was![17]

She also recalled playing the Fairy Dew-Drop with Fay Compton as Aladdin on the radio:

> She was very, very funny. We had such fun. We thought the whole thing was so funny that we giggled and giggled our way through all the rehearsals, much to the despair of the producer who spent most of his time shushing.[18]

In August 1962 Norah's mother Molly died. She was ninety-five. Norah had been a loving and dutiful daughter, visiting often and sharing her news. For decades the need to please her parents had been a major driver in Norah's life and the secret of her inner life had stayed hidden.

Now Norah was able to paste in her scrapbook a cutting from we know not where. In jokey fashion it mentioned a fourth putative marriage to an elderly duke which came to nothing. Nonetheless Norah proudly cut out and stuck in the cutting which affectionately referred to her as 'lesbian actress and comedy star Norah Blaney'.

In December 1963 *Waiting in the Wings* was broadcast on the radio with Norah reprising her role as Maudie. In the same year, having celebrated her seventieth birthday, Norah recorded an intense drama for ITV's Armchair Theatre season. For scheduling reasons it was never broadcast but a copy of *The Bandstand* is available for viewing at the BFI Archive. In it Norah gave the screen performance of her life as a trusting elderly lady who strikes up a relationship with a seemingly kind park-keeper.

Norah's performance in the long tracking shots and close-ups cannot be faulted. It is all the more remarkable because she completely holds her own opposite the brilliant actor Donald Pleasance, who would soon become famous for his portrayal of Blofeld in the 1967 Bond film *You Only Live Twice*.

For Wrexham Theatre Company, touring Wales, Norah played the iconic role of Lady Bracknell in a musical version of Wilde's famous play, rechristened *Half in Earnest* by the well-known composer Vivian Ellis. In March 1965 she played the Nurse in *Hippolytus* at the Hampstead Theatre Club and later that year Ada Doom in *Something Nasty in the Woodshed* at the Theatre Royal Stratford East. In 1966 she appeared as a nun in a television play for BBC Wales, *Behind the Veil* starring Barbara Cavan and Margaret Tyzack. Norah's scrapbook contains several cuttings of Cavan, a handsome woman who also appeared briefly in the TV classic *Doctor Finlay's Casebook*.

Recurring television series provided well-paid work for actors fortunate enough to get a part. In 1966 Norah was cast in a famously ropey TV soap opera, *Crossroads*. A critic wrote at the time:

> It seems unbelievable in 1966 that any company would put this penny-pinching moth-eaten catastrophe on the screen. It is a chilling burlesque of acting, directing and producing. Everybody and everything moves in agonisingly slow motion, dragging every petty incident to the point where it snaps and vanishes. The dialogue is woolly, the acting stilted, the directing stale, the result absurd... But despite it all, Norah Blaney as novelist Miss Leopold puts up a performance far better than the programme deserves.[19]

In 1967 she appeared in a television adaptation of a book by her old friend JB Priestley, *Angel Pavement*. Then onstage she played Madame Desmortes in *Ring Round the Moon* at the Belgrade Theatre, Coventry. The role required her to be pushed around in an antique wheelchair, which was inclined to malfunction. Fellow cast members Auriol Smith and Paul Shelley remember her as a formidable but likeable person who exuded stage presence despite the confines of the part.[20]

The following year she toured in a production of the classic lesbian drama *The Killing of Sister George,* not in the part made famous on film by Beryl Reid, but as Madame Xenia,[21] a fortune teller who lives upstairs.

Norah had her final job in the West End at the Apollo Theatre as an understudy in *Home* by David Storey in 1970. There is no record of whether she went on in the bleak modern drama set in a psychiatric home, but she must have at least rehearsed alongside Sir John Gielgud for she told Derek Hunt, 'It was a lovely experience and a great privilege to play with such a wonderful artist. I've always been one of his most ardent fans. I think he's simply superb... that lovely voice.'[22]

Norah continued to be heard in radio roles, including the Pythian High Priestess in an adaptation of Euripides' play *Ion.* It had been translated and adapted in 1937 by lesbian Imagist poet H.D.[23] and the radio production (in October 1970) received great praise from critic Gillian Reynolds: 'One felt ennobled... inspired by the play, the performances, and this superbly interpretative production.'[24]

The theme of an older woman seeking the son she had abandoned at birth following her seduction by the god Apollo may have struck a chord with Norah. It had parallels with the central story of a mother/son rift in *Waiting in the Wings.* Facing the prospect of loneliness in old age, Norah would later tell Derek that she often wondered about the child she never had.

By now Norah was living in a flat at Highstone Mansions, Camden. She no longer had a dog for company. She still had her grand piano and the portrait of Gwen in prime position on the wall. She turned eighty on 16 July 1973.

Practising a Chopin ballade one day she snapped two tendons in her right had and had to have an operation. She gave up writing the magazine stories, but remained active, going to concerts and the theatre; and particularly admired the opera singer Janet Baker.

It was in 1975 that she made friends with actor and record collector Derek Hunt. They shared a love of the theatre and an irreverent sense of humour. Derek tried to gain more recognition for her by contacting the organisers of the Royal Variety Performance and the producers of the *Michael Parkinson Show*, to no avail. Over several sessions that lasted late into the night, he recorded interviews with Norah about her career. She enjoyed this and, as a thank you, would always insist on paying for Derek to take a taxi home to his flat in Soho.

One day, out of the blue, Norah received a phone call from someone at HMV, inviting her to their studio in Hayes, Middlesex. On the appointed day, a white Rolls Royce arrived to collect her. Derek came too and they were entertained like VIPs. It was the company's way of paying tribute to Norah for the huge number of songs she had recorded on the label – many of them, of course, with Gwen.

In her eighty-fourth year Norah appeared in two series for television. The first was a BBC adaptation of a children's novel by Rumer Godden. *Kizzy* told the story of a group of travellers and centred on an orphan girl. Norah played a none too sympathetic relative. Miriam Margolyes, then thirty-five, was

Norah and Derek go to HMV

also in the cast and she recalled Norah, forty years later:

> She was lovely. We talked a lot – and she spoke about being
> gay, how it had to be hidden, about The Gateways Club
> in Chelsea, about someone riding a horse up the steps of a
> house where there was a party. She seemed totally happy.[25]

Being able to talk openly about her sexuality and share at least
one of her favourite stories about Gwen was a tonic.

Her other television role that year was in the ITV drama
series *Within These Walls*. Norah played Dolly Grey, a sly old-
timer in the prison system, who acts as a cleaner and cleverly
exacts revenge on a new inmate who has been conning old
ladies. She is a recurring figure in Series Four. As the final credits
roll on Episode Three she is seen alone mopping the floor,
loudly humming the tune to her Irving Berlin hit of fifty years
earlier, 'All Alone'.

When filming ended, Norah was depressed. She told Derek
in a letter[26] that while she was flattered the director had written
to tell her she was 'marvellous', she felt tired, lonely and even
suicidal. She feared she would now always be typecast as 'that
old lag Dolly Grey'. She ends the letter jokingly, 'Excuse me
while I shoot myself.'

In most of the letters she is on happier form:

> What funny things people collect these days! While I was in
> 'Makeup' last Wednesday one of the engineers (young, blue
> jeans etc) came in with a bundle of old songs (sheet music)
> with my picture on the covers looking like Theda Bara.[27] So
> I had to autograph them!
> Oh get *me*.
> Poor old Trout[28]

Norah's ability to laugh at herself in these letters is appealing.
They are full of humorous takes on her predicament and she
is always interested to hear Derek's news. She makes a good
correspondent.

She stayed in touch with the Farrar family, who recognised
that she had been important in Gwen's life. Marjorie had died
in 1975, leaving her companion of sixty years, Peggy, to sell

Newbiggin Hall, the large estate in County Durham where they had lived since leaving Chicheley Hall. By 1980 only the youngest Farrar sister, Ella, was still alive. She lived in Warwickshire, where her son and daughter-in-law now had a growing family. Her granddaughter, Olivia, remembers, as a child, being awed by Norah's bangles, bright lipstick, red nail varnish and chain smoking when she came to visit.[29]

Norah said in a letter to Derek, 'If didn't smoke 1,000,000 cigs a day and have a drop of whiskey in the p.m. I'd be okay. But the doubling of my rent is a nuisance.'[30]

Ever money-conscious, in October 1979 Norah moved into Denville Hall, a Victorian Gothic house on Duck's Hill Road, Northwood – the home for retired actors which had been Coward's model for The Wings nursing home. Norah was quick to point out there were few similarities. Here she could live much more cheaply thanks to the home's charitable status. But leaving Highstone Mansions meant reluctantly dispensing with most of her possessions. Sir Gerald Kelly's portrait of Gwen went fittingly to Ella Farrar.

On arrival at Denville Hall, Norah had difficulty finding room for all the clothes she had brought. She had a television in her room and appreciated the little bar downstairs, open for an hour before dinner, where she could buy whiskey and ginger ale for 26p. She wrote: 'The place is beautifully run – food good too, darling.'[31]

She found that she was still much more active than the other residents. 'They all look about 150 and something like a cage of old, very old-looking fowls and no sense of humour at all. I do miss having a giggle.'[32]

By January 1980 she was writing to Derek to say how isolated she felt: 'No one here is any fun at all… Let's face it, we all come here to end our days and no one is immortal, but I do wish [the other residents] would be a bit more cheerful about it.'[33]

Norah and Derek kept up a regular correspondence between his occasional visits. She relieved her boredom by substituting new names for Denville Hall in the address line at the top of her letters: Deathville Morgue, Duck's Arse Road, Wheelchair

Crescent, Boulevard des Corpses, and signing herself off with funny takes on other people's names: 'Hylda Baker, with a Y of course', 'Your mate Mrs Nicholas Parsons', 'Dolly Dandruff', 'Thora Turd'. After suffering a fall and having her foot bandaged she signed herself off 'Anna Pavlova'.

She dreaded Christmas, when 'you can bet your life I shall be expected to be the Court Jester and sit on my arse and sing some old songs the words of which I have completely forgotten – Hell!'[34] but was thrilled to receive a parcel of gifts from Derek.

Another friend and visitor was Graham Newell, a musical theatre enthusiast who delighted her by bringing an antique copy of *Popular Music and Dancing Weekly* with her and Gwen on the front cover. He took her to visit the opera singer Dame Eva Turner, who remembered Norah's act with Gwen, saying, 'You made such an enormous impression.'[35]

Newell acted as an intermediary when author Roger Wilmut interviewed Norah in November 1981 as part of the research for his book about music hall, *Kindly Leave the Stage*. They met in a sitting room at Denville Hall over cups of tea. Norah had been a resident there for two years and by this time she was eighty-eight. Her memory for detail was very good and she had some sheet music, records and articles to show the two men.

She began by presenting a version of her life that almost perversely downplayed the years 1912 to 1923 which were the focus of Wilmut's enquiry. Norah had, to an extent, become institutionalised by Denville Hall. She had started to believe a particular version of herself, developed in the humdrum small talk of hundreds of days of shared meals and communal living. Norah spoke of her irritation when residents were condescending about Blaney and Farrar or treated her as if the partnership was all that her career had amounted to. One can read into her initial responses a sense that Norah was easily marginalised in a place where status and self-esteem depended on past accomplishments and one-upmanship flourished. Another difference between her and the rest was that many had children and grandchildren who visited. Like so many gay people going into care, Norah was obliged to muffle her queer past, re-inventing her personal history and her current behaviour to match other people's conventional memories and the heteronormative assumptions of staff.

But the chance to chat with two sympathetic young men from outside the confines of the Hall soon sparked off the old stories. Norah repeated many of the favourites that she had told Derek: Gwen running away from school, their meeting through Elwes, Gwen gatecrashing Lady Londonderry's ball, and further back, Norah winning her scholarships and playing the piano with Casals.

> I suppose I've had a bit of a lurid life... Nobody ever connects me with anything but Gwen... I adored her of course... she was very funny... we had some wonderful times.[36]

She was quick and funny and utterly lucid, making her visitors roar with laughter by quoting Charlot's comment, 'Gwen had all the lesbians in London to see her.'

A week after this interview, Norah was at her alma mater to receive honorary membership, which is bestowed on 'individuals who have made an exceptional contribution to life at the Royal College of Music and the wider musical community'. She had always felt guilty for 'deserting the primrose path of classical music'. It was marvellous to not only be welcomed back into the fold, but receive the honour from the Queen Mother, who recalled her visit backstage at *The Punch Bowl*, saying, 'You and Gwen were such fun.'

Norah spent Christmas with a cousin twenty years her junior – one of the small boys left motherless in 1918 when Molly's sister-in-law Eunice suddenly died. John Thatcher, now in his late sixties, had returned to the UK after a successful career in the Far East. He had not forgotten how Molly had helped look after him and his brothers when they were little. For Norah, Christmas with John was a welcome day out from Denville Hall.

Early in the New Year, a young American writer, Joel Lobenthal, researching his biography of Tallulah Bankhead, contacted Norah ahead of a visit he hoped to make to Denville Hall to interview her and Leslie Henson's ex-wife Gladys. He recalls:

> I talked to Norah on the phone and she was very responsive, said she had photos of herself with Ziegfeld, then when I mentioned Tallulah, the temperature dropped and she got off quickly... When I had lunch with Gladys, Norah was sitting at a nearby table, loudly declaiming that she had refused to talk to me, that young people didn't go to the theater anymore because it was too expensive. She seemed to be perfectly at ease with her fellow residents – rather booming, however.[37]

This was the front Norah put up to mask her isolation. 'Not a soul here who is any sort of fun at all.'[38]

On 16 July 1983, Norah celebrated her ninetieth birthday. In an interview for the local paper to mark the occasion she described the home as 'bedpan alley'. Regretting that arthritis now prevented her from playing the piano as well as she would like she added, 'But you know I can still play anything with my good left hand. Even here.'[39]

Derek remembers a visit where she sat at the piano and started to play 'What'll I Do?' but couldn't remember the words and dissolved into tears. She wrote her final letter to him in October. She had lost her old birthday book, was confused about friends' birthdays, but (correctly) remembered that his was 'nearby'. She had tried to get him on the telephone three times.

> I have only just come from the hospital a few days ago as I had to have another blood transfusion – such a bore. I have got to have one about every five weeks. Can't write more. Eyes very tiresome and writing not so easy when you are in the 90s.
> Lots of love and hoping to see you soon,
> Your old pal Norah[40]

Norah died at Denville Hall on Wednesday 7 December 1983. Derek Hunt, Graham Newell and John Thatcher, among many others, attended her funeral service at St Matthew's Catholic Church, Northwood, on 15 December. It was followed by a committal at Breakspear Crematorium, where, afterwards, her ashes were scattered in the Garden of Remembrance.

In her final years Norah felt that her past achievements were forgotten. The tapes she made with Derek in 1976 had been a bit of fun, but there would be no lasting memorial to her double act with Gwen once the 78s had gone to the scrap heap and the pages of sheet music had turned to dust. She felt no self-pity, but rather a sense of sadness that the memory of someone as unique and extraordinary as Gwen should die with her.

Norah reckoned without Derek broadcasting the interviews on community radio and the recordings finding their way to the British Library Sound Archive. She could not have imagined the internet, which would make her frolics on a golf course with Gwen available to view the world over.

Norah had watched and absorbed the performances of such great stars as Gertie Millar, Ruth Draper, Ella Shields, Vesta Tilley and Yvette Guilbert. In the lineage of female comedy performers, Norah represents a link between them and the artists who followed. Her resilience, professionalism and versatility are a lesson to any of today's hopefuls seeking fame on a plate. Her act with Gwen can be seen as the precursor to the various queer or female comedy partnerships that followed the Waters Sisters: Hinge and Bracket, Wood and Walters, French and Saunders, Mel and Sue, Rose and Rosie.

The topicality of Blaney and Farrar's material made the act ephemeral, very much of its own time; but the sincerity and precision of the looks, smiles, lyrics and harmonies Gwen and Norah shared make them pioneers of lesbian courage and visibility.

Norah and Gwen in Wonder Bar

Postscript

A hundred years on from the heyday of Blaney and Farrar, the custodians of their memory meet, drawn together by this project thanks to social media and the internet. From as far afield as Melbourne, Jakarta, Johannesburg, Bradford, Warwickshire and Cornwall, they convene on a London townhouse.

There are Gwen's nephew and Norah's friend Derek, both now in their eighties. From the house where Gwen grew up in South Africa comes the St Andrew's Girls' School archivist. She has restored Sir George's grave and ensures the Farrar name still echoes in the corridors of Bedford Court. The son of Norah's cousin, who has spent his life in the forefront of international journalism, brings a tiny yellowing cutting Norah kept from her time with the RSC. A witness to those Stratford performances shares warm testimony of the love Gwen's lesbian friends felt for her long after she was dead, and first-hand insights into Norah's characterful passage to old age.

A key collaborator on this book is there: his curiosity about Gwen's tenancy of a Surrey cottage has led to explorations and exhibitions on Blaney and Farrar and a timely, fascinating study of their good friend Teddie Gerard. An academic shares expertise on intersectionality in early twentieth-century revue. From Australia a connoisseur of early film has tracked down and patiently restored extremely rare Phonofilm footage of both Gwen and Norah. A man who lives in Woodlands, Norah's Bradford home, is drawn to the event by his conviction that if we learn to recognise the richness of diversity in the past, we can appreciate the place of diversity in the present.

There are actors here who connected with Norah on one level when they were starting out in the 1960s, and now recognise themselves as the experienced old-timers on a stage full of youngsters. Our hosts, who did not know their King's Road house had been a centre of the London lesbian demi-monde, have embraced the fact and want a blue plaque to celebrate. Queer people and straight people, academics and laymen, artists and historians come together to champion Gwen and Norah.

The snippets of their lives that were lodged in people's memories or between the pages of fading manuscripts have been brought together into something that gives a fuller version of their lives. It takes the reader to complete the picture by bringing to this story what they know of queer lives lived in secrecy – in Gwen and Norah's case, such secrecy that no letters or diaries remain.

We must draw on a lesbian love affair running concurrently with theirs for words to help our imaginations. Here Vita Sackville-West writes to Virginia Woolf in 1926:

> I just miss you, in a quite simple desperate human way...
> I miss you even more than I could have believed; and I
> was prepared to miss you a good deal. So this letter is just
> really a squeal of pain. It is incredible how essential to me
> you have become. I suppose you are accustomed to people
> saying these things... but oh my dear, I can't be clever and
> stand-offish with you: I love you too much for that. Too
> truly. You have no idea how stand-offish I can be with
> people I don't love. I have brought it to a fine art. But you
> have broken down my defences.[1]

I said in the Foreword that we can naturally exonerate Gwen and Norah from the guilt and shame of forbidden love, but I asked whether the reader would want to forgive the way they treated each other. I hope the answer to that is yes. For the most part they persevered while the world told them their intimacy was wrong, renewing their relationship after each setback. Perhaps the best coda for their love story is this song Norah recorded in 1928:

The song is ended
But the melody lingers on
You and the song are gone
But the melody lingers on

The nights were splendid
And the melody seemed to say,
'Summer will pass away
Take your happiness while you may'

There 'neath the light of the moon
We sang a love song that ended too soon
The moon descended
And I found with the break of dawn
You and the song had gone

But the melody lingers on.[2]

301

The duo in a drawing by Gwen featuring the royal box

ACKNOWLEDGEMENTS

I am enormously grateful to the following people without whose generosity and enthusiasm this book would not have been possible: above all to Jeremy Palmer for his meticulous research and his unflagging encouragement. He has patiently followed up on the smallest of clues and his diligent enquiries have led to the most exciting discoveries. He is a wonderful historian and has become a great friend. Another person essential to this book is Derek Hunt and I thank him for having the foresight to interview Norah in 1976 and the kindness to say she would have liked me and approved of this project. Gwen Farrar's nephew, Sir Andrew Watson, and his wife, Christabel, Lady Watson, have been exceptionally kind hosts and supporters. Charles Duff has shared his memories of Norah and his impressions of Gwen with great warmth and love.

Di Stiff and Phil Cooper of the Surrey History Centre have been outstanding champions of Gwen and Norah's story. James McConnel has been a most helpful intermediary with his father Adrian who very kindly gave us access to Betty Pollock's archive. Philip Jones has been immensely generous with his time and knowledge of Norah in her incarnation as Mrs Basil Hughes. Bev Smith of St Andrew's School, Johannesburg, gave me a wonderful tour of Bedford Court in 2016 and has continued, ever since, to be enthusiastic and supportive. Jonathan Thatcher, Ursula Thatcher and Mark Peters have been very helpful with Norah's family history. I thank Jonathan for reading the manuscript and Mark and Ursula for putting me in touch with Derek Hunt. Andrew Parsons kindly guided me through the London Scottish Regiment archives to the material relating to Albert Lyne. Andy Simons, formerly of the British Library Sound Archive, gave me great encouragement, provided recordings and digitally rescued Derek's frail cassette tapes. John Jefferies, archivist of the Classic Boat Museum, was helpful in providing images of Joe Carstairs.

My heartfelt thanks go to the following people, many of whom kindly read the manuscript and gave me encouraging feedback: Alice Arnold, Sophie Aynsley, David Benson, Geoff Bowden, Alan Brodie, Eddie Bundy, Jennifer Burden, Paul Burston, François Chapon, Charlie, Harry and Tascha Child, Penny and Anthony Clark, Hugh Comerford, Gill Cook, Kate Crane, Claire Crookenden, Ann Dieckmann, Mark Eccleston, Jennifer Froude, Fani Galinou, Caroline Gonda, Sue Gorbing, Lucinda Gosling (the head of research at the Mary Evans Picture Library, who has been amazing), Ailsa Grant Ferguson, Jenny Hammerton, Sal Hampson, Barney and Olivia Hatch, Steve Holland, Jane Hoy, Norman Jacobs, Vicky Lewis, Lisa Lipman, David Linton, Sarah Lloyd, Chris Long, Tom and Victoria Lowther, Miriam Margolyes, Lucy McCann, Duncan McLaren, Carole Newman, Jamie Niven, Kevin Nyakairu, Nuala O'Sullivan, Kay Palmer, Naomi Paxton, Wendy Pearce, Liz and David Pettifer, Jan Pimblett, Maroussia Richardson, Peter Roscoe, Freddie Rowe, Veronica and Bob Schroter, Ginny Sennett, Paul Shelley, Auriol Smith, Howard Spencer, Clare Summerskill, Sue Trebilcock, Debbie Turner, Rachel Whitbread, Ilsa Woloszko, Charlotte Wright, Sarah Wyatt and Diney Zalk.

I am grateful to the Society for Theatre Research for a grant which has helped pay for picture licences.

Roger Wilmut shared his 1981 interview with Norah, for which I am most thankful. Other writers who have engaged with me on the subject of Gwen and Norah and encouraged this endeavour are: Val Brown, Peter Bradshaw, Peter Dickinson, Charles Duff, Travis Elborough, Maureen Emerson, Joel Lobenthal, Joan Schenkar, Kate Summerscale, Jane Traies, Helena Whitbread, and especially Jill Gardiner and Diana Souhami.

My editor and publisher Helen Sandler at Tollington Press

has worked tirelessly, prompting me to make innumerable, cleverly observed improvements, with great patience, tact, humour and a shared passion for lesbian history.

Andrew Kay has designed a succession of beautiful front covers for this book. The one we chose represents just a fraction of his immensely encouraging and creative input on this project for which I am extraordinarily grateful.

Rosie Wakley has been infinitely patient, understanding and supportive.

I am grateful to the following for permission to quote material:

'All Alone' and 'The Song is Ended', words and music by Irving Berlin © 1997 Irving Berlin Music Corp. Universal Music Publishing Limited. All Rights Reserved. International Copyright Secured. Used by permission of Hal Leonard Europe Limited. 'If Love Were All' by Noel Coward from the operetta *Bitter Sweet* by Noel Coward © 1929 BC Aventales AG. Used with permission.

Extract from Introduction to *Coward: Plays, Five*, Sheridan Morley, reprinted by permission of Bloomsbury Publishing Plc. Extract from *Daphne du Maurier and Her Sisters* reprinted by permission of HarperCollins Publishers Ltd © Jane Dunn 2013. 'Faire-Part' by Natalie Clifford Barney is quoted by kind permission of Monsieur François Chapon.

Extracts from his interview with Norah, her scrapbook and her letters to him, reproduced by kind permission of Derek Hunt. Extracts from his interview with Norah Blaney and from *Kindly Leave the Stage* reproduced by kind permission of Roger Wilmut.

For certain newspaper images, successor copyright holders are unknown. With thanks to the British Newspaper Archive (www.britishnewspaperarchive.co.uk).

Other credits are included in the List of Illustrations, Foreword and Notes. Every effort has been made to trace and contact copyright holders. Any omissions or errors will be corrected at the earliest opportunity.

NORAH BLANEY

Looking back, 1926

NOTES

Foreword

1   The best version of this footage can be found on the British Pathé website: www.britishpathe.com/video/the-stars-off-stage-miss-norah-blaney-and-miss-gwe
2   *Leeds Mercury*, 17 December 1931
3   'Tell Me I'm Forgiven,' lyrics by Roland Leigh, sung by Carl Brisson in the revue *Wonder Bar* at London's Savoy Theatre in 1930-31

Chapter 1: The Champion Baby

1   *South Wales Daily News*, 20 June 1894
2   *Guernsey Star*, 21 June 1894
3   'Partners and Pals,' Norah Blaney, *Popular Music and Dancing Weekly*, 8 March 1924 (No.7, Vol.1)
4   Norah Blaney in conversation with Derek Hunt, 1976
5   Norah Blaney in conversation with Roger Wilmut, 1981
6   Norah in conversation with Derek Hunt, 1976
7   Sir Henry Wood's Promenade Concerts were held at the Queen's Hall in Langham Place until it was destroyed by a German bomb in 1941.
8   Norah in conversation with Derek Hunt, 1976
9   George Thalben-Ball later became organist and choirmaster at the Temple Church and was behind the world-famous 1927 recording of Mendelssohn's 'Hear My Prayer' in which Ernest Lough sang the solo, 'O for the Wings of a Dove'.

Chapter 2: One Per Cent Talent, Nine Per Cent Luck and Ninety Per Cent Hard Work

1   The chapter title borrows Jan Paderewski's formula for success, quoted in *Masters of the Keyboard* by Donald Brook, 1947.
2   *My Young Years* by Arthur Rubinstein, 1973
3   Norah in conversation with Derek Hunt, 1976
4   A humorous reference to *Peter Pan*
5   *Yorkshire Post*, 21 February 1912
6   Norah in conversation with Derek Hunt, 1976
7   *Ibid.*

8 *Era*, 11 February 1914

9 *Royal College of Music Magazine*, May 1914

10 The Band of Hope was a temperance organisation for working-class children, which preached the evils of drink and organised constructive activities such as choirs and music competitions.

11 As late as 15 October 1936 Clarkson Rose was reminiscing about Albert Lyne's 'perfect playing' in 'Peradventure', his column in the *Stage*.

12 Almost twenty years later, after a career singing in recitals and oratorios, Labbette surprised the opera world by appearing at the Royal Opera House as Mimì in *La Bohème,* performing under the Italian-sounding pseudonym 'Lisa Perli'. She took the name from her birthplace, the London suburb of Purley. In her conversations with Derek Hunt, Norah recalled seeing this performance ('and very charming she was too') and going backstage for a 'girlish gossip' with Dora. The two women enjoyed catching up so much that when Labbette's lover, the distinguished conductor Sir Thomas Beecham, popped his head around the door because he wanted to go home, Labbette retorted, 'Go away! Can't you see I'm chatting to Norah?'

13 *Eastbourne Gazette*, 30 June 1915

14 *Hull Daily Mail*, 19 June 1916

15 'My Experiences at the Front,' Norah Blaney, unknown publication, undated cutting, Norah's scrapbook

16 *Ibid.*

17 *Ibid.*

18 Letter from Lieutenant Kenneth Mackenzie, 13 June 1917, quoted in *The Imperial War Museum Book of the Western Front* by Malcolm Brown, 1993

19 'My Experiences at the Front,' *op. cit.*

20 *Middlesex Chronicle*, 11 November 1916

21 *Ibid.*

Chapter 3: Those Maddening Bits We Could Not Remember

1 Biography of Sir George Farrar by Muriel, Viscountess Lowther, unpublished, Bodleian Library Special Collections

2 Gwen was officially named Gwendoline – perhaps after the eponymous heroine of the 1886 opera by Emmanuel Chabrier. Although Gwen was known, ever after, by the shortened form of her name, it seems she already had something in common with Norah, whose middle name, Mignon, was the title of an 1866 opera by Ambrose Thomas.

3 A myth persists that Gwen was born in 1899 and nearly every published source maintains this, but all the official records and her birth certificate concur with 14 July 1897.

4 Park Street seems to have been the location of choice for immensely

wealthy mothers visiting London to give birth. Gwen was born at number 108. Less than three years later Marion (Joe) Carstairs was born at number 115.

5 Biography of Sir George by Muriel
6 *Ibid.*
7 *Ibid.*
8 *Ibid.*
9 *Johannesburg Star*, 1 December 1905
10 Biography of Sir George by Muriel
11 *Transvaal Leader*, 21 April 1911
12 *Johannesburg Star*, 8 April 1911
13 *South African Sunday Times*, 24 May 1910
14 *Rand Daily Mail*, 11 March 1907

Chapter 4: Well Done Miss Gwen!

1 Biography of Sir George by Muriel
2 Undated letter from Sir George to Helen
3 *Sunday Post*, 9 May 1920
4 Norah in conversation with Derek Hunt, 1976
5 Biography of Sir George by Muriel
6 *The Well of Loneliness* by Radclyffe Hall, 1928
7 'Conversation With Zara Nelsova' by Tim Janof, Internet Cello Society website: www.cello.org/Newsletter/Articles/nelsova.htm

Chapter 5: Drink to Me Only

1 'Partners and Pals,' Norah Blaney, *Popular Music and Dancing Weekly*, 8 March 1924
2 Norah in conversation with Roger Wilmut, 1981
3 'My Romantic Career: Theatrical Star's Remarkable Secret Revealed,' *Sunday Post*, 9 May 1920
4 *Ibid.*
5 'Partners and Pals,' *op. cit.*
6 'My Romantic Career,' *op. cit.*
7 John Addington Symonds, an early writer on homosexual love, showed in 1884 that every line matches Epistle 33 by Philostratus.
8 'Partners and Pals,' *op. cit.*
9 'My Romantic Career,' *op. cit.*
10 Letter from Gervase Elwes to to his wife Winefride, 4 July 1917
11 'My Experiences at the Front,' Norah Blaney, cutting, Norah's scrapbook
12 *What Is Found There: Notebooks on Poetry and Politics* by Adrienne Rich, 2003

13 *The Well of Loneliness* by Radclyffe Hall, 1928

14 *Modern Troubadours* by Lena Ashwell, 1922

15 *Ibid.*

16 *Ibid.*

17 Letter from Gervase Elwes to his wife Winifrede, 4 July 1917

18 Norah in conversation with Roger Wilmut, 1981

19 'Partners and Pals,' *op. cit.*

20 'My Romantic Career,' *op. cit.*

21 Letter from Gervase Elwes to his wife Winifrede, 9 July 1917

22 'Partners and Pals,' *op. cit.*

23 Norah in conversation with Roger Wilmut, 1981

24 *Eat My Dust: Early Women Motorists* by Georgine Clarson, 2008

25 'Dressing-Room Dialogues: Gwen Farrar in Grease Paint,' Pamela Travers, *South African Pictorial*, 21 February 1925

26 'The Life of Albert Nobbs' in *A Story-Teller's Holiday* by George Moore, 1918

27 *Ibid.*

28 'My Romantic Career,' *op. cit.*

29 'Partners and Pals,' *op. cit.* (They first appeared at the London Palladium on 19 August 1917.)

30 *Ibid.*

31 *Leeds Mercury*, 29 March 1924

32 Norah in conversation with Roger Wilmut, 1981

33 'Partners and Pals,' *op. cit.*

34 *Top Hat and Tails* by Michael Marshall, 1978

35 *Don't Fence Me In* by Renée Houston, 1974

36 *Financier*, undated cutting, Gwen's scrapbook

37 Unattributed cutting, circa October 1918, Gwen's scrapbook

38 *Leeds Mercury*, 29 March 1924

Chapter 6: A Swing of the Pendulum

1 'My Romantic Career,' *Sunday Post*, 9 May 1920

2 *The Sweet and Twenties* by Beverley Nichols, 1958

3 Norah in conversation with Derek Hunt, 1976

4 *Here Lies the Heart* by Mercedes de Acosta, 1960

5 *Gluck* by Diana Souhami, 1988

6 *Ballads and Poems* by Alfred Noyes, 1928

7 *The Paying Guests* by Sarah Waters, 2014

8 'Partners and Pals,' Norah Blaney, *Popular Music and Dancing Weekly*, 8 March 1924

9 Norah in conversation with Derek Hunt, 1976

10 *Scrapbook for the Twenties* by Leslie Baily, 1959

11 Norah told this story in conversation with Derek Hunt in 1976. There

really was an artist billed as the Royal Sussex Dwarf in the 1870s.

12 'Shall I Have It Bobbed or Shingled?' by Robert Weston and Bert Lee

13 *The Feminine Middlebrow Novel, 1920s to 1950s* by Nicola Humble, 2001

14 *Stage,* 6 February 1919

15 'Palladium Pleasantries,' Palladia, *Pall Mall Gazette,* 5 November 1919

16 Norah in conversation with Derek Hunt, 1976

17 *Scrapbook for the Twenties, op. cit.*

18 *Sunday Post,* 9 May 1920

19 *The Sweet and Twenties, op. cit.*

20 *Harrogate Herald,* undated cutting, Gwen's scrapbook

21 Letter to the editor from Virginia Woolf, *New Statesman,* 16 October 1920

22 'We Don't Want to Get Married' by Myrtle Boland, James Brennan and William Jerome

23 *Pall Mall & Globe,* 23 October 1921

24 'Just a Rag!', Margaret Chute, unknown publication, cutting, Gwen's scrapbook

25 Norah in conversation with Derek Hunt, 1976

26 *The Wandering Years: 1922-39* by Cecil Beaton

27 *Here Lies the Heart* by Mercedes De Acosta, 1960

28 Earl of Malmesbury, House of Lords, *Hansard,* 18 August 1921

29 Lord Desart, *ibid.*

30 Lord Chancellor, Earl of Birkenhead, *ibid.*

31 *Mrs Keppel and Her Daughter* by Diana Souhami, 1996

32 *Gluck* by Diana Souhami, 1988

33 *Western Daily Press,* 12 March 1921

Chapter 7: Suitors

1 Prince Edward would take the throne briefly as Edward VIII in 1936 before abdicating, his brother Bertie succeeding him as George VI. Their bisexual younger brother George sometimes partied with Edward and was another fan of Gwen and Norah. He was also a close friend of Noel Coward and, it is rumoured, was arrested in drag with him late one night in central London before being let off by police.

2 Norah in conversation with Derek Hunt, 1976

3 *Ibid.*

4 The Hippodrome is now refurbished as a spectacular casino.

5 Letter from Lady Ella Farrar to Helen Turner, 31 November 1921

6 'The Black Sheep of the Family' by Fred Barnes

7 *Sunday Post,* 6 November 1921

8 Norah in conversation with Derek Hunt, 1976

9 Pathé website https://www.britishpathe.com/video/the-midnight-follies-and-some-of-the-steps-we

10 Norah in conversation with Roger Wilmut, 1981

11 *Every Other Inch a Lady* by Beatrice Lillie, 1972

12 *A Star Danced* by Gertrude Lawrence, 1945

13 *Pall Mall Gazette*, 24 April 1922

14 *Manchester Evening Chronicle*, 28 March 1931 – the paper is recalling the event nine years later in a report on Norah's divorce from Durham.

15 *Hampshire Advertiser*, 29 April 1922

16 *Belfast Telegraph*, 20 March 1931

17 *Ibid.*

18 *Hampshire Advertiser*, 9 September 1922

19 *Near East*, 29 June 1922

20 Alfred Lester can be seen in a Pathé clip, in a sketch set on Clapham Junction Station: https://www.britishpathe.com/video/nibbles-from-rats-at-the-vaudeville-theatre-london/query/alfred+lester

21 *Bystander*, 28 March 1923

22 *Stage*, 4 October 1923

23 *Pall Mall Gazette*, October 1923

Chapter 8: Friends

1 *The Times*, 27 December 1944

2 Anton Dolin quoted in *Tallulah!* by Joel Lobenthal, 2008

3 *Ibid.*

4 Norah in conversation with Derek Hunt, 1976

5 *It's Only the Sister* by Angela du Maurier, 1951

6 *Charley's Woods* by Charles Duff, 2018

7 *Noel Streatfeild* by Angela Bull, 1984

8 Norah in conversation with Roger Wilmut, 1981

9 *Ibid.* Norah also recorded this story for Derek; and it found its way into the memoir of the great drag performer Douglas Byng and a book by Beverley Nichols, so it must have been notorious.

10 *Motor Boating Magazine*, October 1929

11 Angela du Maurier's diary, 29 October 1924, quoted in *It's Only the Sister, op. cit.*

12 *Ibid.*

13 *Daphne du Maurier and Her Sisters* by Jane Dunn, 2013 (letter to Tod dated 2 January 1925)

14 *Old Maids Remember* by Angela du Maurier, 1966

15 *It's Only the Sister, op. cit.*

16 *Ibid.*

17 As reported by actress Una Venning to Joel Lobenthal, quoted in email to the author from Lobenthal, 20 November 2018

18 *People*, 6 July 1924

19 Coward uses the phrase in his 1930s play *Private Lives*.

20 *Crazy Pavements* by Beverley Nichols, 1927

21 Joe Carstairs in conversation with Jacqueline Rae, c.1989

22 *Daily News*, July 1930, cutting, scrapbook

23 *The Queen of Whale Cay* by Kate Summerscale, 1997

24 *Dundee Evening Telegraph*, 14 April 1924

25 *Step-daughter of Imperial Russia* by Natalia Mamontova Majolier, 1940

26 *Young in the Twenties* by Ethel Mannin, 1971

27 *The Diaries of Evelyn Waugh*, 3 July 1924

28 *Ibid.*, 23 June 1924

29 *Autobiography*, Augustus John, 1975

30 Pathé News website. With permission. https://www.britishpathe.com/
   video/the-stars-off-stage-miss-norah-blaney-and-miss-gwe

31 *For Ladies Only? Eve's Film Review Pathé Cinemagazine 1921-33* by Jenny
   Hammerton, 2001

32 'Dressing-Room Dialogues: Gwen Farrar in Grease Paint,' Pamela
   Travers, *South African Pictorial*, 21 February 1925

33 *Ibid.*

34 On 14 June 1924 the *Yorkshire Post and Leeds Intelligencer* reported
   on Gwen's collision some weeks earlier with a taxi: 'The court was
   told, Miss Farrar, with two other ladies, was sitting in front, with the
   chauffeur in the dickey behind, and was driving at a speed which
   competent witnesses estimated about 35 to 40 miles an hour.' She
   was fined five pounds, with five guineas costs, and banned for three
   months. Joe Carstairs was one of the passengers and had herself been
   banned for two years the previous September.

35 *The Sweet and Twenties* by Beverley Nichols, 1958

36 Years later, when Audry Carten and her partner Caroline were bringing
   up Caroline's little boy together, he was given a diary containing a
   quote from Shakespeare for every day of the year. 'Look up Gwen's
   birthday,' they told him. Charles duly read out the quote: '14 July –
   Kill all the lawyers!' Audry and Caroline burst out laughing – it was
   the ideal quote for Gwen, perfectly capturing her anti-authoritarian
   stance. (Author's conversation with Charles Duff, 17 November 2015)

37 Private diaries of Una Troubridge, in the Lovat Dickson papers,
   accessed online through the Canadian Research Knowledge Network
   at: http://heritage.canadiana.ca/view/oocihm.lac_reel_h1196

38 *Tallulah* by Tallulah Bankhead, 1952

39 Letter from Romaine Brooks to Natalie Clifford Barney, 5 June 1924,
   Department of Special Collections and University Archives, McFarlin
   Library, University of Tulsa

40 *The Well of Loneliness* by Radclyffe Hall, 1928

41 *The Trials of Radclyffe Hall* by Diana Souhami, 1998

42 Norah Blaney in conversation with Derek Hunt, 1976. Arthur
   Roberts (1852–1933) was a music hall performer famous for playing
   pantomime dames and for coining the word 'spoof'.

Chapter 9: Dressing-Room Dialogues

1   *The Unsinkable Hermione Baddeley* by Hermione Baddeley and Muriel Burgess, 1984
2   Norah in conversation with Derek Hunt, 1976
3   'Dressing-Room Dialogues: Gwen Farrar in Grease Paint,' Pamela Travers, *South African Pictorial*, 21 February 1925
4   *The Footlights Flickered*, W MacQueen-Pope, 1959
5   'Dressing-Room Dialogues,' *op. cit.*
6   *Ibid.*
7   *Era*, 21 February 1925
8   Norah in conversation with Derek Hunt, 1976
9   *Ibid.*
10 *Northern Whig*, 11 October 1924
11 *Scrapbook for the Twenties* by Leslie Baily, 1959
12 'Percy's Posh Plus Fours Are Priceless' by Robert Weston and Bert Lee
13 *Tallulah!* by Joel Lobenthal, 2008
14 'Lookin' Out the Window Wearin' Out the Carpet' by Clarence Gaskill
15 Norah in conversation with Derek Hunt, 1976
16 This was either Dorothy Todd who held the post until 1926 or Alison Settle who succeeded her.
17 Norah in conversation with Derek Hunt, 1976
18 It was shattered by a bomb in World War Two.
19 *Mr Selfridge in Chicago* by Gayle Soucek, 2015
20 'It Ain't Gonna Rain No More' by Wendell Hall
21 Sebastian Barry mentions Gwen singing this lyric in his novel *The Secret Scripture*, 2015
22 *Bradford Telegraph*, 1 November 1928
23 *The Ziegfeld Touch* by Richard and Paulette Ziegfeld, 1993
24 'Exchange is No Robbery,' *Tatler*, 3 March 1926
25 *London Evening News*
26 In 2016 as a Marriott, at the corner of Lexington and 49th Street, it was dwarfed by the Manhattan skyline.
27 *World* newspaper, undated cutting, Norah's scrapbook
28 *New York Morning Post*, undated cutting, Norah's scrapbook
29 *New York Daily Graphic*, undated cutting, Norah's scrapbook
30 Advertisement, *New York Times*, 29 December 1925
31 *Sheffield Mail*, 29 September 1928
32 *Ibid.*
33 *The Big Sea* by Langston Hughes, quoted in *Encyclopaedia of Lesbian Histories and Cultures* ed. Bonnie Zimmerman, 2013
34 Norah in conversation with Derek Hunt, 1976
35 *New York Morning Telegraph*, undated cutting, Norah's scrapbook
36 Undated cutting, Norah's scrapbook

37 American *Vogue*, 15 March 1926
38 *New York Sunday News*, 14 February 1926
39 *Ibid.*
40 *London Evening News*, undated cutting, Norah's scrapbook
41 Norah in conversation with Roger Wilmut, 1982

Chapter 10: If You Hadn't Gone Away

1   Norah in conversation with Roger Wilmut, 1981
2   'If You Hadn't Gone Away,' words and music by Lew Brown, Billy Rose and Ray Henderson
3   'You Flew Away From the Nest' by Al Jolson
4   *Sunday Post*, 27 June 1926
5   *Northern Whig*, 3 July 1926
6   'In My Gondola,' words by Bud Green and music by Harry Warren
7   *Tatler*, 7 July 1926
8   'Yes Sir, I Prefer Brunettes' by Robert Weston and Bert Lee
9   Norah in conversation with Derek Hunt, 1976
10 Since demolished, on the site of what is now the Gillian Lynne Theatre
11 Lyrics from the 'Huguette Waltz' from *The Vagabond King*, words by Brian Hooker, music by Rudolf Friml
12 *Crystal*, October 1927, cutting, Norah's scrapbook
13 Norah in conversation with Derek Hunt, 1976
14 *Exeter and Plymouth Gazette*, 29 July 1926
15 *Screening Sound: A Compilation of Film-Sound Examples*, Women's Film and Television History Network website: https://womensfilmandtelevisionhistory.files.wordpress.com/2017/02/btsb-lunchtime-programme-june-2016.pdf
16 *Gloucester Journal*, 25 August 1928
17 *Folkestone, Hythe, Sandgate and Cheriton Herald*, 11 December 1926
18 Jill Mayerl in conversation with Peter Dickinson, 11 August 1981, quoted in *Billy Mayerl*, presented by Dickinson, BBC Radio 3, 25 August 1996
19 *Radio Times*, 22 October 1926
20 *Sunday Post*, 26 December 1926
21 *Divertissement* by Anton Dolin, 1931
22 Billy Mayerl, 'They Gave Me "The Bird" in Birkenhead,' *Tit-bits*, 3 July 1937, quoted in *Marigold* by Peter Dickinson, 1999
23 'I'm a Little Blackbird looking for a Bluebird,' words by Grant Clarke and Roy Turk, music by Arthur Johnston and George W Meyer
24 *Graphic*, 11 June 1927
25 *Tatler*, 17 August 1927
26 'Side By Side' by HM Woods
27 *Stage*, 28 July 1927

28 *Illustrated London News*, 30 July 1927
29 *Era*, 7 December 1927
30 *Weekly Despatch*, 11 December 1927
31 *Ibid.*
32 *Daily Herald*, 12 December 1927
33 *Radio Times*, 21 June 1928

Chapter 11: A Rendezvous of the Fast and Smart Set

1 *Sermons, Soap and Television* by John Logie Baird, 1988
2 Gwen and Audry were friendly with Polly Stapleton-Cotton, who lived in Opio with Elisabeth Parrish Starr and Winifred (Peggy) Fortescue. See *Escape to Provence* by Maureen Emerson, 2009
3 'We Can't Blame the Bobbies for That' – this topical song may have been written by Weston and Lee, or possibly Farrar and Mayerl themselves.
4 *Cheltenham Chronicle*, 11 August 1928
5 *Bedfordshire Times and Independent*, 23 November 1928
6 *Britannia and Eve*, 26 October 1928
7 CID Special Report 614265, 31 July 1928
8 *Ibid.*
9 CID Inspector's Report, 28 July 1928
10 Report from Sir Haldane Porter, 28 August 1928
11 *Derby Daily Telegraph*, 20 September 1928
12 *Graphic*, 27 October 1928
13 *Tallulah* by Tallulah Bankhead, 1952
14 *Ibid.*
15 *Bystander*, 31 October 1928
16 Quoted in *Tallulah* by Tallulah Bankhead
17 *Stage*, 28 November 1929
18 *Era*, 17 December 1930
19 *Ibid.*
20 Information from Maurice Bottomley's 'Cocktails with Elvira' website: elvirabarney.wordpress.com
21 *Western Mail*, 13 November 1929
22 *Dover Express*, 22 November 1929
23 *The Weeping and the Laughter* by Viva King, 1976
24 *The Queen of Whale Cay* by Kate Summerscale
25 *Radio Times*, 18 July 1936
26 *Sketch*, 18 January 1928
27 'Psychogenic Factors in Overt Homosexuality,' George W Henry, in *American Journal of Psychiatry*, January 1937, vol. 93, no. 4, quoted by Jonathan Ned Katz on the website www.outhistory.org
28 Available to view online via the BFI website. Sadly, when viewed in

2019, the film was reproduced slightly too fast, making Norah sound like a chipmunk.

29 Norah in conversation with Derek Hunt, 1976

30 *Sheffield Mail*, 28 September 1928

31 *Ibid.*

32 'A Book That Must Be Suppressed,' James Douglas, *Sunday Express*, 19 August 1928

33 *Ibid.*

34 *Tatler*, 5 September 1928

35 *Manchester Dispatch*, 7 December 1928

36 *Leeds Mercury*, 31 December 1929

37 *Yorkshire Evening News*, 27 December 1929

38 *Yorkshire Evening Post*, 7 January 1930

39 *Yorkshire Observer*, 27 December 1929

40 Unknown publication, undated cutting, Norah's scrapbook

41 *Leeds Mercury*, 31 December 1929

42 *Ibid.*

43 *Ibid.*

44 'I'll Keep Off The Grass No More,' words and music by WJ Stafford

45 *Yorkshire Post and Leeds Intelligencer*, 27 December 1929

46 *Sheffield Mail*, 11 March 1930

47 *Ibid.*

48 *Daily Sketch*, undated cutting, Gwen's scrapbook

Chapter 12: We'll Cling Together

1 Norah and Gwen rented rooms at the Hotel Splendide at 105 Piccadilly and at the Berkeley to conduct interviews following their reunion, but it is unclear if or why Norah stayed in a hotel on her return from Leeds.

2 *Evening News,* 2 March 1930

3 Unknown publication, undated cutting, Gwen's scrapbook

4 *Ibid.*

5 Louis McQuilland in *Everybody's Weekly*, 1930

6 *Illustrated Sporting and Dramatic News*, 29 October 1932

7 *Liverpool Post*, 15 May 1930

8 Norah in conversation with Derek Hunt, 1976

9 *Sheffield Independent*, 16 May 1930

10 'They All Fall in Love' by Cole Porter

11 'Moanin' For You,' words by Dan Dougherty, music by Edmund Goulding

12 *Ibid.*

13 'The Moon is Low' by Nacio Herb Brown from the film *Montana Moon*

14 'Don't Tell Her What Happened to Me' by Ray Henderson, Buddy G De Sylva and Lew Brown

15 *Loveliest of Friends* by G Sheila Donisthorpe, 1931, quoted in *The Spinster and Her Enemies* by Sheila Jeffreys, 2003

16 Ironically, demand for *Loveliest of Friends* came, in no small part, from lesbians, hungry to see their lives acknowledged and depicted in some way, even if it had to include the damning disclaimer.

17 *Sunday Dispatch*, 15 June 1930

18 *Evening News*, 14 June 1930

19 'I'm Alone in a Crowd' lyrics by Roland Leigh

20 *Illustrated Sporting and Dramatic News*, 20 December 1930

21 In 1934 *Wonder Bar* was adapted into a very successful Warner Brothers movie. It featured a famous queer moment when a male dancer cut into a man and woman on the dance floor asking 'May I?' and proceeded to partner the man, to the woman's surprise, prompting the observation, 'Boys will be boys,' from Al Jolson.

22 Norah in conversation with Roger Wilmut, 1981

23 *Yorkshire Observer*, 1930, cutting, Norah's scrapbook

24 'If I Had a Girl Like You' by Louis McDermott

25 *Stage*, 1 January 1931

26 *Era*, 3 January 1931

27 *Bradford Telegraph and Argus*, 27 December 1930

28 *Ibid.*, January 1931, cutting, scrapbook

29 Norah in conversation with Roger Wilmut, 1981

30 *Yorkshire Evening News*, January 1931

31 Rowland Leigh (1902-1963) was later part of George Cukor's gay Hollywood set. See: www.ronnisanlo.com

32 Norah in conversation with Roger Wilmut, 1981

33 *Bradford Telegraph and Argus*, 26 January 1931

34 *Ibid.*, 27 February 1931

35 'Just a Little Longer' by Irving Berlin

36 Norah in conversation with Roger Wilmut, 1981

37 *Loveliest of Friends, op. cit.*

38 Norah in conversation with Roger Wilmut, 1981

39 Norah in conversation with Derek Hunt, 1976

40 Dorothy Wilding was later to take the iconic portrait of Elizabeth II that was used on British postage stamps between 1952 and 1967

41 *Photography Magazine*, 15 March 1933, quoted in *Dorothy Wilding* by Terence Pepper, 1991

42 Cecil Beaton, quoted in *Dorothy Wilding, ibid.*

43 *Stage*, 8 June 1931

44 Norah in conversation with Derek Hunt, 1976

45 *Yorkshire Post and Leeds Intelligencer*, 15 February 1932

46 *Nottingham Journal*, 15 February 1932

47 *Yorkshire Post and Leeds Intelligencer*, 22 February 1932

Chapter 13: After Dinner

1   *Leeds Mercury*, 21 April 1932
2   Basil's homes had unimaginative names: Moorlands was followed, confusingly, by Woodlands.
3   'A Yorkshire Woman's Notes,' Joyce Mather, *Leeds Mercury*, 31 April 1932
4   *Hampshire Telegraph*, 11 November 1932
5   British Pathé, *Off-License*, 30 June 1932: https://www.britishpathe.com/video/off-license-1/query/Gwen+Farrar
6   Sir Hugh Smiley married Cecil Beaton's sister Nancy in January 1933.
7   Edward Chichester, 6th Marquess of Donegall, was a journalist and jazz lover.
8   Lance Lister had been the partner of legendary drag performer Douglas Byng and with him recorded the delightfully camp song 'The Cabaret Boys' in 1928.
9   *Leeds Mercury*, 29 September 1932
10 *Hampshire and Sussex County Press*, 30 September 1932
11 'A Yorkshire Woman's Notes,' Joyce Mather, *Leeds Mercury*, 27 September 1932
12 *Ibid.*
13 *Ibid.*
14 Surmised from unrecorded conversation between Norah and Derek Hunt
15 *Birmingham Evening Dispatch*, 4 October 1932
16 'Fashions from Stage and Stalls' by Florence Roberts, *Illustrated Sporting and Dramatic News*, 29 October 1932
17 *Sunday Graphic and Sunday News*, 30 October 1932
18 *Sunday Dispatch*, 23 October 1932
19 *Sunday Referee*, 10 March 1933
20 'A Yorkshire Woman's Notes,' Joyce Mather, *Leeds Mercury*, 13 October 1932
21 *Ibid.*, 13 December 1932
22 *Children in Uniform* by Christa Winsloe
23 'Low Notes and High Jinks,' *Bystander*, 29 March 1933
24 *Stage*, 15 June 1933
25 Florrie Forde was a music hall artist famous for leading sing-along songs such as 'Hold Your Hand Out Naughty Boy'
26 Joyce Mather, *Leeds Mercury*, 1 April 1933
27 *Stage*, 19 August 1933
28 *Sunderland Daily Echo and Shipping Gazette*, Friday 20 October 1933
29 *Leeds Mercury*, 8 December 1933
30 Denys was the mother of a toddler who would grow up to be the screen star and activist Virginia McKenna.
31 English translation by Jessica Walker from her show about Solidor, *All I Want Is One Night*

32 *Sketch*, 13 December 1933

33 Harold Lloyd, like Charlie Chaplin and Buster Keaton, was a huge star of silent-era films.

34 *Yorkshire Evening Post*, 16 October 1934

35 'Keep Young and Beautiful' by Al Dubin and Harry Warren

36 'A Talent to Amuse' by Noel Coward

37 'Another One Gone' by Beverley Nichols

38 Recording in the collection of the Effingham Local History Group

39 Originally released as HMV B8321, the tracks can now be heard as MP3 downloads from musichallcds.co.uk (WindyCDR54)

40 'What'll I Do?' by Irving Berlin

41 'Maybe I'm Wrong Again,' words by Jo Trent, music by Jack Bennett

42 *Surrey Mirror and County Post*, 5 April 1935

43 *Kensington Post*, 19 July 1935

44 *Era*, 4 December 1935

45 The film was remastered and rereleased in 2015 in Volume 7 of the Ealing Studios Rarities Collection.

46 *Truly Wilde* by Joan Schenkar, 2000

47 *Ladies Almanack* by Djuna Barnes, 1928

48 *Leeds Mercury*, 12 January 1937

49 *Daily Herald*, 7 June 1937

50 Sir Howard Kingsley-Wood was Minister of Health in Neville Chamberlain's Conservative Government.

51 *Era*, 13 January 1937

52 *The Queen of Whale Cay* by Kate Summerscale, 1997

53 *Ibid.*

Chapter 14: Submerged

1   Joe Carstairs recalled how they prefaced the news in a 1980s interview.

2   *Yorkshire Evening Post*, 2 September 1937

3   *Tatler*, 3 November 1937

4   *The Well Of Loneliness* by Radclyffe Hall, 1928

5   Letter from Gwen Farrar to Natalie Clifford Barney, 12 February 1938. Gwen's and Dolly Wilde's letters to Natalie are held in the Barney archive, Bibliothèque Littéraire Jacques Doucet, Paris.

6   *Ibid.*

7   *Someone To Dinner* by Inez Holden and *Nothing Ever Happens* by Eda Clarke

8   *Stage*, 16 December 1937

9   The *New York Times* had compared Gwen and Norah to the Duncan Sisters in 1925

10 *Daily Mirror*, 25 April 1938

11 Letter from Dolly Wilde to Natalie Barney, 5 November 1938

12 *Ibid.*

13 *Yorkshire Evening Post*, 9 July 1938

14 *English Journey* by JB Priestley (1934)

15 Could be any of Lady Farrar's sisters: Maud Bell, Hermione Waylen or Daisy Adamson

16 Dolly to Natalie, 3 August 1938

17 *Ibid.*

18 Dolly to Natalie, 5 November 1938

19 Dolly to Natalie, 13 December 1938

20 Pamela 'Honey' Harris was, coincidentally, the granddaughter of Mabel Batten, a key lover, pre-Troubridge, of Radclyffe Hall.

21 Honey Harris to Natalie Clifford Barney, 28 May 1939

22 Dolly to Natalie, 28 January 1939

23 *Ibid.*

24 Dolly to Natalie, 16 February 1939

25 Dolly to Natalie, date hard to decipher, probably 25 February 1939

26 Gwen to Natalie, 15 August 1939

27 Joyce Grenfell was a comedy monologist and TV star. Victoria Wood was one of those who cited her as an important influence.

28 *Stage*, 8 June 1939

29 *Yorkshire Post and Intelligencer*, 12 December 1939

30 *Ibid.*

31 Letter from Harold Holt to AH Brown at BBC Bristol, 24 May 1940

32 *Ibid.*

33 *Daily Mirror*, 28 June 1940

34 *Ottawa Citizen*, 17 August 1940

35 'Peradventures' by Clarkson Rose, *Stage*, 5 June 1941

36 *Ibid.*

37 Letter from Norah to Leslie Baily, 23 August 1937

38 Norah in conversation with Derek Hunt, 1976

39 Grizel was an older sister of the film star David Niven. She had been an actress but became a successful sculptor, famous for 'Bessie', the statuette awarded annually to the winner of the Women's Prize for Fiction.

40 An adaptation of *A Lady Reflects*

41 Letter from Enid Bagnold, 1 October 1940, held in Papers of Sir Cecil Beaton, St John's College Library, University of Cambridge (viewed online through Janus portal)

42 *Bedfordshire Times and Independent*, 10 January 1941

43 *Truly Wilde* by Joan Schenkar, 2000

44 'Faire-Part' by Natalie Clifford Barney from *In Memory of Dorothy Ierne Wilde*, ed. Barney, 1951

45 *The Weeping and the Laughter* by Viva King, 1976

46 *Charley's Woods* by Charles Duff, 2018

47 Letter from Radclyffe Hall to Evguenia Souline, 24 August 1927, collected in *Your John*, Radclyffe Hall, ed. Joanne Glasgow, 1997

48 *Tatler*, 11 June 1941

49 *So Far, So Good* by Adrian McConnel, 2015
50 James Lonsdale in conversation with Christabel Watson, May 2005, from an account written by Watson
51 *Noel Streatfeild* by Angela Bull, 1984
52 In 1947 Joan Griffiths became the first female presenter of the iconic BBC Radio 4 programme *Woman's Hour.*
53 *The Sweet and Twenties* by Beverley Nichols, 1958
54 *The Times*, 27 December 1944
55 *Ibid.*, 11 January 1945
56 *Beaton in Vogue* by Cecil Beaton, ed. Josephine Ross, 2012
57 Originally a term for a bald-headed man, otherwise a figure of fun
58 *Autobiography* by Augustus John, 1975

Chapter 15: I Was Known as Norah Blaney

1   Letter from Norah to Thurstan Holland, 29 September 1951
2   Freddie Rowe in conversation with the author, 14 March 2019
3   Card from Daphne du Maurier to Basil and Norah Hughes, December 1950, in Norah's archive
4   Letter from Daphne du Maurier to Ellen Doubleday, 1 October 1951
5   St Austell Players website: www.staps.co.uk
6   Norah in conversation with Derek Hunt, 1976
7   *Ibid.*
8   Letter from Norah to Norman Carrell, 17 July 1954
9   Letter from Norman Carrell to Norah, 9 September 1954
10 Internal BBC memo signed by Alastair Scott-Johnston, 23 November 1954
11 *At Your Peril* by Hugh Cudlipp, 1962
12 'Nora and Tilly' by Norah Hughes, *Woman and Home*, April 1964
13 Possibly the wording 'night' is significant. Barbara Back may have been a lover of Norah's in the mid to late 1950s.
14 Norah in conversation with Derek Hunt, 1976
15 Audio recording of *Mainly For Women Twice Twenty* broadcast on BBC Television, 9 October 1957
16 'All Alone,' words and music by Irving Berlin
17 'Cottage for Sale' by Willard Robinson
18 Letter from Norah to Gale Pedrick, 24 February 1954
19 *Ibid.*, 14 March 1954
20 *The Classic British Telefantasy Guide* by Paul Cornell, Martin Day, Keith Topping
21 *Radio Times*, 29 November 1957
22 *Shields Daily News*, 5 December 1957
23 Quoted in *The Classic British Telefantasy Guide, op. cit.*
24 *The Sweet and Twenties* by Beverley Nichols, 1958

Chapter 16: Waiting in the Wings

1 Norah in conversation with Roger Wilmut, 1981
2 Letter from Peggy Webster to Noel Coward, 21 February 1960
3 *Ibid.*, 25 July 1960
4 *Stage*, 4 August 1960
5 Noel Coward, quoted in the Introduction to *Coward: Plays, Five*, Sheridan Morley
6 Sheridan Morley, *ibid.*
7 Noel Coward, *ibid.*
8 *Ibid.*
9 *Don't Put Your Daughter on the Stage* by Margaret Webster
10 Norah in conversation with Derek Hunt, 1976
11 Norah wrote thanking Audry, Caroline and Charles for their second visit to see *Macbeth* and the flowers they had brought, signing herself off 'The Bitchy Witch'.
12 Email to the author from Charles Duff, 12 November 2018
13 Email to the author from Maroussia Frank, 21 January 2015
14 Review by Caryl Brahms, unknown publication, undated cutting, kept by Norah
15 Quoted in *Charley's Woods*, Charles Duff, 2018
16 Email to the author from a representative of Diana Rigg's agent, Dalzell Beresford, 6 July 2015
17 Norah in conversation with Derek Hunt, 1976
18 *Ibid.*
19 *Daily Mirror*, 21 June 1966
20 Author's phone conversations with Paul Shelley and Auriol Smith, April 2019
21 In the 1968 film this part was changed to something quite different. The movie also made use of the Gateways Club, an iconic underground lesbian venue, which Norah evidently knew, barely a stone's throw from the house in Chelsea.
22 Norah in conversation with Derek Hunt, 1976
23 Hilda Doolittle (H.D.), American poet, had a relationship with the English writer Annie Winifred Ellerman (Bryher) that lasted from 1918 to H.D.'s death in 1961.
24 Review by Gillian Reynolds, *Guardian*, October 1970, quoted in *Radio Times*, 17 December 1970
25 Email from Miriam Margolyes to the author, 22 November 2015
26 Letter from Norah to Derek Hunt, 21 August 1976
27 Theda Bara had been a popular silent film star in 'vamp' roles.
28 Postscript to an undated letter from Norah to Derek, c.1979
29 Author's conversation with Olivia Hatch, 5 March 2019
30 Letter from Norah to Derek, undated
31 *Ibid.*, 20 October 1979

32 *Ibid.*
33 *Ibid.*, 18 January 1980
34 *Ibid.*, 10 November 1980
35 Eva Turner, quoted by Graham Newell in conversation with Norah and Roger Wilmut, 1981
36 Norah in conversation with Roger Wilmut, 1981
37 Email from Joel Lobenthal to the author, 21 August 2018
38 Letter from Norah to Derek, 10 November 1980
39 *Telegraph and Argus*, 16 July 1983
40 Letter from Norah to Derek, 11 October 1983

Postcript

1 Vita Sackville-West to Virginia Woolf, January 1926
2 'The Song Is Ended,' words and music by Irving Berlin

BIBLIOGRAPHY

Ashwell, Lena, *Modern Troubadours*, Gyldendal, 1922

Baddeley, Hermione and Burgess, Muriel, *The Unsinkable Hermione Baddeley*, Pan, 1984

Bailey, Paul, *Three Queer Lives*, Penguin, 2002

Baily, Leslie, *Scrapbook for the Twenties*, Frederick Muller, 1959

Baird, John Logie, *Sermons, Soap and Television*, Royal Television Society, 1988

Bankhead, Tallulah, *Tallulah Bankhead: My Autobiography*, Victor Gollancz, 1952

Barnes, Djuna, *Ladies Almanack*, private printing, 1928

Barnes, Djuna, *Nightwood*, Faber, 1936

Barry, Sebastian, *The Secret Scripture*, Faber, 2015

Beaton, Cecil, ed. Ross, Josephine, *Beaton in Vogue*, Thames & Hudson, 2012

Beaton, Cecil, *The Wandering Years: 1922-39*, Weidenfeld & Nicolson, 1961

Brook, Donald, *Masters of the Keyboard*, Rockliff, 1947

Brown, Erica, 'The Rise and Fall of "The Original Bright Young Thing",' *Review of English Studies*, Vol. 66, Issue 273, Febuary 2015

Brown, Malcolm, *The Imperial War Museum Book of the Western Front*, Sidgwick & Jackson, 1993

Bull, Angela, *Noel Streatfeild: A Biography*, Collins, 1984

Byng, Douglas, *As You Were*, Duckworth, 1970

Castle, Terry, *The Apparitional Lesbian: Female Homosexuality and Modern Culture*, Columbia University Press, 1993

Castle, Terry, *Noel Coward and Radclyffe Hall*, Columbia University Press, 1996

Clarson, Georgine, *Eat My Dust: Early Women Motorists*, John Hopkins University Press, 2008

Cohen, Lisa, *All We Know*, Farrar, Straus and Giroux, 2012

Cornell, Paul, Day, Martin and Topping, Keith, *The Classic British Telefantasy Guide*, Gateway, 2015

Coward, Noel, ed. Morley, Sheridan, *Coward: Plays, Five*, Methuen, 2014

Cudlipp, Hugh, *At Your Peril*, Weidenfeld & Nicolson, 1962

De Acosta, Mercedes, *Here Lies the Heart: A Tale of My Life*, Andre Deutsch, 1960

Dickinson, Peter, *Marigold: The Music of Billy Mayerl*, OUP, 1999

Doan, Laura, *Disturbing Practices: History, Sexuality and Women's Experience of Modern War*, University of Chicago Press, 2013

Doan, Laura, *Fashioning Sapphism: The Origins of a Modern English Lesbian Culture*, Columbia University Press, 2001

Dolin, Anton, *Divertissement*, Sampson Low Marston, 1931

Donisthorpe, G Sheila, *Loveliest of Friends*, Old Royalty, 1931

Duff, Charles, *Charley's Woods: Sex, Sorrow and a Spiritual Quest in Snowdonia*, Zuleika, 2018

Du Maurier, Angela, *It's Only the Sister*, Peter Davies, 1951

Du Maurier, Angela, *Old Maids Remember*, Peter Davies, 1966

Du Maurier, Daphne, *Gerald: A Portrait*, Victor Gollancz, 1934

Dunn, Jane, *Daphne du Maurier and Her Sisters*, Harper, 2013

Elborough, Travis, ed., *Our History of the 20th Century: As Told in Diaries, Journals and Letters*, Michael O'Mara, 2017

Elwes, Winifrede, *Gervase Elwes*, Grayson, 1935

Emerson, Maureen, *Escape to Provence*, Chapter and Verse, 2009

Faderman, Lillian, *Surpassing the Love of Men*, William Morrow, 1981

Forster, Margaret, *Daphne du Maurier*, Doubleday, 1993

Freeman, Elizabeth, *Time Binds: Queer Temporalities, Queer Histories*, Duke University Press, 2010

Gale, Maggie, *West End Women: Women and the London Stage 1918–1962*, Routledge, 1996

Hall, Radclyffe, *The Well of Loneliness*, Jonathan Cape, 1928

Hall, Radclyffe, ed. Glasgow, Joanne, *Your John: The Love Letters of Radclyffe Hall*, New York University Press, 1997

Hammerton, Jenny, *For Ladies Only? Eve's Film Review Pathé Cinemagazine 1921-33*, Projection Box, 2001

Houston, Renée, *Don't Fence Me In*, Pan, 1974

Humble, Nicola, *The Feminine Middlebrow Novel, 1920s–1950s*, OUP, 2001

Jeffreys, Sheila, *The Spinster and Her Enemies*, Spinifex, 2003

John, Augustus, *Autobiography*, Jonathan Cape, 1975

King, Viva, *The Weeping and the Laughter*, Book Service, 1976

Lavery, Bryony, *Tallulah Bankhead,* Absolute, 1999

Lawrence, Gertrude, *A Star Danced,* WH Allen, 1945

Leask, Margaret, *Lena Ashwell: Actress, Patriot, Pioneer,* University of
    Hertfordshire Press, 2012

Lillie, Beatrice, *Every Other Inch A Lady,* WH Allen, 1972

Lobenthal, Joel, *Tallulah! The Life and Times of a Leading Lady,* Harper
    Collins, 2008

Love, Heather, *Feeling Backwards,* Harvard University Press, 2009

Lynn, Olga, *Oggie: The Memoirs of Olga Lynn,* Weidenfeld and Nicolson, 1955

MacQueen-Pope, WJ, *The Footlights Flickered,* Herbert Jenkins, 1959

Mamontova Majolier, Natalia, *Step-daughter of Imperial Russia,* S Paul, 1940

Mannin, Ethel, *Young in the Twenties,* Hutchinson, 1971

Marshall, Michael, *Top Hat and Tails,* Elm Tree, 1978

McConnel, Adrian, *So Far, So Good,* Book Empire, 2015

Moore, George, 'The Life of Albert Nobbs,' in *A Story-Teller's Holiday,*
    Cumann Sean-eolais na hÉireann, 1918

Moore, James Ross, *André Charlot: The Genius of Intimate Musical Revue,*
    McFarland, 2005

Nesbitt, Cathleen, *A Little Love and Good Company,* Faber, 1975

Nichols, Beverley, *Crazy Pavements,* Jonathan Cape, 1927

Nichols, Beverley, *The Sweet and Twenties,* Weidenfeld & Nicolson, 1958

Nicholson, Virginia, *Singled Out,* Penguin, 2007

Noyes, Alfred, *Ballads and Poems,* William Blackwood, 1928

Oram, Alison, *Her Husband Was a Woman,* Routledge, 2007

Pepper, Terence, *Dorothy Wilding,* National Portrait Gallery, 1991

Priestley, JB, *English Journey,* Harper, 1934

Rich, Adrienne, *What Is Found There: Notebooks on Poetry and Politics,*
    WW Norton, 1994

Rubinstein, Arthur, *My Young Years,* Knopf, 1973

Schenkar, Joan, *Truly Wilde: The Unsettling Story of Dolly Wilde, Oscar's
    Unusual Niece,* Virago, 2000

Shanke, Robert A and Marra, Kim, eds., *The Gay and Lesbian Theatrical
    Legacy,* University of Michigan Press, 2005

Soucek, Gayle, *Mr Selfridge in Chicago: Marshall Field's, the Windy City and
    the Making of a Merchant Prince,* History Press, 2015

Souhami, Diana, *Gluck: Her Biography,* Pandora, 1988

Souhami, Diana, *Mrs Keppel and Her Daughter,* Harper Collins, 1996

Souhami, Diana, *The Trials of Radclyffe Hall,* Weidenfeld & Nicolson, 1998

Souhami, Diana, *Wild Girls: Paris, Sappho and Art: The Lives and Loves of Natalie Barney and Romaine Brooks*, Weidenfeld & Nicolson, 2004; republished as *Natalie and Romaine*

St Clair, Angela, Lady Erskine, *Fore and Aft,* Jarrolds, 1932

St Pierre, Paul Matthew, *Songs and Sketch Transcripts of British Music Hall Performers Elsie and Doris Waters,* Edwin Mellen, 2003

Summerscale, Kate, *The Queen of Whale Cay,* Viking, 1997

Waters, Sarah, *The Paying Guests,* Little Brown, 2014

Waugh, Evelyn, ed. Davie, Michael, *The Diaries of Evelyn Waugh,* Penguin, 1979

Waugh, Evelyn, *Vile Bodies,* Chapman & Hall, 1930

Webster, Margaret, *Don't Put Your Daughter on the Stage,* Knopf, 1972

Wilmut, Roger, *Kindly Leave the Stage: The Story of Variety 1919–1960,* Methuen, 1985

Wyndham, Francis, *Mrs Henderson and Other Stories,* Jonathan Cape, 1985

Ziegfeld, Paulette and Richard, *The Ziegfeld Touch: The Life and Times of Florenz Ziegfeld, Jr,* Harry N Abrams, 1993

Zimmerman, Bonnie, ed., *Encyclopaedia of Lesbian Histories and Cultures,* Routledge, 2013

Index

About the Author

Alison Child holds a degree in history from Cambridge University and a masters in research from the University of Brighton. She is the creative director of Behind The Lines Theatre Company and for them has devised three plays, *All the Nice Girls*, *Deep in the Heart of Me* and *Fall of Duty*. As a member of the Cambridge Footlights she co-wrote and performed in two revues, touring nationally. Her most recent acting role was as Sappho in *Sappho Singing*, a film shot in Skala Eressos, Lesvos, where Alison lives with her partner, Rosie, when they are not at home in Brighton.